SEVEN LIFETIME SPORTS

A Handbook for Skill Development
Revised Edition

by

Jerry F. Clark, Ed.D.
Chairman of HPER Department
Oral Roberts University
Tulsa, Oklahoma

eddie bowers publishing, Inc.
2600 Jackson Street
Dubuque, Iowa 52001

This book is dedicated to the one who supported me and helped me put it all together -- my wife Nancy.

eddie bowers publishing, inc.
2600 Jackson Street
Dubuque, Iowa 52001

ISBN 0-945483-17-1

Table of Contents

List of Illustrations

Chapter 5   PICKLE-BALL

Chapter 6   RACKETBALL

Chapter 7   TENNIS

Preface

This book contains seven chapters covering dual and individual sports activities. These seven sports are the ones most often selected by our students at Oral Roberts University. There is currently no book that covers all of these sports and few that cover most of them. This book was developed to incorporate all seven of these sports activities into a single comprehensive teaching text that would meet the needs of both students and teachers. These particular sports are considered "Lifetime Sports." It is important that students learn the fundamentals properly in order to play them successfully and thus continue to participate and enjoy them throughout their lifetime.

This handbook is designed for the beginning participant and contains indepth instruction of the basic fundamentals, correction of errors and practice drills for each sport. These sections are written to provide the beginner with simple and clear directions for learning and practicing the basic skills in a sequential and progressive order. It is intended to facilitate the class instructor, but is also basic enough to be used for self-instruction. Each chapter contains information pertaining to the history, benefits, terminology, rules, equipment, basic fundamentals, errors and corrections, drills, and skills test for each sport.

Acknowledgements

As with all authors, the completion of a book comes as a result of the contributions of many people. I would like to acknowledge Elaine Drain in our Word Processing Center. Her initiative in correcting obvious errors we had missed, as well as her patience and understanding as we submitted the many re-writes and corrections was greatly appreciated. Janet Doty of our Graphics Department supplied the many drawings found throughout this book. Her time and effort on the illustrations, as well as her dedication to designing such an attractive book cover, greatly enhanced the book. Lori Black and Mark Maskell gave unselfishly of their time to pose for several of the photo illustrations. My thanks to all of them.

CHAPTER 1

ARCHERY

HISTORY

The exact date of the invention of the bow and arrow is unknown; however, archaeologists estimate that they were used around 100,000 years ago. The discovery of archery ranks along with the invention of the wheel, the discovery of fire, and the development of speech as one of the most important cultural advances in the history of the human race. It was a major factor in man's rise above the earth's creatures since he was no longer forced into hand-to-hand combat. Archery skill became of vital importance for mankind's survival for thousands of years. The bow and arrow was the primary weapon of the American Indians as well as many foreign countries. It was the chief weapon of warfare throughout most of the world until the battle of the Spanish Armada in 1588. The English used firearms in that defeat and the bow gradually became obsolete as a weapon of war. It is still used by a few of the aboriginal races in remote parts of the world, primarily Africa and South America, as both a weapon of war and for hunting game and fish.

The sport of archery is probably more popular today in the United States than any time in our history. The fascination of the bow and arrow often carries over from childhood and results in many adults taking up the sport. Bow hunting has become so popular that most states currently have special "archery only" seasons for game such as deer, elk, bear, and turkey. Most cities and numerous rural "hunting communities" throughout the land have bow and arrow enthusiasts who have formed archery clubs. These groups often have field and tournament ranges to simulate the local hunting conditions and for membership tournaments.

BENEFITS

Archery is one of our "lifetime sports" that can continue to provide exercise, excitement, and fun for most or all of our lives. It develops good muscle tone in the arms, shoulders, and back muscles. The constant contracting of the abdominal and back muscles along with the stretching of the chest muscles is also useful in the development and maintenance of good posture. It can also be quite beneficial psychologically since it is relatively easy to learn and usually rewards the participant with rapid progress.

It is an excellent sport for men, women, and children. Although women often must use a bow with less bow weight than men, they soon discover that they can become equally as proficient. There are many social benefits to be derived from couples or groups practicing together at targets, playing archery games, participating in archery tournaments, or bow hunting. A family of bow hunters is common today in many areas of the United States. The joy of bow in hand, being in the forest on a beautiful October morning, and "taking in" all that nature has to offer is a pleasure that has to be experienced to be truly understood. So get the bow and arrows and head for the outdoors to enjoy the sport for the entire family!

TERMINOLOGY

Anchor point   To place the index finger of the drawing hand under the chin or at the corner of the mouth at full draw.

Archery golf   The game that is played and scored like golf, but using a bow and arrow.

Arm guard   A protective device to prevent the bow string injuries on the inside of the bow forearm.

Arrow plate The vertical point of contact, usually made of leather, that the arrow crosses.

Arrow rest The support arm upon which the arrow lies when it is nocked on the string.

Back The part of the bow away from the archer.

Blunt An arrow with a blunt tip instead of a pointed one. Used primarily for small game hunting.

Bow arm The arm which supports the bow when shooting.

Bowsight A mechanical device placed on the bow to allow you to aim directly at the center of the target.

Bowstring The string of the bow, usually made of Dacron or Kevlar.

Bow Tip Protector A small cap that is placed on the tip of the lower limb of the bow to protect it from contact with the ground or floor.

Bracing The act of stringing a bow.

Broadhead A broad, sharply pointed arrowhead used for hunting.

Canting Tilting the bow out of the vertical position as you shoot.

Cast The speed and distance a bow can propel an arrow.

Clout shooting A game in which ground targets are used for long-distance shots. The target is 48 ft. in diameter and the shooting distances vary from 120 to 180 yds.

Cock feather (index feather) The odd colored feather which is perpendicular to the bow when the arrow is shot.

Composite bow A bow made of two or more materials, such as wood and fiberglass.

Compound bow A bow that uses a system of pulleys and cables to gain an added mechanical advantage.

Creeping Allowing the string hand to move forward as the arrow is being released.

Crest The colored hands around the shaft of the arrow which aid in its identification.

Draw To pull the bowstring back to the anchor point.

Draw weight The weight measured in pounds, used to bring the bow to full draw.

End A designated number of arrows, usually six, that are shot in succession before retrieving.

Face The surface of the bow towards the bowstring.

Field Captain Man in charge of an archery tournament.

Finger tab, finger glove Leather devices or covering used to protect the three fingers on the bowstring.

Fletching The feathers or vanes on an arrow which stabilize the flight of the arrow.

Flight shooting Shooting an arrow for distance.

Flu-flu Arrow with extra large feathers to slow it down rapidly; used in shooting at targets in the air or hunting.

Follow-through Maintaining good form after the arrow has been released. "Pose for a picture" until the arrow hits the target.

Full draw The position of the archer when the bowstring has been drawn and the bowhand is at the anchor point.

Grip Handle of the bow.

Ground quiver A device that is stuck in the ground to hold arrows and bow.

Group To shoot arrows in a pattern. A good grouping means the arrows are in close proximity.

Hen feathers The two identical colored feathers on the arrow that parallel the nock.

Holding Holding an arrow at full draw while aiming.

Instinctive shooting Aiming and shooting a bow without the aid of a bowsight or other mechanical means. Requires learned judgment. Also called bare bow shooting.

Kisser button An indicator placed on the string so it touches the lips when the archer is at full draw. Helps to reinforce the anchor position.

Lady Paramount Woman in charge of an archery tournament.

Limb Upper or lower part of the bow that bends when the bowstring is drawn.

Mat (also called butt) The circular disc of straw to which the target face is attached.

Nock To place the arrow on the string. Also the attachment found on the fletched end of the arrow which is placed on the bowstring.

Nock locator (nocking point) A device that indicates where the arrow is to be nocked on the bowstring.

Overbowed An archer who is drawing too strong a bow.

Overdraw Drawing an arrow beyond the inside face of the bow or using a longer arrow than the bow was designed to handle.

Overstrung The bowstring is too short for the bow.

Petticoat The edge of the target outside of the scoring area.

Pile The tip, head, or point of the arrow.

Quiver A device used to hold arrows.

Range The distance to be shot; the place where shooting takes place.

Recurve bow A bow with curved tipped limbs that bend away from the archer when the bow is held in the shooting position.

Release To allow the string to leave the fingers.

Riser The center part of the bow that includes the handle.

Round Shooting a prescribed number of ends at prescribed distances.

Roving Archery game which involves shooting at random targets such as paper, cans, etc. Good for bowhunting practice.

Scatter Opposite of grouping, arrows are scattered on target.

Self bow Bow made of one kind of material.

Serving The thread reinforcement on the center of the bowstring. It helps protect it from wear.

Shaft The body of the arrow, excluding the point, nock, and fletching.

Sight window The cut-out section of the bow above the handle that allows a clear view of the bowsight.

Spine The stiffness-flexibility combination of an arrow. Arrows should be spined according to the bow weight.

Stabilizer Extending a rod or rods from a bow to help to maintain its stability when shooting.

Stacking A characteristic in some bows that make them disproportionately more difficult to pull as you draw back.

Tackle An inclusive name for archery equipment.

Timber Term used in field archery to warn others that an arrow is being shot; same as "fore" in golf.

Torque An undesirable twisting of the bow by the bowhand, or the bowstring by the string hand

Toxophilite A lover of the bow, an archer.

Trajectory The path of an arrow in flight.

Understrung A bow that has a string that is too long. The distance is too short between the handle and the string.

Vane The feather or plastic fletching on an arrow.

Wobble The erratic action of an arrow in flight.

EQUIPMENT

The only archery tackle that is really necessary is a bow and some arrows. If the bow has a string and the arrows are long enough, then you are in business. However, for safety and comfort it is desirable to also have an arm guard, finger tabs or glove, and some type of quiver.

Bows--They are either self bows or composite bows depending on how they are made. A self bow is made of a single material like wood, metal, or fiberglass. A composite or laminated bow is constructed by cementing two or more materials together. Wooden and metal self bows are not as popular as those made of fiberglass. Fiberglass bows are low in cost and very durable, making them attractive for teaching beginners in schools and camps. For the more experienced archer, however, composite bows are more popular. They combine beauty, stability, and arrow speed to make them desirable for both target and field shooting. The composite limbs are usually made from a lamination of hardwood and fiberglass strips. A layer of wood with strips of fiberglass laminated on both sides is the common construction technique. Graphite is being used more and more in the process. Generally speaking, the more wood and the better the quality of the wood that is used in the composite, the greater the cost of the bow.

The most popular and common bow design for the target archer today is the recurve bow (Figure 1.1). This bow takes its name from the fact that the tips of its limbs are bent or curved away from the archer. This is different from the longbow, which has limbs that bend towards the archer. This design provides for greater arrow speed than is possible with a longbow. The recurve design has made it possible to construct shorter bows without losing the cast or speed in which the arrow can be released. The newer designs also help to prevent "stacking," which is common with recurves. This is the abnormally increased pull needed to draw the bow string back to the anchor point or shooting position. Most tournament archers use the composite working recurve bow. A less expensive model that has gained popularity in school and camp settings is the semi-recurve.

In recent years the latest and most revolutionary advances in bow technology have given us the compound bow. This type bow utilizes a system of pulleys, cables, and cams to gain a mechanical advantage. The major advantage of the compound is that it's much easier to shoot accurately. The eccentric wheel and cable system lets you draw and hold a heavier draw weight bow with much less effort than a recurve or straight bow. It is hard to pull until you reach about one-half of the draw, then it releases and becomes easier. It is quite common to have only one-half of the tension or pull that is experienced at full draw of other types of bows of the same peak weight. You can, therefore, shoot a much stronger bow and a heavier arrow with greater ease and accuracy than with other types of bows. For these reasons the compound bow has enjoyed phenomenal popularity in a relatively few short years. Bow hunting has made greater gains in the number of participants in the USA than most other adventure sports, in large measure because of the compound bow.

Most tournaments involving target archery still restrict the types of bows to recurves or longbows. The Olympics will only allow recurve style bows. There are, however, more tournaments each year that include compounds and virtually all field archery tournaments, where there are choices, find compounds as the heavy favorite.

Once you have decided on the type of bow, you next need to determine your best draw weight. This is the bow poundage that you can draw and hold without undue strain for 6-10 seconds. An important consideration here is that as your shooting skills improve and your draw strength increases, you will probably want a bow with more poundage. You might want to delay buying your own equipment until you have acquired some basic skills and strength. All standard bows are measured for weight at a 28-inch draw length. Your bow weight will change by approximately $2\frac{1}{2}$ pounds for every inch that your draw length is above or below 28 inches. Therefore, if you have a 26 inch draw length and a 30 pound bow, you are really only drawing 25 pounds.

Beginning archers should choose a bow that they can draw with ease. A bow that is too heavy will prevent you from developing good shooting form. Learning to shoot will be much harder if the act of drawing the bow takes all of your strength. As a general rule, beginning women archers should choose a bow between 15-25 pounds, and men between 25-35 pounds.

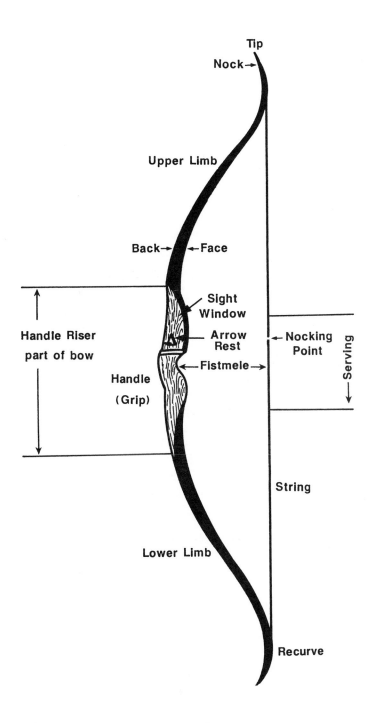

Figure 1.1 Parts of a Recurve Bow

Many compound bows have draw weights that are adjustable. The weight setting may vary by 20 pounds or more. This can be extremely useful for bow hunters who may start out practicing at the 50 pound setting and when the hunting season approaches, adjust the bow to 70 pounds. This provides for greater arrow cast and a corresponding minimal trajectory adjustment for shots in the field.

Arrows--The length of arrows that you should use is directly related to the length of your arms. A practical and effective way to determine the correct arrow length is to stretch your arms in front of your body with the palms together. Place the fletched end of the arrow against your sternum. With the arms outstretched and using both hands, place the point end of the arrow between your hands. To be the correct length the arrow should extend from one-half inch to two inches past your fingers. For the beginner, it is not critical if the arrow is slightly long, but the arrow should <u>never</u> be too short. (Figure 1.2)

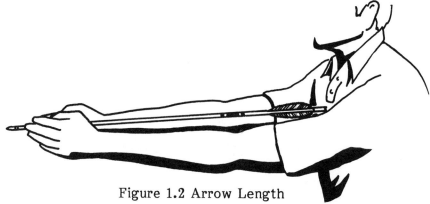

Figure 1.2 Arrow Length

Arrow shafts are made from either wood, fiberglass, a combination of graphite and fiberglass, or aluminum. Wood arrows are the least expensive and the best ones are made of cedar. The primary disadvantages of wood are breakage, splintering, and warping. They are, however, suitable to develop skill, especially if they are matched. Matched arrows are those that are identical in weight and spine to each other. Fiberglass arrows are more expensive, but they are also more durable and provide a much truer flight than wood. Aluminum arrows are the best on today's market. They have a greater degree of flexibility, strength, and balance than other types of arrows. They are difficult to break or bend under normal shooting conditions, and are impervious to weather conditions. Most tournament archers and bow hunters use aluminum arrows. Hunting arrows differ only in that they require more fletching and the inclusion of a broadhead point.

Arrow fletching (feathers) come in a variety of forms. The two materials used almost exclusively are feathers and plastic. The shape and size of the vanes differ widely and usually are a matter of preference based on your particular style and ability in shooting. The feather which is at right angles to the groove in the nock, and is the odd colored one, is called the cock feather. The other two feathers are called hen feathers. (Figure 1.3)

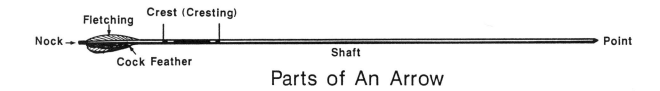

Parts of An Arrow

Figure 1.3 Parts of An Arrow

Your choice of a bow and arrows is extremely important in order for you to properly develop your archery skill. With this in mind you should choose a bow that best meets your present ability, and shoot arrows that are uniform in spine and weight.

<u>Bowsight</u>--This is a mechanical device that attaches to the bow and allows you to aim directly at the center of the target. Sights are very helpful to beginners since the technique is so similar to shooting a gun. Shooting instinctively without sights requires exceptional depth perception, visual acquity, and the ability to adjust your aim. There

are two basic types of bowsights; one for hunting and one for target shooting. The hunting bowsight has multiple pin settings for different distances since the exact shooting distance is unknown. The target bowsight has a single pin setting that can be calibrated for the known distances that are to be shot.

Finger Tabs or Gloves--These are commonly used to protect the fingers. They help protect the middle three drawing fingers. The force of the string can cause soreness and blisters, especially for beginning archers, if one is not worn. Generally speaking, gloves are preferred by hunters and tabs by target archers.

Arm Guard--These have two primary functions; first, to protect the arm from the slap of the bowstring, and second, to hold loose fitting clothing so that it will not interfere with the path of the bowstring. The string slap against the inner side of the forearm can cause considerable pain and discoloration. A good arm guard can not only prevent this, but can also prevent the "flinching" that occurs when you expect the string to bite.

Quiver--This is a device to hold arrows while you are shooting. There are many types to choose from depending on your needs: ground quivers, back quivers, hip quivers, bow quivers, and others. Ground quivers, which usually hold both the bow and arrows are very helpful in a group setting. The most popular quiver for field and target archery is the hip or side quiver. Most bow hunters use a bow quiver. These quivers are mounted on the bow with individual arrow slots to both prevent noise and serve as a cover to protect the broadheads.

RULES AND ETIQUETTE

RULES

- The officials in a tournament are the Field Captain for the men and the Lady Paramount for the women.
- The primary responsibilities of archery officials are: certify field conditions, enforce safety procedures, maintain order on the shooting line, enforce all rules for shooting and scoring, penalize unsportsmanlike conduct, and make final decisions necessary at the targets.
- Archers must wait for a signal from the official before shooting.
- Any type of bow can be used, except a crossbow or a compound bow.
- Any type of arrows may be used except those that will cause unreasonable damage to the target.
- Any archer who demonstrates poor sportsmanship is removed from the tournament after receiving one warning from the field official.
- The archer straddles the shooting line.
- After shooting an end, the archer should step back several feet behind the shooting line until all archers have finished shooting.
- To shoot a round means to shoot a certain number of ends from a given distance.
- When more than one distance is used, each distance in the round is called a range.
- Archers are not allowed to practice at various ranges while shooting in a tournament.
- The longest range is shot first and then each other range progressively to the shortest.
- Archers must wait for a signal from the official before retrieving.
- As a courtesy you should remain on the shooting line until your partner has finished shooting.

SCORING

The target face has five concentric circles and is 48 inches in diameter. The scoring values beginning with the center circle are as follows:

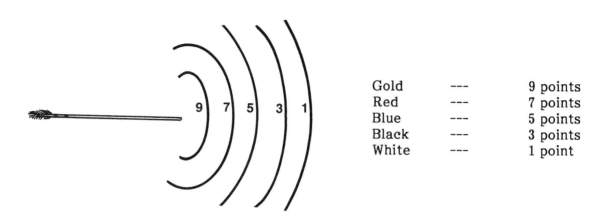

Gold	---	9 points
Red	---	7 points
Blue	---	5 points
Black	---	3 points
White	---	1 point

Figure 1.4 Scoring

The target petticoat (outside the white ring) is 0. An arrow that cuts-the-line between two colors is given the higher value. An arrow that bounces off the target after hitting the scoring area, if witnessed, counts seven points. It also is scored as seven if an arrow passes through the target and is witnessed. Each archer is responsible for seeing that arrows are called correctly, recorded properly, and turned into the officials.

SAFETY RULES

1. Never release the bowstring without an arrow on it. (Called dry-firing and could break the bow.)
2. Be sure the arrows are long enough. An arrow should never be drawn past the arrow-rest of the bow. This could cause the arrow to shatter and go any direction, or possibly be driven into the bow hand.
3. If an arrow falls off of the arrow rest while at full draw, do not attempt to place it back until you let the bow down. If released in this position it would likely travel astray.
4. The bow should be braced only in the direction that it was designed to bend.
5. Never shoot an arrow straight up in the air.
6. Keep the bow-arm elbow turned out to avoid slapping it with the bowstring.
7. Do not shoot if anyone is near the target, behind it, or between you and the target.
8. When pulling arrows from the target, make certain that no one is directly behind you.
9. Never start shooting until the instructor or an official gives the command.
10. To pull an arrow from the target, place one hand against the target, palm out, with the arrow between the fingers. With the other hand hold the arrow near the target surface and pull it out the same angle it went in. (Figure 1.5)
11. Never cross the shooting line to retrieve until the instructor or an official gives the command.

Figure 1.5 Pulling Arrows from Target

FUNDAMENTALS OF ARCHERY

Archery is truly a sport for the entire family. The skills to be mastered are few when compared to most other sports. It does not require extraordinary power, strength, or neuromuscular development to become proficient. The primary archery skills are based on the scientific principles of physics, kinesiology, and anatomy. Along with good form, relaxation and concentration are important elements of good shooting. It is quite common to achieve a surprising amount of success in the initial stages of instruction and practice. In time, this rapid improvement may slow down to the point where your scoring ability is at a standstill. This is when soundness of technique, along with the ability to be graceful and consistent, will gradually allow you to move forward. Let's get a good start on these fundamentals.

Good Archery begins with common sense--You should always be aware of the lethal potential of the bow and arrow. It's only dangerous, however, when the one using it becomes careless or irresponsible. You must show a healthy respect for your tackle and a safety-conscious attitude toward others when shooting in any type of setting.

If you are in an organized group for shooting, it is vital that your rules incorporate good common sense with the concept of always being aware of the whereabouts of your fellow archers. The most basic safety concept of all is that once an arrow is placed on the bow, it should only be pointed in the direction of the intended target. Archery safety rules and procedures are discussed in another section.

Another common problem that arises when you begin shooting is the type of clothing worn. Target archery is unique among the action activities in that there are no distinctive clothing or footwear requirements. Coats and loose-fitting long-sleeved shirts, blouses, and sweaters, however, often cause shooting errors. This type of clothing can become entangled in the bowstring after it is released, thus causing an erratic arrow flight. It is also a good practice to remove jewelry, watches, and pens or other objects from the pockets prior to shooting. These, too, can be caught by the bowstring.

You should follow a set routine of inspecting the bow and arrows at the beginning of each session. Examine the bow to determine that it is not cracked or warped, check the string for fraying, and be assured that the arrows are not cracked, are fully fletched, and are straight. These simple observations can help to eliminate potential problems and lead to greater success and fun.

BRACING THE BOW

Bracing is simply stringing the bow in preparation for shooting. This procedure usually becomes automatic after a few practices, but can present problems for a few and even cause damage to the bow. The use of a bowstringer is the safest and best method for bracing the bow. This device works on the principle of even pull pressure on the limbs by using a single string that is attached to the limb tips by small leather cups. The string is then held down with a foot while the hand pulls up on the bow grip. This allows the archer to slide the loop into the notch at the end of the bow. If bowstringers are not available, the bow can be safely braced manually.

The step-through method (see Figure 1.6), is the safest manual way to string the bow. Caution should be taken, however, because if this method is not performed correctly, it could result in a twisting of the bow limbs and possible breakage. The chance of this occurring can be reduced by checking to make sure that the bottom loop of the bowstring is properly seated in the string groove on the lower limb. A rubber band or bow tip protector around the string and bow will usually eliminate this problem. To perform this technique, you should step through or between the bowstring and the face of the bow with one leg. The same leg is against the upper part of the riser section, while the recurve of the lower bow limb curls around the other ankle. The bowside arm then bends the upper limb, getting resistance from the leg, while the other hand moves the string loop into the upper notch of the bow. After slipping the string into place you should check both bow nocks to see that the string is properly inserted into each before releasing the tension on the bow. Failure to insert them properly is a major cause of twisting and breaking of a bow. To unstring the bow, simply reverse this process.

The push-pull method for stringing lightweight bows is quick, and is a technique that is sometimes used by experienced archers. This method is not recommended because of numerous injuries that have resulted from using this technique.

Figure 1.6 Step-Through Method

THE STANCE

A good stance forms the base on which good shooting form is built. The stance for most archers should be at right angles to the target. In this position, called the square stance, the toes are on a line with each other and with the center of the target. The feet should be spread approximately shoulder-width apart, with even weight distribution that provides a feeling of solidity. With the body erect but relaxed, you simply turn your head toward the target. This should be the body position throughout the delivery of the arrow. Any swaying or shifting of weight forward or backwards will result in a weakened foundation for shooting. (Figure 1.7)

The open stance allows the front foot to drop back several inches from the rear foot. This stance is a little more difficult to master, since the hips and shoulders are not aligned with the center of the target. It does allow for more freedom of movement of the bow arm, which is advantageous to some archers.

NOCKING THE ARROW

This is the placement of the arrow in the shooting position on the bowstring. This is followed by the positioning of the fingers on the string in preparation for the draw. In nocking the arrow, the bow is held horizontal to the ground next to the hip nearest the target (Figure 1.8). The arrow, with the cock feather pointing up, is then placed on the bow and string with the rear hand. The nock of the arrow is placed across the string at the nocking point. This point must be established and marked. It is located on the bowstring slightly above perpendicular to the arrow rest of the bow--from 1/8 inch to 3/16 inch above (Figure 1.1). Metal nock locators can be purchased to mark this point, or articles such as string, tape, or rubber bands could suffice. It is essential that the nocking point remain constant with every arrow or there will be elevation differences in arrow placement on the target. The nock locator should be positioned so that the arrow nock will rest below and against it, thus insuring a consistent nocking point. Some archers prefer double nock locators in which the arrow is placed between them. After the arrow is nocked, you will observe that the arrow is angling slightly downward from the nocking point to the arrow rest on the bow. This position is more conducive to a smooth arrow release and flight than one in which the arrow is placed at right angles to the string and arrow rest.

Figure 1.7 Stance

Figure 1.8 Nocking Arrow

THE GRIP and DRAW

"Gripping the bow" is a misleading statement for good archery technique. It refers to the position of the bow hand on the bow grip. You should not actually grip the bow as the draw and release are performed. The bow is held or gripped while nocking the arrow and after the arrow hits the target. During the draw and release phase of shooting, the bow hand and arm could be compared to placing a forked stick at the pivot point of the bow to achieve stability and consistency with each shot. As the draw is begun, the bow hand pushes the bow, at its pivot point, toward the target. As shown in (Figure 1.9), the bow is placed between the thumb and index finger. Keeping the wrist straight and firm, not overly flexed or extended, let the bow set the hand position. This simply means if the arm, wrist, and hand are properly aligned, the bow will move to the correct hand position rather than placing the hand on the bow, gripping it, and forcing it to stay in that position. The bow will come to rest along the inner side of the thumb muscle and the Y formed by the thumb and index finger. If any other part of the palm touches the grip, it should be only lightly with no pressure. The other three fingers are completely relaxed, and none of the fingers apply any pressure to any part of the bow. For consistent shooting, it is essential to place the bow hand exactly the same way for each arrow.

Figure 1.9 Gripping Bow

Figure 1.10 The Draw

Drawing is performed by pulling the bowstring back to an anchor point on your face. This begins after the arrow is nocked and the bow is held horizontal by the bow hand. With the string hand, place the index finger above the nock and the next two fingers below the nock. The string should lie across the crease of the first joints of these three fingers. The string fingers form a hook to pull the string, while the thumb and little finger are relaxed and curl around similar to the Boy Scout salute. From this position the bow is moved up to a vertical-to-the-ground alignment. The bow is then simultaneously pushed by the bow hand and pulled by the string hand. It is important to mention here that the string arm, hand, and fingers should serve primarily as a rod and hook to pull the string back. The draw is accomplished by utilizing the shoulder and back muscles and not the muscles of the hand and arm. The back of the hand should remain flat and in line with the arm. The arm and hand should be in an approximate straight line with the arrow (Figure 1.10).

The little finger and thumb do not touch the bow string and the wrist never flexes or hyperextends during the draw and release. Both shoulders should be kept down throughout the draw, and you should feel the shoulder blades squeezed together. The draw ends when the string hand has reached an anchor point on the face.

THE ANCHOR POINT

The "anchor point" indicates the place on your face where the forefinger or index finger will be placed for each full draw. You should select a spot which feels natural and comfortable and stay with it consistently. This is one of the most important considerations for uniform shooting results. You must draw to the same anchor point regardless of the distance to be shot. If the anchor point is inconsistent, then the shots will have varying degrees of power imparted to them, and consistent shooting will be impossible. Many field archers, bow hunters, and instinctive shooters use a high anchor point. The low anchor point is used most often by those that utilize a bow sight for aiming.

The high anchor point that is most widely used involves placing the index finger at the corner of the mouth (see Figure 1.11). This is a good reference point that can be easily achieved, and easily observed, with each draw. Others may choose to anchor as high as the bone beneath the eye. They feel that by anchoring this near the eye they can aim instinctively, yet have almost the same view as you would aiming a rifle.

With the low anchor point the index finger is placed under the chin, and a slight pressure is exerted on the mandible. This position allows the bow string to bisect and touch the chin, lips, and nose (Figure 1.12). With three reference points, this anchor is excellent for consistency, thus explaining why it is so popular for sight aiming. It is not as popular for instinctive shooting because it places the arrow at a greater distance beneath the eye. This makes it more difficult, kinesthetically, to adjust the line of vision and the position of the arrow.

Both types of anchor points can be used effectively for any kind of shooting. You ultimately should use the one which feels most comfortable and is most consistent with good scoring. Whatever anchor you select, just remember that an exact anchor establishes the velocity of the arrow.

Figure 1.11 High Anchor Point

Figure 1.12 Low Anchor Point

AIMING

When full draw has been reached, there should be a slight pause or holding period during which the aiming occurs. It is important to note here that when the string is drawn and anchored, the eye nearest the string should be lined up directly over the shaft of the arrow and looking down the arrow toward the target. If the string is drawn to the side of the face, away from the eye, then the directional aiming adjustments become much more difficult. For <u>instinctive aiming</u> the arrow will only be seen out-of-focus; your primary focus will be on the center of the target. The instinctive shooter needs to have good eyesight and depth perception and keep both eyes open throughout the shot. As you peer over the arrow point toward the target, you will see a gap or space between the point of the arrow and the intended point of landing on the target. You must learn to concentrate on the center of the target and let the bow arm adjust instinctively for the range. It involves natural coordination between the eyes and bow arm, the eyes judging the distance to the target, and the bow arm positioning the arrow for that particular distance. As you continue to practice shooting instinctively, you will gradually begin to disregard the arrow almost entirely and concentrate more and more on the center of the target. While you are improving your archery fundamentals, you will also develop greater kinesthetic and visual awareness which will enable you to adjust rapidly from varying distances.

The <u>bow sight</u> technique for aiming will usually enhance your ability to hit the intended target. When using this method, you must establish a bow sight setting on the bow for each shooting distance. This requires you to shoot a number of ends at each sight for each distance. The line of sight for this technique is to open only the eye nearest the string and place the aiming point, or opening, directly on the intended target (Figure 1.13). This is similar to a rifle scope in which the crosshair is placed on the target. There are situations, such as opposite eye dominance, that would greatly distort the position of the target if only one eye were used for aiming. In this case it would be preferable to keep both eyes open, however, it is still imperative that you aim only with the eye that is looking directly down the arrow shaft to the target. The important part of this aiming technique is the steadiness and time that you keep the bow sight in the center of the target. When the sight becomes steady in the middle of the gold, then it's time to release the string.

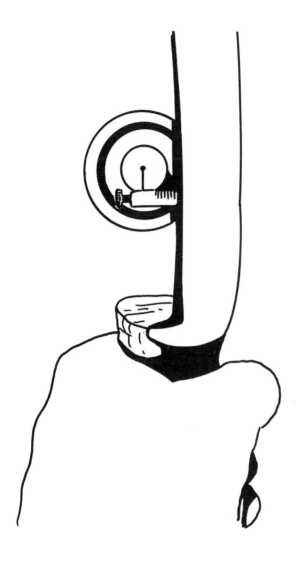

Figure 1.13 Aiming with Bowsight

RELEASE AND FOLLOW-THROUGH

Releasing the arrow is the most important technique to master in archery. Paradoxically, the key elements are relaxation and concentration. A good release is one that gets the fingers off the string without any adverse effect on the flight of the arrow. Often it becomes difficult to relax and release when most of your energy is focused on concentrating on the center of the target. Both of these elements must be controlled, however, to achieve any real degree of archery success. The proper release is a normal reaction of the drawing hand moving back, with the string rolling off the fingers as they are relaxed. This hand reaction is caused by the back muscles and not by pulling the fingers off the string. When the message to release is passed from the brain, the back muscles give a final squeeze, and the string fingers relax. The bow string will literally brush the fingers away from its path if the fingers have been relaxed sufficiently.

If this action of releasing is performed correctly, the follow-through will occur naturally as the hand with fingers relaxed, moves back along the neck (Figure 1.14). The faulty form, where the release hand moves out from the face rather than straight back can only be corrected by the method of tightening the back muscles during the hold and release. As a beginner, you should avoid the habit of trying to release the arrow strictly with the hand muscles or by hyperextending the wrist. This usually results in a "plucking" of the string and produces very erratic shooting results. The follow-through for the bow arm is to hold it still while the arrow travels toward the target. The string hand should remain under the ear near the neck, and the bow arm and hand should stay in the exact release position until the arrow strikes the target. You should think of the follow-through phase, from the release to the arrow striking target, as "posing for a picture." This is also a good opportunity to evaluate your performance and try to improve on areas of poor technique.

Figure 1.14 Follow-Through

ERRORS AND CORRECTIONS

Illustrations of the <u>MOST COMMON</u> errors and how to correct them

<u>ERROR</u>   <u>ILLUSTRATION</u>
Gripping the bow tightly--poor hand
position

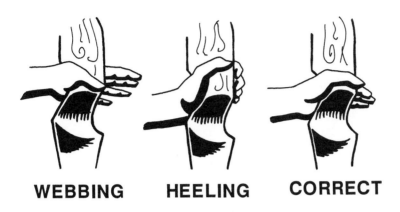

WEBBING   HEELING   CORRECT

Figure 1.15

RESULTS AND CORRECTION
-   Arrows tend to go left for a right-handed archer--tension causes a lack of control.
-   <u>Correct</u> this by using only the index finger and the thumb to control the bow grip. Keep other fingers relaxed and away from the grip.

<u>ERROR</u>   <u>ILLUSTRATION</u>
Rotation of the bow wrist into
or away from bow

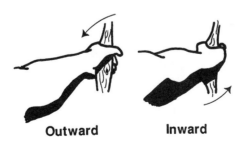

Outward   Inward

Incorrect Wrist Rotations

Figure 1.16

RESULTS AND CORRECTION
-   Causes bow to twist on release, resulting in a loss of control. Inconsistent shooting results.
-   The wrist must be kept firm and in a straight line with the arm. Remember the bow arm, wrist, and hand acts as a forked rod to hold the bow in a set position.

Drawing with the finger and hand muscles,
evidenced by a cupped hand

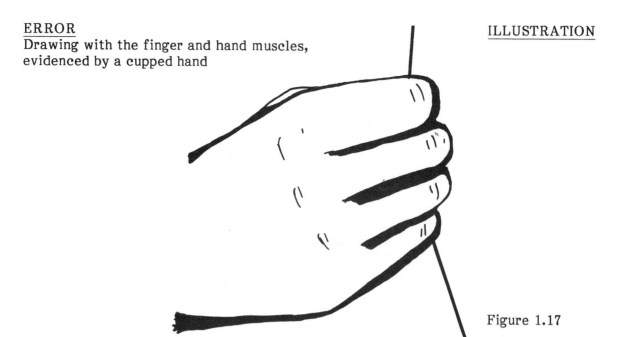

Figure 1.17

RESULTS AND CORRECTION

- Arrow may fall off the arrow rest; rough release that often sends arrows to the left for a right-handed shooter.
- Correct this by keeping the back of the hand flat and using the shoulder and back muscles to draw the string.

ERROR
Allowing the arrow to "creep" forward
during the aiming period

ILLUSTRATION

Figure 1.18

RESULTS AND CORRECTION

- Arrows will vary in elevation, mostly low.
- Correct this by maintaining your anchor point until release and utilizing your back muscles to hold and release the arrow.

ERROR
Moving bow in any direction as
the arrow is released

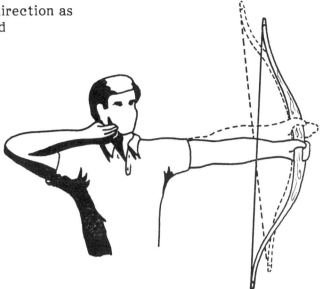

Figure 1.19

RESULTS AND CORRECTION

-    Arrows are pushed off the target line in the direction the bow is moved.
-    Keep the bow arm in the aim and release position until the arrow strikes the target. Remember, "pose for a picture."

OTHER PROBLEM AREAS:

	ERROR	RESULT	CORRECTION
1.	Nocking the arrow too high or too low	Causes arrow to hit the target either high (if nocked low), or low (if nocked high).	Always use a nock locator in the correct position.
2.	Heeling the bow (putting pressure on lower part of thumb and part of palm)	Arrows will usually be high; erratic shooting because of wrist movement.	Extend the hand, wrist, and arm straight toward the target and let the bow fit in naturally.
3.	Bow elbow bent too much	Poor stability in drawing and aiming--inconsistent results.	Elbow and wrist must be straight and firm. If the string is hitting your arm, try rotating the elbow slightly away from the string.
4.	Rotation of the bow shoulder inward toward the string (hunched shoulder)	This causes a poor alignment and is very inconsistent with a smooth and relaxed aim and release. Often shoot to the left for a right-handed shooter.	Keep a balanced and relaxed stance, keep the shoulders down throughout the draw and release.

5.	Using the hand and forearm to draw the string, evidenced by the arm and elbow hugging the chest	Poor stability and strength with the improper muscles drawing. Will often shoot low, very inconsistent.	You should feel the shoulder blades moving together as the arrow is drawn. Let the arm and fingers simply hook the string to the stronger ba muscles.
6.	Use of the thumb as a hook behind the jaw bone	This prevents a smooth consistent release. Often causes an erratic vertical pattern.	Allow the thumb and lit finger to curl and relax under the palm.
7.	Loose-fitting clothing on bow arm	Unless held down with an arm guard, causes string to catch, resulting in a loss of power. Arrows usually land low and to the left for a right-handed shooter.	Short-sleeved or tight-fitting clothes should be worn so they will not interfere with the string
8.	Not holding the aim long enough	Snap shooting; inconsistent pattern over entire target.	Aiming requires total concentration on the center of the target. Y must allow the time to perform a steady aim. may need a lighter bow.

IMPROVEMENT DRILLS AND GAMES

1. STARTER DRILL (1) (NO TARGET FACE)

   -- Begin shooting from 10 yards at a 48" target.
   -- Shoot 3 ends at this distances then move to 15 yards and shoot 3 ends.
      -- Concentrate on form throughout Drill.
      -- Review Fundamentals prior to shooting each end.
      -- Upon release of each arrow, hold position and analyze for technique.
      -- [Review Errors and Corrections]

   STARTER DRILL (2) (WITH TARGET FACE)

   -- Continue to review form and have qualified archer check it. Correct faults immediately.
   -- Shoot the same as the first starter drill--aim for the center gold of target.
   -- Analyze shooting form and results on target face.
   -- [Review Errors and Corrections]

2. BLUE DRILL

   -- Shoot 5 ends at 20 yards.
   -- Concentrate on form and review Fundamentals and Errors and Corrections.
   -- Attempt to keep each end within the blue (from blue ring to center of the gold).
   -- Analyze each arrow that hits outside the blue to determine the cause. (Attempt to score a minimum of 30 points on each end.)

3. SHOOT THE ARCHERY SKILLS TEST (SEE ARCHERY SKILLS TEST)

-- Analyze for form and results after each shot.
-- Remember that seemingly minor errors and deviations at the shorter distances will be magnified as you move farther from the target.
-- Attempt to keep the arrows inside the blue at 20 yards and inside the black at 30 yards.

ARCHERY SKILLS TEST

GENERAL INFORMATION

Purpose — To Measure the player's ability to shoot arrows accurately at various distances from the target.

Facilities/ Equipment — An open field 60 yards long, regulation 48" targets, regulation target faces, regulation bows and arrows, arm guards, finger tabs. A student may use his/her personal bow and arrows or school-owned equipment. However, students may not borrow equipment from other students.

Directions — The student will shoot 24 arrows at a 48" target from two different distances as specified below:

2 ends at 20 yards
2 ends at 30 yards

Students may shoot two practice arrows for each distance. All official rules governing the sport of target archery are enforced.

Scoring—Arrows in the target face shall be evaluated as Gold-9; Red-7; Blue-5; Black-3; White-1. Maximum Score: 24 x 9 = 216 points.

ARCHERY
Skills Test Score Sheet

_____ Male/Female Date_____ Instructor _____
                          circle

_____ Section_____ Day/Time_____

TEST ITEM	RAW SCORES	RECORDER'S SIGNATURE

20 Yds.

```
        _____
              Arrows
   End   1 2 3 4 5 6    Total
    1    _____
    2    _____

                       ____        _____
```

30 Yds.

```
        _____
              Arrows
   End   1 2 3 4 5 6    Total
    1    _____
    2    _____

                       ____        _____
```

Total _____

T-Score _____   Grade _____

ARCHERY SKILLS TEST NORMS

| | *20 YDS. | | *30 YDS. | |
T-Score	Men	Women	Men	Women
76	118	94	124	79
74	114	90	118	75
72	110	86	112	71
70	106	82	106	67
68	102	78	100	63
66	98	74	94	59
64	94	70	88	55
62	90	66	82	51
60	85	62	76	47
58	81	58	70	43
56	77	54	64	39
54	73	50	58	35
52	69	46	52	31
50	65	42	46	27
48	61	38	40	23
46	57	34	36	19
44	53	30	32	15
42	49	26	29	12
40	45	22	25	9
38	41	18	21	6
36	37	12	17	3
34	33	8	13	2
32	29	↓6	↓9	1

(left margin labels: ed, ...ediate, ...ing)

23

ARCHERY
Skills Test Score Sheet

_____ Male/Female Date_____ Instructor _____
                        circle

_____ Section_____ Day/Time_____

TEST ITEM   RAW SCORES   RECORDER'S SIGNATURE

20 Yds.
                   _____
                        Arrows
                   End 1 2 3 4 5 6   Total
                    1   _____
                    2   _____

                                       _____   _____

30 Yds.
                   _____
                        Arrows
                   End 1 2 3 4 5 6   Total
                    1   _____
                    2   _____

                                       _____   _____

                   Total _____

                   T-Score _____   Grade _____

ARCHERY SKILLS TEST NORMS

		*20 YDS.		*30 YDS.	
	T-Score	Men	Women	Men	Women
	76	118	94	124	79
	74	114	90	118	75
	72	110	86	112	71
	70	106	82	106	67
	68	102	78	100	63
ced	66	98	74	94	59
	64	94	70	88	55
	62	90	66	82	51
	60	85	62	76	47
	58	81	58	70	43
mediate	56	77	54	64	39
	54	73	50	58	35
	52	69	46	52	31
	50	65	42	46	27
	48	61	38	40	23
ning	46	57	34	36	19
	44	53	30	32	15
	42	49	26	29	12
	40	45	22	25	9
	38	41	18	21	6
	36	37	12	17	3
	34	33	8	13	2
	32	29	↓6	↓9	1

ARCHERY
Skills Test Score Sheet

_____ Male/Female Date_____ Instructor _____
               circle

_____ Section_____ Day/Time_____

TEST ITEM   RAW SCORES   RECORDER'S SIGNATURE

20 Yds.
                  Arrows
        End 1 2 3 4 5 6 Total
        1
        2

30 Yds.
                  Arrows
        End 1 2 3 4 5 6 Total
        1
        2

        Total _____

        T-Score _____   Grade _____

ARCHERY SKILLS TEST NORMS

| | *20 YDS. | | *30 YDS. | |
T-Score	Men	Women	Men	Women
76	118	94	124	79
74	114	90	118	75
72	110	86	112	71
70	106	82	106	67
68	102	78	100	63
66	98	74	94	59
64	94	70	88	55
62	90	66	82	51
60	85	62	76	47
58	81	58	70	43
56	77	54	64	39
54	73	50	58	35
52	69	46	52	31
50	65	42	46	27
48	61	38	40	23
46	57	34	36	19
44	53	30	32	15
42	49	26	29	12
40	45	22	25	9
38	41	18	21	6
36	37	12	17	3
34	33	8	13	2
32	29	↓6	↓9	1

ced

mediate

ning

ARCHERY
Skills Test Score Sheet

_____ Male/Female Date_____ Instructor _____
                         circle

_____ Section_____ Day/Time_____

TEST ITEM	RAW SCORES	RECORDER'S SIGNATURE

20 Yds.

End	Arrows 1 2 3 4 5 6	Total
1		
2		

_____

30 Yds.

End	Arrows 1 2 3 4 5 6	Total
1		
2		

_____

Total _____

T-Score _____   Grade _____

ARCHERY SKILLS TEST NORMS

	T-Score	*20 YDS. Men	Women	*30 YDS. Men	Women
	76	118	94	124	79
	74	114	90	118	75
	72	110	86	112	71
	70	106	82	106	67
	68	102	78	100	63
ced	66	98	74	94	59
	64	94	70	88	55
	62	90	66	82	51
	60	85	62	76	47
	58	81	58	70	43
mediate	56	77	54	64	39
	54	73	50	58	35
	52	69	46	52	31
	50	65	42	46	27
	48	61	38	40	23
ning	46	57	34	36	19
	44	53	30	32	15
	42	49	26	29	12
	40	45	22	25	9
	38	41	18	21	6
	36	37	12	17	3
	34	33	8	13	2
	32	29	↓6	↓9	1

29

ARCHERY
Skills Test Score Sheet

_____ Male/Female Date_____ Instructor _____
                          circle

_____ Section _____ Day/Time _____

TEST ITEM   RAW SCORES   RECORDER'S SIGNATURE

20 Yds.   _____
              Arrows
           End 1 2 3 4 5 6   Total
            1 _____
            2 _____

                              _____   _____

30 Yds.   _____
              Arrows
           End 1 2 3 4 5 6   Total
            1 _____
            2 _____

                              _____   _____

           Total _____

           T-Score _____   Grade _____

ARCHERY SKILLS TEST NORMS

| | *20 YDS. | | *30 YDS. | |
T-Score	Men	Women	Men	Women
76	118	94	124	79
74	114	90	118	75
72	110	86	112	71
70	106	82	106	67
68	102	78	100	63
66	98	74	94	59
64	94	70	88	55
62	90	66	82	51
60	85	62	76	47
58	81	58	70	43
56	77	54	64	39
54	73	50	58	35
52	69	46	52	31
50	65	42	46	27
48	61	38	40	23
46	57	34	36	19
44	53	30	32	15
42	49	26	29	12
40	45	22	25	9
38	41	18	21	6
36	37	12	17	3
34	33	8	13	2
32	29	↓6	↓9	1

ced

mediate

ning

31

ARCHERY
Skill Analysis Score Sheet
(20 points)

Name _____   Date _____

Class _____   Evaluated By _____

POINT GUIDE

2 points -- Student appears competent
1 point -- Occasionally correct or minor errors
0 points -- Needs more attention before ready to
                play

	POINTS SCORED		
	0	1	2
1. Brace the Bow *1) Step through technique 2) Protect the bow	_____	_____	_____
2. Proper Stance & Arrownock *1) Square stance 2) Bow horizonal-lay the arrow	_____	_____	_____
3. Grip the Bow/Draw the String *1) "Forked stick"technique (Grip) 2) 3 Finger draw 3) Shoulder & back-arm align- ment	_____	_____	_____
4. Touch the Anchor Point *1) High anchor point 2) Consistency is the key	_____	_____	_____
5. Aiming the Arrow *1) Instinctive shooting 2) Sight shooting	_____	_____	_____
6. Releasing the Arrow *1) Concentrate and relax	_____	_____	_____
7. Follow - Through *1) Hand under ear 2) "Pose" for picture	_____	_____	_____
8. Choosing a Bow & Arrows *1) Bow weight/arrow length	_____	_____	_____
9. Safety in Archery *1) Do's and don't's 2) "Common Sense" approach to shooting	_____	_____	_____
10. Results *1) Archery skill test results 2) General envaluation	_____	_____	_____

* Points for evaluation

TOTAL SCORE _____

ARCHERY
Skill Analysis Score Sheet
(20 points)

Name _____   Date _____

Class _____   Evaluated By _____

POINT GUIDE

2 points -- Student appears competent
1 point -- Occasionally correct or minor errors
0 points -- Needs more attention before ready to
            play

	POINTS SCORED		
	0	1	2
1. Brace the Bow	____	____	____
*1) Step through technique			
2) Protect the bow			
2. Proper Stance & Arrownock	____	____	____
*1) Square stance			
2) Bow horizonal-lay the arrow			
3. Grip the Bow/Draw the String	____	____	____
*1) "Forked stick"technique (Grip)			
2) 3 Finger draw			
3) Shoulder & back-arm alignment			
4. Touch the Anchor Point	____	____	____
*1) High anchor point			
2) Consistency is the key			
5. Aiming the Arrow	____	____	____
*1) Instinctive shooting			
2) Sight shooting			
6. Releasing the Arrow	____	____	____
*1) Concentrate and relax			
7. Follow - Through	____	____	____
*1) Hand under ear			
2) "Pose" for picture			
8. Choosing a Bow & Arrows	____	____	____
*1) Bow weight/arrow length			
9. Safety in Archery	____	____	____
*1) Do's and don't's			
2) "Common Sense" approach to shooting			
10. Results	____	____	____
*1) Archery skill test results			
2) General envaluation			

* Points for evaluation

TOTAL SCORE _____

CHAPTER 2

BADMINTON

HISTORY

Most historians agree that badminton was once played in India and was called poona after the town of Poona. It was played by that name until the 1870's. Our modern day version of the game came from England where it was first played around 1870. The English played the game at Badminton, the country estate of the Duke of Beaufort in Gloucestershire, England. Hence the name badminton became the official name.

Before 1901 when the present court dimensions were adopted, courts varied considerably, with the most common shape being that of an hour-glass. When the Duke of Beaufort introduced the game, it was played in a room that had two large doors opening inwards on the side walls. In order to allow nonplaying guests to enter and leave the room without disturbing the game, it was decided to narrow the court at the net, thus providing the "hour-glass" shaped court. Variations of court shape and dimensions were common for 30 years following its beginning in England.

Badminton first came to the United States in 1878 at the 71st Regiment Armory Club in New York City. The American Badminton Association was founded in 1936. The name was changed to the United States Badminton Association in 1977.

Many of the countries that are affiliated with the International Badminton Federation compete against each other in international matches. The Thomas Cup is the championship for men's competition. This cup was named for Sir George Thomas, the late president of the Federation. The Uber Cup is the international championship for women. This cup was started by Mrs. H. S. Uber, one of the finest mixed doubles players to play the game. The Thomas Cup was inaugurated in 1948 and the Uber Cup in 1957. Both are played at three year intervals.

Most of the top players in the world still come from the far east, where badminton is considered to be the national sport. Malaysia, Indonesia, and Thailand consistently produce many world champions. The United States has never won the Thomas Cup but has won the Uber Cup on several occasions.

BENEFITS

Many young and old still find badminton to be an ideal game to play. Even beginners find that it's not too difficult to keep the shuttlecock or "bird" sailing back and forth over the net. It's a unique game in that it can be played fast or slow, hard or easy, inside or outside, by anyone with or without skill. More advanced players, however, find that badminton is one of the fastest and most active sports available. A good hard aerobic workout is not only possible, but is likely, with two good players competing in singles. The game has a range of speed greater than any other sport. From the softly touched drop shot to the hard-hitting smash that travels over 100 mph, it is a game that can adjust to any player's skill level.

The social-recreational opportunities that are found in playing doubles, along with the improvement of hand-eye coordination, would be the greatest benefits for most badminton participants. For the more advanced player there are many added physical benefits such as speed, agility, strength, endurance, and aerobic development that occur through regular participation.

TERMINOLOGY

Alley The 1½' extension on both sides of the court used in doubles play.

Attacking Clear An offensive shot that is hit over the opponent's reach, deep into the back court.

Back Alley Area between the back boundary line and the long service line in doubles.

Backhand The nonracket side of the body. If the player plays right handed, the left side is the backhand.

Balk Any deceptive movement which disconcerts an opponent before or during service.

Base The spot approximately in the center of the court to which a player tries to return after each shot.

Bird The commonly used term for shuttlecock or shuttle.

Clear A high, deep shot hit to the back of the opponent's court.

Court The area of play. For singles it is 44' x 17' and for doubles it is 44' x 20'.

Crosscourt Shots Shots hit diagonally from one side of the court to the other.

Double Hit Hitting the bird twice in succession on the same stroke. It is illegal.

Drive A hard-driven, horizontally hit shot that flys low over the net.

Drop Shot A shot which just clears the net and immediately starts to fall in the opponent's court.

Fault Any infraction of the rules, the penalty for which is the loss of the serve or the point.

First Service A term used in doubles to indicate that the team has both its serves.

Forehand The racket side of the body.

Game The number of points necessary to win the game. It consists of 15 points for men's singles and all doubles games, and 11 points for women's singles.

Hairpin Shot A dropshot made from below and close to the net. The flight of the bird is up and barely over the net, and then straight down. The name comes from the path of the bird's flight.

Hand-In Term used to show that the player serving still retains the service.

Hand-Out Term used to show that one player in doubles has lost his service.

Inning Term of service. Time during which a player or team holds the service.

Kill A fast, downward shot that usually cannot be returned.

Let A legitimate stoppage of play due to interference from outside the court. It can also be called after a rally if a player or team served or received in the wrong court (depending on who wins the rally). It is replayed.

Love A term that is more common to tennis which means there is no score. Love all means the score is 0-0.

Match A match is usually the best two out of three games.

Match Point The point which, if won by the serving team, ends the match.

Overhead A striking pattern where the point-of-contact is well above the head.

Passing Shot A shot that goes past your opponent to one side, as opposed to going over their head.

Poona Many historians believe that the original name for badminton was "poona," the name coming from Poona, India.

Rally The exchange of the bird back and forth over the net.

Receiver The player who receives the service.

Round-the-Head-Shot A shot using a forehand overhead striking motion where the point-of-contact is over the player's backhand shoulder.

Rush-the-Serve A quick move toward the net by the receiver after the serve has been struck. A very effective way, mostly in doubles, to put away a weak short serve.

Serve The act of putting the bird in play.

Service Court The area of the opponent's court where the bird must be delivered in serving.

Setting The method of extending the game by playing additional points when the score is tied at specific scores in a game. The player or team reaching the score first has the option of "setting."

Short Service Line The line 6½' from the net that serves must cross to be legal.

Shuttlecock The official name for the bird or shuttle which is usually made from nylon or goose feathers.

Side-in The side whose turn it is to serve.

Side-Out This occurs when the side that is serving loses the serve and becomes the receiving team.

Smash A hard overhead shot that is angled toward the floor in the opponent's court.

Stroke The action for striking the bird with the racket.

Underhand A stroke which is made when the bird is contacted below the level of the shoulders.

U.S.B.A. The United States Badminton Association. This is the badminton governing body in the U.S.A., previously known as the American Badminton Association.

Wood Shot A shot in which the bird is struck by the frame of the racket and not the strings. This is a legal shot.

EQUIPMENT

Provided the court is already marked, the only equipment needed to play is a net and standards, a racket, and a shuttlecock or "bird." Many gymnasium floors in elementary, middle schools, high schools, and colleges have permanent badminton floor markings, which greatly simplify things.

The playing court for doubles is the entire court which is indicated by the outside lines. The court measures 44 feet long by 20 feet wide. The singles court is also 44 feet long, but is only 17 feet wide. The service court for doubles is short and wide, whereas the service court for singles is longer and narrower (Figure 2.1). The alleys on both sides of the court are used in playing doubles but are out-of-bounds in singles, the same as tennis. The net is five feet one inch on the sides, and five feet in the center of the court.

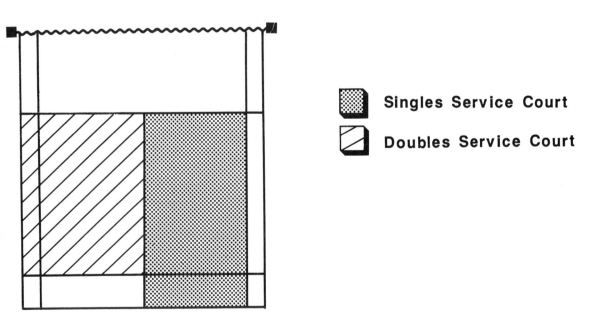

Singles Service Court

Doubles Service Court

Figure 2.1 Service Courts

The racket in badminton is very light and quite fragile. Most good rackets vary between 3.5 and 4.2 ounces. The best rackets were once made of laminated wood.

Although these are still considered excellent rackets, they are being replaced by composite metals in the same way that wooden tennis rackets were replaced. Many players prefer the lighter rackets for greater maneuverability. The weight of the racket should be evenly balanced or slightly lighter in the head.

Most rackets are strung with nylon. It is inexpensive, relatively immune to moisture, and is long lasting. These factors make it ideal for class use and beginners. Gut strings are more expensive, but because of the "feel" are preferred by many advanced players and tournament players. You should select your racket on the basis of balance, weight, type and size of grip, whipping action, and tension of strings, rather than looks.

The shuttlecock or shuttle is more commonly called the "bird." There are two kinds of birds that are used for most play; the nylon bird and the feather bird. The nylon birds are best suited for class and recreational play because they are inexpensive and do not require special care. They are quite durable and commonly last from three to six weeks in a class setting. There are several types of feather birds, and the price varies depending on the quality of the feathers and the construction of the bird. Most are made from goose feathers, and birds of this quality need to be kept in a moist environment to prevent them from drying out. These birds are used in most badminton tournaments because of their trueness and consistency of flight and response. They are, however, impractical for school programs because of their higher cost and due to the fact that after playing several games, the bird must be discarded.

RULES AND ETIQUETTE

The game is started by a toss or spinning the racket. The winning side has the option of choosing (a) service, (b) sides of the court, or (c) to receive. The losing side has the remaining options.

The scoring for most games is 15 points. In women's singles, 11 points constitute a game. It is permissible, by prior arrangement, to play only one game and for it to consist of 21 points. A scoring procedure that is unique to badminton is called "setting" the game. In a 15 point game, when the score is 13 all, the side which first reaches 13 has the option of "setting" the game to five, or when the score is 14 all, the side which first reached 14 has the option of "setting" the game to three. After the score is "set" it is called "love all," and the side which first scores five or three points, depending on the set, wins the game. In either case the "set" must be made before the next service is delivered after the score has reached 13 all or 14 all. In women's singles, where the game is 11 points, the game can be set to three after the score is tied at nine all, or set to two when the score is ten all. If the game is played to 21 points, then the setting is the same as for a 15 point game except that it now occurs at 19 and 20 points instead of 13 and 14.

You change ends of the court at the start of the second game, and also the start of the third, if it's needed. In the third game you change ends when the leading score reaches 8 in a 15 point game, six in an 11 point game, and 11 in a 21 point game. If you forget to change at the designated score, you still change when the mistake is realized, and the existing score stays the same.

In doubles play the first serve is always started from the right side of the court. The bird is served diagonally over the net to the opponent's right court. If the serving team wins the rally, then the server moves to the left side for the next serve. The partner of the serving or "in" team moves to the opposite side from the server as long as they continue to score points. When the "in" side makes a fault, the serve is then begun by their opponents on the right side of the court. On the first serve or first "inning," the serving team receives only one service, i.e., only one team member gets to serve. From then on, each team member is allowed to serve before the side is "out." Each time a point is scored, the players on the serving team exchange courts. This is the only time and situation that players on either team change courts during service. <u>Points are only scored by the serving team or while the side is "in."</u>

In <u>singles play</u> the rules are basically the same. The primary difference would be that when a point is scored, both the server and receiver change sides of the court. The <u>score</u> determines the side of the court in which the service starts each time. Therefore, when the server's score is even, the service would be from the right side and when it's odd, from the left side.

SERVING RULES AND REGULATIONS

1. No player can receive two consecutive services in the same game.

2. When a player <u>serves</u> out of turn or from the wrong service court and wins the rally, a "let" is called. The let is called only if the mistake is discovered before the next serve. When a player <u>receives</u> the serve in the wrong service court and the receiving side wins the rally, a let is called. If the rally is lost, the new playing position is not changed.

3. The server and receiver must stand within the serving and receiving court areas. In doubles, the receiver is the only one who can return the serve. Partners of the server and receiver may stand anywhere within the court.

4. Both the server and receiver must have both feet touching the floor until the serve is delivered.

5. If in serving the server misses the bird, there is no penalty and the serve can be taken over. If, however, the bird is touched, then it counts as an attempted serve.

6. At the point of contact on the serve, the head of the racket must clearly be below the server's <u>hand</u>. The bird must also be below the server's <u>waist</u> at the point of contact.

7. Unlike other net sports, a serve that touches the net and lands in the proper service court is good and must be played.

8. A serve that does not land in the proper service court, but lands wide, long, or short is considered a fault.

9. Any bird that lands on a <u>line</u>, whether in serving or during play, is <u>good</u>.

OTHER RULES AND REGULATIONS

1. The bird cannot be contacted until it has passed over the net. A player's stroke can, however, follow through over the net.

2. A player cannot touch any part of the net with the racket or body.

3. The bird must be clearly hit and cannot be carried on the racket or slung by the racket.

4. A player cannot hit the bird twice in succession, nor can two team members hit the bird twice in succession before it crosses the net.

5.   A player cannot contact the bird with any part of the body while it is in play. The bird can be hit with any part of the racket.

6.   A player cannot attempt to block the bird by placing the racket near the net. The player can, however, protect himself by placing the racket in front of his face.

ETIQUETTE

1.   Courtesy, as in tennis, should be based on good sportsmanship. You should never stoop to "needling" your opponent. If you think you might have committed a foul at the net, then you should call it on yourself.

2.   Balks in serving, movements or noise distractions that are done to obtain an advantage during the serve or during play, are unsportsmanlike and illegal.

3.   The serve should not be delivered until the receiver is obviously ready to play. If, however, the receiver attempts to return the bird, then the receiver is considered ready.

4.   Each side in singles or doubles is responsible for making calls on their side of the court. Your opponent should always be given the benefit-of-the-doubt on a close call, or on a shot that you or your teammate did not clearly see. This is basic to badminton and other sports, such as tennis and pickle-ball. Honesty and integrity are more important than winning the game.

FUNDAMENTALS OF THE GAME

Badminton is a sport in which it is easy to learn some basic skills but is very difficult to master. It can be fun for all ages, simply hitting the bird in a high arc back and forth over the net. To develop a high degree of skill, however, you must be prepared to practice as much as for golf and tennis. A skilled player has not only learned the strategy of the game, but has improved his/her hand-eye coordination, agility, balance, kinesthetic awareness, muscular strength, and aerobic fitness. Good players learn to anticipate shots which gives them the edge on reacting to the best position for the return shot. If you wanted to pick one phrase to characterize good badminton it would be "quick movement for good position."

Get Set to Move--Research studies of movement have shown that a badminton player uses more arm movement in one game than an average baseball pitcher does in a nine-inning baseball game. Also, that a top-flight badminton player runs more in one game than a running back or end does in a 60-minute football game (Armbruster 1979). As you develop your skill in badminton, you will be amazed at just how vigorous an evenly matched game can be.

GRIPPING THE RACKET

There are three basic types of grips used in badminton: forehand, backhand, and frying pan. The two grips used most of the time are the forehand and backhand. Some players find they can use the forehand grip for all shots since it often becomes difficult to change grips when the action is occurring rapidly. Most players, however, do change their thumb slightly on the backhand. The key for each player is the wrist action that can be generated for each stroke. Good wrist action permits more power and control with much less effort. This is totally contradictory to the tennis stroke that calls for an "arm swing" with a firm wrist. Since the shuttlecock is so lightweight, the wrist can remain cocked until the last moment before impact.

To assume the correct forehand grip, hold the racket by the shaft with the non-racket hand, keeping the racket face perpendicular to the court and pointing away from the body. Now simply shake hands with the grip of the racket. The index finger should be slightly separated from the other fingers and the "V" formed between the thumb and index finger should be directly on top of the handle (Figure 2.2). The grip should be loose to allow for maximum wrist action. A tight grip creates tension in the wrist muscles which restricts the movement of the wrist joint.

Many players use a slight variation for the backhand known as the "thumb-up" grip. From the forehand grip, turn the racket slightly to the right, for a right-handed player, and place the thumb along and parallel to the back side of the handle (Figure 2.2). This thumb position produces more power by providing for a more forceful wrist-snap from the backhand side. Another advantage of this grip is that by making this slight change, less body turn is required for many backhand strokes. Often when using the same grip for the forehand and backhand, a backhand stroke requires more arm and shoulder turn to provide the needed power. By using the thumb-up backhand grip and cocking the wrist and thumb toward the elbow, the required power can be provided without as much shoulder rotation.

The change from a forehand to a backhand grip can be made without the assistance of the non-racket hand. The turn is slight enough that by quickly manipulating the grip with the fingers, the "thumb-up" position is set.

The "frying pan" grip is used almost exclusively in doubles play, for service and service returns (Figure 2.2). The short serve is used mostly in doubles. When the serve is higher than desired, the frying pan grip is useful to allow the receiver to quickly punch it downward over the net.

forehand grip

Figure 2.2 Racket Grips

backhand grip

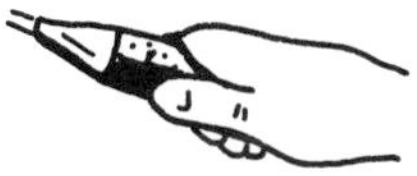

frying pan grip

BODY POSITION--STANCE, FOOTWORK, AND POSITION

It is essential that you start from and return to a "ready position" for each badminton shot. In singles this position is approximately the center of the court, and in doubles, the center of your side. As the term "ready position" indicates, you should be prepared to move in any direction. The knees should be slightly bent and the weight on the balls of the feet. The racket should be held comfortably away from the body at approximately head height and aligned across the center of the body. You should concentrate on the type of stroke made by your opponent and the direction of the bird, to enable you to move and set up as quickly as possible. For example, it's obvious if he/she hits a forceful stroke, aiming upward, that it's a deep clear shot and you should be moving toward the back of the court. A majority of the time your opponent will hit the bird as far away from you as possible. That is why a giant step toward developing badminton skill is improving your ability to recognize a shot, and then to quickly move and set up for the return.

When making a stroke in badminton, especially as a beginner, the body should be at a right angle to the net; i.e., on a forehand shot the non-racket side and foot should be nearer the net than the racket side. In this position, the body weight will be on the rear foot on the backswing and transferred to the front foot at impact and follow-through. Such a weight transfer adds power to the stroke and allows for better control. Movements made sharply to either side or backwards are most easily performed by pivoting on one leg in the direction of the intended movement, then utilizing short quick steps in a skipping or sliding motion. When moving backwards to return a clear shot, whenever possible, maneuver to a position that places the bird on the forehand side. This is <u>always</u> an easier stroke than a deep backhand. <u>Remember</u> that the last step before the bird is struck should always be taken with the <u>racket foot</u>. Good footwork is the <u>key</u>, for you can neither hit the bird efficiently nor control your opponent if you cannot get into position to hit.

STROKING THE BIRD

Badminton strokes may be classified according to the flight of the bird. They are performed with any combination of overhand and underhand, and forehand and backhand strokes. The resulting patterns and names are as follows:

(1) drive (2) clear (3) drop (4) smash

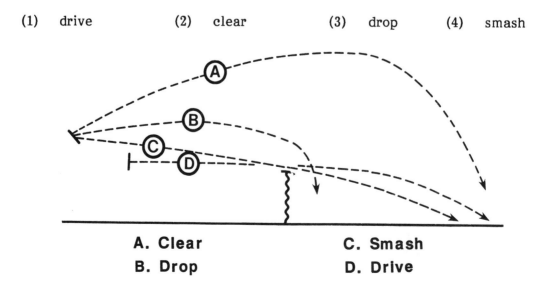

A. Clear **C. Smash**
B. Drop **D. Drive**

Figure 2.3 Stroke Patterns

FOREHAND OVERHEAD STROKES

When the bird is hit to the racket side, you should take a position for a forehand stroke. If the bird is high, then you have a choice of the four shots above (Figure 2.3). The preparation for the forehand should be the same for all shots except for the direction the racket head is pointing on the backswing. By using nearly the same motion for all forehand shots, the opponent cannot anticipate and thus prepare for it, until it's actually hit. This also applies to backhand strokes.

Body Position--As previously mentioned in Stance, Footwork, and Position, for either the forehand or backhand strokes, you should move to a sideways position to the net. For the forehand backswing the weight should be on the rear foot. The racket arm is bent at the elbow, and the hand is close to the shoulder with the wrist cocked.

Point of Contact--The stroke is then made by throwing the racket hand toward the desired point of contact with the bird. At this point the weight has shifted to the front foot and the wrist is snapped forward with a force which depends on the type of shot to be made; i.e., a smash would be very forceful, whereas, a drop shot would require little force. Since the racket and bird are both lightweight, the wrist action and resulting speed of the racket face, can impart excellent bird speed. To gain the maximum benefit, the wrist must remain cocked until just before the contact. This is especially true of the smash and clear shots that usually require power for greater effectiveness.

Follow-Through--The weight is forward and the arm and body move in the direction the bird is traveling. The arm and racket should continue to move down and around to the non-racket side as the rear foot is moved forward and even with the front foot. It is completed by facing the net in the "ready position."

The differences in the execution of the four shots are determined by the point-of-contact, angle of the racket face, and the amount of force used. The overhead clear shot is used to force the opponent deep in the back court (Figure 2.4). The point-of-contact is over the racket shoulder and nearly as high as you can reach with the racket. The bird should be contacted with the racket face moving upward just prior to the peak of its arc. The stroke requires a full swing and a forceful wrist break through the bird in an upward path.

The smash is a crisply hit shot that travels from high to low into the opponent's court (Figure 2.5). This is the glamour shot of badminton that abruptly ends many rallies. It can be hit with either a forehand or a backhand overhead, but is much easier and most often hit with a forehand. The body motion for the smash is quite similar to hitting a clear. The major difference being that the contact point is approximately 6 inches in front of the contact point for a clear. This allows you to meet the bird slightly in front of the racket shoulder and stroke it diagonally down. The closer to the net that you make the stroke, the greater the downward angle you would attempt. Proper execution of the smash requires full body extension and contacting the bird at the peak of your reach.

Figure 2.4 Overhead Clear   Figure 2.5 Smash

The overhead <u>drop shot</u> should begin with the same body and arm motion as the clear and the smash. As previously stated, it is important that you don't "give away" prematurely, the type and placement of your shots. The ideal drop shot will barely clear the net and drop sharply to the court. (Figure 2.3) The point-of-contact is slightly forward of the point for a clear. The force of the wrist break, and thus the racket speed, is quickly reduced just prior to contact in order to accommodate a landing point just over the net. This shot requires a lot of touch and good judgment on the force of the stroke. If it's hit badly, it will either not clear the net or be too long and allow the opponent an easy smash return.

The <u>drive</u> shot can be hit from the overhead position or from a lower side stroke position. The shot should be hit with good power. It is characterized by its path of travel, which is parallel to the court (see Figure 2.3). The drive is often used as a defensive shot when the smash or drop shot cannot be executed. It is used offensively when your opponent is out-of-position and you want to hit to the open court area. Occasionally, a well-placed drive shot; i.e., one hit directly to the opponent's head or body, can force a weak return and a good chance to put-it-away.

BACKHAND OVERHEAD STROKES

<u>Body Position</u>--When the bird is on the non-racket side, the backhand stroke is used. The racket-side is turned to the net with the weight on the rear foot. The arm is brought across the body so that your racket shoulder is pointing toward the net and the wrist is cocked.   At the completion of the backswing, the racket hand should be approximately at the neck level with the head of the racket angling down. On the foreswing the weight is shifted to the front foot and the upper arm is moved up and toward the bird with the elbow leading the forearm and racket.

<u>Contact Point</u>--As with the forehand stroke, the cocked wrist is released through the bird at contact. As the front leg straightens and the body extends up to meet the bird, the racket arm extends and the wrist snaps the racket face into the descending bird. The point-of-contact will depend on the type of shot to be hit. The bird position for a <u>clear</u> should be approximately even with the rear shoulder, whereas for the <u>drop shot</u> and <u>smash</u>, the bird should be between the head and front shoulder.

<u>Follow-Through</u>--The trunk should continue to rotate toward the net as the racket and arm travels in the direction of the shot. The racket arc completes its path down and

toward the racket side as you quickly reassume the "ready position." The same basic principles that are used for the smash, drop, drive, and clear shots on the forehand side are used for the backhand.

On both the backhand and forehand strokes the backswing must be started early enough to allow for a smooth, rhythmical, and unbroken swing. This is why good footwork is such a vital part of the game, since good positioning allows you sufficient time to "set up" and to make fundamentally sound strokes.

OTHER BADMINTON STROKES

Underhand Shots--The underhand stroke is used when the bird has dropped below the net. The shot can be hit with either a forehand or backhand stroke. The non-racket foot is forward supporting most of the weight for a forehand and the racket foot is forward for the backhand. The two shots that can be hit underhanded are the clear and the drop shot. The clear allows you to gain time to recover the center "ready position" by forcing your opponent to the back court. The underhand clear is similar to the long serve (see Serving). The underhand drop shot is often used to return a short serve or return a low shot. It is most successful when hit from your forecourt and stroked so that it passes within a foot of the net and quickly drops into the opponent's forecourt. The fundamentals of the stroke are almost the same as for the short serve. The underhand drop shot is an excellent alternative to the underhand clear. The cross-court drop shot forces the opponent to cover a wide area and to try and return a low shot. It is very effective when the opponent is moving to one side of the court and the shot is hit to the opposite court.

Round-the-Head Stroke--This is an overhead stroke that is contacted above the head and slightly to the non-racket side of the body. It is sometimes used in place of the backhand since greater velocity can be achieved with it. The execution of the stroke is similar to a smash except that the body and arm will bend more toward the position of the bird. The racket is swung in a half-circle arc above the non-racket shoulder, and the wrist should stay cocked until the instant just prior to contact.

SERVING

The serve is the underhand stroke that begins play. For a serve to be legal, the bird must be hit below the server's waist, and all of the racket head must be below the server's hand. There are several types of serves depending on how the bird is put into play. The out-of-hand serve is the easiest to learn, since as the name implies, the bird is virtually hit from the hand (Figure 2.6). The drop serve requires greater concentration and coordination because the bird is struck as it drops to the court (Figure 2.7). The backhand serve is a more advanced serve that is currently used by many tournament players.

Since the serve is basically a defensive shot, it is important for you to use as much deception as possible to try and keep the receiver off-balance. You should use the same serving motion for every serve regardless of the type of flight attempted. The three types of serves according to their flights are: (1) the short serve which should barely clear the net and land in the service court just beyond the short service line; (2) the long, high serve which should travel higher than the opponent's reach and land just inside the back of the service court; and (3) the drive serve that is hit up and hard into the receiver or into a desired area of the court.

Figure 2.6 Out-of-Hand Serve

Figure 2.7 Drop Serve

THE SERVING STROKE

Body Position--The starting point for the server in singles is about 2 paces behind the short service line and as close to the center line as possible. For doubles the server stands approximately one pace behind the short service line and slightly away from the center line. The serve is executed by facing the opponent and placing the non-racket foot forward. Most of the weight is placed on the forward foot. The bird is held by the feathers and is positioned out in front of the body below the waist. The backswing is a full arm movement with the wrist cocked and the racket pointing backward, parallel to the court. On the forward swing the arm is brought forward in a pendulum arc and the wrist remains cocked.

Contact Point--For the out-of-hand serve the bird is released just before contact is made. The wrist breaks forcefully at the contact point for the long serve, and not as forcefully or not at all for the short serve. The point of contact should be between the knee and the waist at about arm's length in front of the front foot. For the drop serve the bird is released at about shoulder height and slightly to the racket side of the front foot. Contact is made with the racket arm fully extended at approximately knee height. The wrist action is the same for both types of serves.

Follow-Through--It will depend on the type of stroking action that is used. The short serve will have very little follow-through, whereas the long serve will have trunk and shoulder rotation. Since the long serve requires a forceful wrist break, the arm will finish high and to the nonracket side. The trunk will rotate to the same side with all of the weight on the front foot. Immediately following the serve, you must return to a "ready position" for the return.

SERVING STRATEGY

For the short serve the bird should be stroked just hard enough to allow it to clear the net and fall in the service court. This requires considerable practice with the correct combination of wrist and arm action. If the serve is too high, it allows for an easy smash or drive return by your opponent. If it's too low, then it will not clear the net. As previously mentioned, it is important to utilize the same serving motion for the low, high, or drive serves. This prevents the opponent from anticipating a type of serve and thus gaining an advantageous position. A long serve to the opponent's backhand side can be very effective. This forces the opponent to return a shot from deep in the court and from his/her weaker side. In singles long serves are desirable most of the time.

48

Occasionally a combination of short and long serves is useful to keep your opponent off-balance and force him/her to return different types of shots. On the long serve, you should hit it high enough so that it drops straight down close to the back line. This forces your opponent deep, and because of the angle, is difficult to return. The short serve is used mostly in doubles play because of the service court area. There are times, however, when a long serve, or a drive serve hit directly at your opponent can be very effective in doubles.

SINGLES PLAYING STRATEGY

The basic strategy in singles is to maneuver your opponent up and back with drop and clear shots until you can force a weak return or an error. Smashes should be used when a return is high and short but very seldom from deep in your court. Often such a long smash allows your opponent to return with a drop shot for a winner.

Usually the best return of a short serve is a clear to your opponent's backhand side. There are times, however, when a well-placed drop shot can catch the opponent moving backwards expecting a clear return. Variation is essential on returns to prevent your opponent from anticipating your shots.

After every shot it is vital that you return to a good court position. You should avoid making shots that will not allow you time to get back to this position. On the other hand, if your opponent is moving to cover an open area of the court, hit the bird to the area that he/she is leaving. It is very difficult for someone to stop and reverse their direction and then play a good return.

Try to build your game with the ability to alternately execute drop shots and clear shots and then smashes and drives when the opportunity is right. Keep moving your opponent from front to rear and side to side until either an error is made or you are presented an easy put-away.

DOUBLES

Doubles is a fun, fast-paced game that requires not only all of the skills of singles, but also good teamwork. The major difference between doubles and singles is that someone is now covering half of the court, but which half? This will depend on what type of formation you and your partner decide on prior to the start of the game. Without a plan or formation you will find yourselves running over each other and/or have both of you in one area of the court and the remainder of the court open. The following two formations, side-by-side and front and back, are recommended for beginning badminton players (Figure 2.8). A combination formation can be used as you become more proficient.

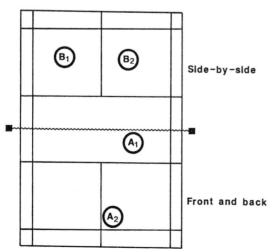

Side-by-side

Front and back

Figure 2.8 Doubles Formations

Side-by-side Formation--In this formation each partner is responsible for his/her half of the playing court. The base position for each player is midway between the center service line and the side boundary line of his/her side of the court, and approximately four feet behind the short service line. (Figure 2.9)

This formation is probably best suited for beginning players because it clearly defines the area that each partner has to cover. Another advantage is that the formation represents a good basic defensive position since there are no obvious open areas on the court. The primary disadvantage is in the type of coverage responsibility of each partner. It's advantageous to know your exact area to cover, but the problem is that in covering one-half of the court, you must cover 22 feet from the net to the rear boundary. It often becomes quite difficult to move forward and backwards to return drop shots and clears. Another disadvantage to playing side-by-side is the common indecision over who should play a shot that is hit near the center line.

Front-and-Back Formation--In this alignment one member covers the front of the court, and the other back half of the court. The base for the front partner should be in the center of the court just behind the short service line, and the back partner should start at the center line just in front of the rear doubles service line. (Figure 2.10) The front player is responsible for all drop shots and other shots that can be easily reached and potentially hit with a better return than the deeper partner. The back player takes all long shots and others that the front partner cannot easily reach. This alignment is well suited for mixed doubles because it's usually easier for the lady to cover the front shots and the man to cover the rear and hit the longer shots that require greater force. Another advantage of this formation is that it provides the opportunity for more offensive shots since both partners are in better positions for drop, smash, and drive returns. Other than the obvious problem of uncertainty as to who should take some shots, the major disadvantage is that the center alignment affords poor defense against smashes and drives that are near the sidelines.

Combination Formation--This alignment combines the best of the other two formations and is constantly changing according to the game situation. Basically it utilizes the side-by-side formation for defense and the front-and-back formation for offensive attack. The primary disadvantage is that it requires considerable game experience to play it effectively, and it becomes easier the more you play with the same partner.

Figure 2.9
Side-by-Side Formation

Figure 2.10
Front-and-Back Formation

50

DOUBLES PLAYING STRATEGY

When playing against a side-by-side formation, it is good strategy to hit a shot deep to the opponent's backcourt and hit a drop shot the next shot on the same side of the court. Against the front-and-back alignment, you should frequently hit shots down the side alleys.

Always work toward setting your partner up for a winning shot. Try to make shots that will require the type of return that allows your partner to hit his/her best shot. Conversely, avoid hitting shots that leave your partner open to smash returns or returns that force him/her to "scramble around" to retrieve them.

Rush short serves often by stepping forward as soon as the bird is served and keeping the racket face parallel to the net. If the bird is high enough, simply "punch it" at a downward angle. You will not need either power or a backswing for this shot.

Try to consistently make attacking shots, shots hit down. When you smash or drop from the backcourt, your partner should move forward to protect against drop shot returns. Make placements to the least obvious spots or to where they are more difficult to return such as the backhand side.

ERRORS AND CORRECTIONS

Illustrations of the <u>MOST COMMON ERROR</u>, and how to correct them

<u>ERROR</u>   <u>ILLUSTRATION</u>
Hitting bird too high or inconsistent
on short serves

too high over net on short serve

Figure 2.11

<u>RESULTS AND CORRECTION</u>
- This is often caused by using too much wrist-action in the swing resulting in the bird flying too high over the net, and an easy put-away return for the opponent.
- <u>Correct</u> this by keeping the wrist cocked throughout the swing. Bend the arm at the elbow and <u>sweep</u> or <u>push</u> the bird over the top of the net without a wrist break.

<u>ERROR</u>   <u>ILLUSTRATION</u>
Hitting bird high but only to
about half court on the long serve

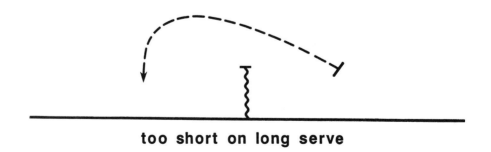

too short on long serve

Figure 2.12

<u>RESULTS AND CORRECTION</u>
- This type of short serve sets your opponent up for a smash return.
- Bring the racket face into the bird at an angle of approximately 45° to 60°, instead of 60° to 80°, which takes much greater force to send it deep

enough. Avoid swinging only with the arm since this makes it very difficult to generate enough force to hit the bird into the back of the court. Practice breaking the wrist and bringing the racket face into the bird at the proper angle.

ERROR
Improper court position in
relation to bird

ILLUSTRATION

Figure 2.13

RESULTS AND CORRECTION

- This usually results in drives and clears that are too high and too short, many shots that are not well placed, and drops that carry too far over the net.
- Good position is essential for good strokes. Try to get behind all shots, especially deep clears and serves. If you don't move quickly and set up behind these shots, the results are usually either a high short clear or a poorly placed shot.

ERROR
Inability to hit bird deep
into the opponent's court
and/or hit it hard on a smash

ILLUSTRATION

Figure 2.14

<u>RESULTS AND CORRECTION</u>

- The results are similar to #3 in that returns that allow your opponent to take the offensive places you in a weakened defensive position.
- To achieve power on a shot, the nonracket shoulder should be toward the net as the swing is begun. The sequential rotation of the trunk, shoulders, and finally arm and wrist break, are critical for a forceful stroke. The non-racket foot, and not the <u>racket foot</u>, should step forward on the stroke, and the wrist should break forcefully through the bird at contact.

OTHER PROBLEM AREAS

ERROR	RESULT	CORRECTION
1. Barely touching bird on long serve--probably caused by holding bird too long before dropping it, or not watching it in the beginning stage of serving.	Fault, opponent becomes server.	Bird should be dropped before the swing starts for the "drop serve." Drop the bird out in front of the body and <u>watch it</u> as you stroke it
2. Backhand clears that do not carry deep enough into the opponent's court.	Results in an excellent smash opportunity for your opponent.	It is essential to get a good shoulder turn with the racket foot forward. As with the forehand, yo start the swing with a forward weight shift, trunk and shoulder rotation, and finally a strong wrist break.
3. Serving to the same spot repeatedly.	Opponent can anticipate the serve and move to a better return position as soon as the bird is struck.	Develop <u>proficiency</u> in the long, short, and the drive serves. Keep your opponent guessing as to which serve is coming ar where it will be placed.
4. Allowing bird to drop too low before stroking it.	This results in a shot that is hit upward. A defensive shot that often allows your opponent to take the offensive.	On overhead smashes an drives, attempt to conta the bird as high as possible. The greater th downward angle you can hit, the better your chances of the opponent missing or hitting a wea defensive return.

ERROR	RESULT	CORRECTION
5. Same foot is forward and/or feet are together for all shots.	Often with beginners the nonracket foot is kept forward for forehand and backhand shots, or the feet are placed evenly for the backhand. Usually results in weakly hit shots from the backhand.	Practice turning sideways to the net, with the nonracket foot forward on the forehand, and the racket foot forward on the backhand.

IMPROVEMENT DRILLS AND GAMES

1. BASIC RACKET CONTROL DRILL (FOREHAND AND BACKHAND)
   - Attempt to keep the bird traveling upward by stroking it with the forehand stroke. Keep the bird "in play" by continually hitting it straight upward approximately 10-15 feet high.
   - Hit as many strokes as possible without missing.
   - Try to reduce the area that you must move to keep bird in flight. (Concentrate on hitting bird straight upward.)
   - Concentrate on watching bird and coordinating arm and wrist action.
   - Use same drill with backhand stroke.

2-5. SKILLS TEST ITEMS (DRILLS)
   - Practice each item, then have a partner score you on the test.
     2. Short Serve
     3. Long Serve
     4. Drop Shot
     5. Clear

6. SMASH DRILL
   - Two birds and four students per court
   - Two students on one end of the court setup the two students on the other end for smash returns.
   - Player one hits the bird high to player two who smashes the bird. Player two stays in the center of his/her half of the court. Players three and four do the same on the other half of the court.
   - There is no rallying. Players change roles after 10 smash attempts.

7. DRIVE RALLY DRILL
   - Two students take positions on each side of the net approximately five or six feet behind the short service line in the center of the court.
   - Put the bird in play with a drive serve and then attempt to drive the bird back and forth to each other's forehand.
   - Do not try to hit winners--try to hit it straight, horizontal, and to a spot that allows your partner to return it.
   - Try to increase the number of times the bird is struck during each rally.
   - Avoid hitting arcing shots; try to keep bird on a flat trajectory.
   - Vary drill by hitting forehand to backhand, and backhand to backhand.

8. DROP SHOT RALLY DRILL
   - Two students take a position on both sides of the net at the short service lines.
   - After putting the bird in play with a short serve, try to rally using drop shots only.

9. DROP SHOT GAME
   - This game is played between the short service lines, except that a short serve is used to begin each rally. The game is scored like singles and played like a singles game.
   - Any shot, after the serve, that goes past the short service line is out of court and counts as a fault.
   - This game develops "touch" for the short game in badminton.

10. CLEAR AND DROP COMBINATION DRILL
    - Student A stand just behind the short service line--Student B is across the net, midway between the short service line and the baseline.
    - Student A hits clears to Student B who returns, first with a drop and then a deep clear.
    - Student A continues to hit clears until student B has hit 20 total shots--players then rotate.

BADMINTON SKILLS TEST

GENERAL INFORMATION

The following test is designed for the beginning badminton player. It is designed to objectively assess ability in various situations.

1. French Short Serve
2. Drop Shot
3. French Clear
4. High Serve

I.   FRENCH SHORT SERVE

Purpose--To measure the player's ability to serve the short serve accurately and low into the opposite court.

Facilities/Equipment--A regulation badminton court properly marked (See Figure 2.15), regulation height badminton net, rope, racket, several shuttlecocks in good condition.

Directions--The student stands anywhere in the regulation right court for serving and serves 10 times into the opposite right service court. The shuttlecock must go under the rope placed 20 inches above the net and parallel to it and must otherwise be a legal serve. Repeat the described procedures in the left court. The student should aim toward the areas counting the higher point values (See Figure 2.15). A total of 20 short serves are attempted. Two practices on the right side only are allowed.

Scoring--Score each serve by the numerical value of the area in which it first lands (5, 4, 3, 2, 1). Shuttlecocks which land on a line will score the higher value. Illegal serves and serves which fail to go between the rope and net will score "0." The final score is the sum of 20 serves. Maximum score is 100.

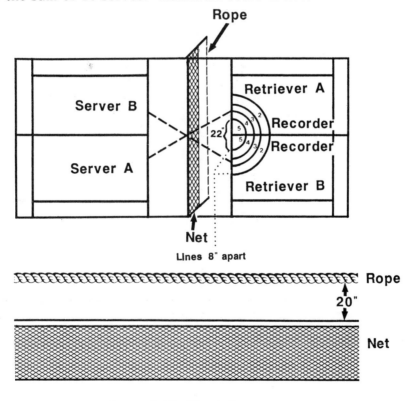

Figure 2.15 Short Serve

Scott, M. Gladys, Aileen Carpenter, Esther French, and Louise Kuhl: Achievement Examinations in Badminton, Research Quarterly, 12, 242-253, May 1941.

II. DROP SHOT

Purpose--To measure the player's ability to execute the drop shot.

Facilities/Equipment--A regulation badminton court properly marked (See Figure 2.16), regulation height badminton net, rope, racket, several shuttlecocks in good condition.

Directions--The student stands anywhere behind the short service line on the court opposite the target to receive 20 served shuttlecocks, which he will attempt to send back across the net, under the rope, using a drop shot. The short serve must be legal and go under the rope. Serves not meeting the criteria may be re-served. Otherwise, all serves are to be played by the student.

Scoring--Score each drop shot by the numerical value of the area in which it lands (5, 4, 3, 2, 1). Shuttlecocks that land on a line will score the higher value. Drop shots which go above the rope, out-of-bounds, or in the net will count "0." The final score is the sum of 20 drop shots. Maximum score is 100.

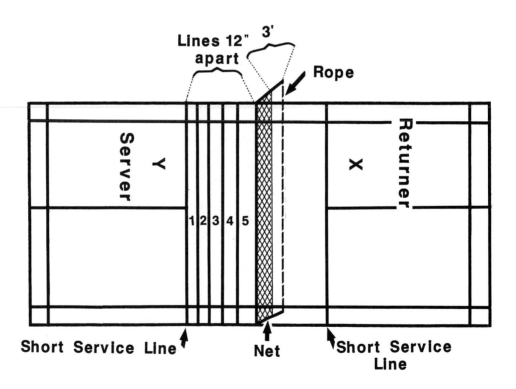

Figure 2.16 Drop Shot

III.   FRENCH CLEAR

Purpose--To measure the player's ability to execute the clear shot for distance and accuracy.

Facilities/Equipment--A regulation badminton court properly marked (See Figure 2.17), a rope, rackets, and shuttlecocks in good condition.

Directions--The student shall stand five feet behind the short service line on the court opposite the target and receive 20 shuttles, which he will attempt to send, by means of a clear stroke, <u>above the eight foot rope</u> so that the shuttle lands on the target. The server may stand anywhere behind the short service line and must serve the shuttle with enough force and height that it will carry beyond the short service line, above the student's head, and within one step in any direction of the student. A shuttle that is carried or slung counts "0." Two practices are allowed.

Scoring--Score each clear shot by the numerical value of the area in which it first lands. Shuttles which land on a line will score the higher value. Clears which fail to go over the rope or otherwise illegal according to badminton rules will count "0." The final score is the total of the values made by 20 shuttles. Maximum score is 100.

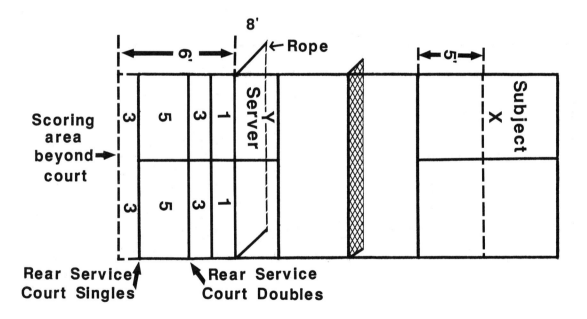

Figure 2.17   French Clear Test

French, Esther and Evelyn Stalter: Study of Skill Tests in Badminton for College Women, Research Quarterly, 20, 257-272, October 1949 (modified by ORU).

IV. HIGH SERVE

Purpose--To measure the player's ability to serve a high serve with distance and accuracy into the opposite court.

Facilities/Equipment--A regulation badminton court properly marked (See Figure 2.18), regulation height badminton net, racket, several shuttlecocks in good condition. A rope 8' high and 14' from the net is used to ensure proper height of the shuttlecock.

Directions--The student stands anywhere in the regulation right court for serving and serves 10 times into the opposite right service court for the singles game. The shuttlecock must be legally served. Repeat the described procedures in the left court. The student should aim toward the areas counting the higher point values (See Figure 2.18). A total of 20 high serves are attempted. Two practices on the right side only are allowed.

Scoring--Score each serve by the numerical value of the area in which it first lands (5, 3, 2, 1). Shuttlecocks which land on a line will score the higher value. Serves which are served illegally will score "0." The final score is the sum of 20 serves. Maximum score is 100.

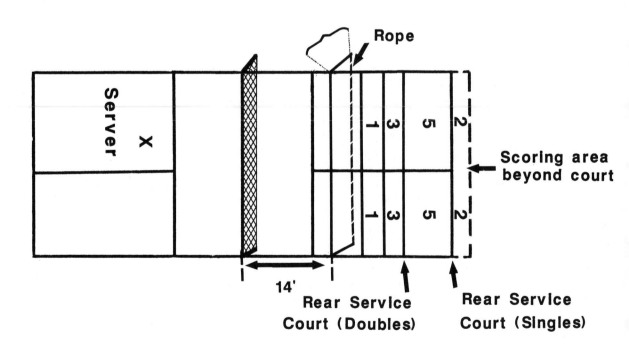

Figure 2.18 High Serve

Hutcheson, Sigrid: Activity Proficiency Program (New York: Syracuse University, 1977), p. 31.

BADMINTON
Skills Test Score Sheet

_____ Male/Female Date_____ Instructor _____
circle
Section _____ Day/Time

TEST ITEM		TRIALS	TOTAL SCORE	T-SCORE	RECORDER'S SIGNATURE

Short Serve   Right: __ __ __ __ __

Left: __ __ __ __ __

__ __ __ __ __   [   ] _____ _____

Drop Shot   __ __ __ __ __

__ __ __ __ __

__ __ __ __ __   [   ] _____ _____

Clear Test   __ __ __ __ __

__ __ __ __ __

__ __ __ __ __   [   ] _____ _____

High Serve   Right: __ __ __ __ __

Left: __ __ __ __ __

__ __ __ __ __   [   ] _____

Total _____   Average _____

Grade _____

BADMINTON SKILLS TEST -- NORMS

T-Score	Long Serve		Clear Shot		Short Serve		Drop Shot	
	Men	Women	Men	Women	Men	Women	Men	Women
76	69	57		99	84	76	86	78
74	67	56	100	96	81	73	84	76
72	65	54	98	93	78	70	82	74
70	63	52	96	90	75	67	80	72
68	62	50	94	87	72	64	78	70
66	60	48	92	84	69	61	76	68
64	58	47	90	81	66	58	74	66
62	56	45	88	78	63	55	72	64
60	55	43	86	75	60	52	70	62
58	53	41	84	72	57	49	68	60
56	51	40	82	69	54	46	66	58
54	49	38	80	66	51	43	64	56
52	48	36	78	63	48	40	62	54
50	46	34	76	60	45	37	60	52
48	44	30	74	57	42	34	58	50
46	42	29	72	54	39	31	56	48
44	41	27	70	51	36	28	54	46
42	39	25	68	48	33	25	52	44
40	37	23	66	45	30	22	50	42
38	35	22	64	42	27	19	48	40
36	34	20	62	39	24	16	46	38
34	32	18	60	36	21	13	44	36
32	30	16	58	33	18	10	42	34
30	29	15	56	30	15	8	40	32
28	27	13	54	27	12	6	38	30
26	25	11	52	24	9	4	36	28
24	24	9	50	21	6	2	34	26

ced 66

mediate 56

ning 46

BADMINTON
Skills Test Score Sheet

_____ Male/Female Date_____ Instructor _____
                           circle
_____ Section_____   Day/Time _____

		TRIALS	TOTAL SCORE	T-SCORE	RECORDER'S SIGNATURE

EST ITEM

Short Serve   Right: __ __ __ __ __

               Left: __ __ __ __ __
                         __ __ __ __ __   [   ]   _____   _____

Drop Shot   __ __ __ __ __
                         __ __ __ __ __
                         __ __ __ __ __   [   ]   _____   _____

Clear Test   __ __ __ __ __
                         __ __ __ __ __
                         __ __ __ __ __   [   ]   _____   _____

High Serve   Right: __ __ __ __ __
                         __ __ __ __ __
               Left: __ __ __ __ __
                         __ __ __ __ __   [   ]   _____
                                            Total   _____   Average _____
                                                            Grade   _____

BADMINTON SKILLS TEST -- NORMS

T-Score	Long Serve Men	Women	Clear Shot Men	Women	Short Serve Men	Women	Drop Shot Men	Women
76	69	57		99	84	76	86	78
74	67	56	100	96	81	73	84	76
72	65	54	98	93	78	70	82	74
70	63	52	96	90	75	67	80	72
68	62	50	94	87	72	64	78	70
66	60	48	92	84	69	61	76	68
64	58	47	90	81	66	58	74	66
62	56	45	88	78	63	55	72	64
60	55	43	86	75	60	52	70	62
58	53	41	84	72	57	49	68	60
56	51	40	82	69	54	46	66	58
54	49	38	80	66	51	43	64	56
52	48	36	78	63	48	40	62	54
50	46	34	76	60	45	37	60	52
48	44	30	74	57	42	34	58	50
46	42	29	72	54	39	31	56	48
44	41	27	70	51	36	28	54	46
42	39	25	68	48	33	25	52	44
40	37	23	66	45	30	22	50	42
38	35	22	64	42	27	19	48	40
36	34	20	62	39	24	16	46	38
34	32	18	60	36	21	13	44	36
32	30	16	58	33	18	10	42	34
30	29	15	56	30	15	8	40	32
28	27	13	54	27	12	6	38	30
26	25	11	52	24	9	4	36	28
24	24	9	50	21	6	2	34	26

ced 66

nediate 56

ning 46

BADMINTON
Skill Analysis Score Sheet
(20 points)

Name _____   Date _____

Class _____   Evaluated By _____

POINT GUIDE
2 points -- Student appears competent
1 point -- Occasionally correct or minor errors
0 points -- Needs more attention before ready to
            play

	POINTS SCORED		
	0	1	2
1. Gripping the Racket *1) Forehand/Backhand (thumb placement)	____	____	____
2. Maintaining Good <u>position</u> *1) Good footwork - stroke position 2) The "ready position" - court coverage	____	____	____
3. Overhead Shots *1) Forehand(position/contact/ follow-through) 2) Backhand(position/contact/ follow-through)	____	____	____
4. Underhand Shots *1) Position and best choices	____	____	____
5. Good <u>Serves</u> *1) Long serve technique 2) Short serve technique	____	____	____
6. The Basic Strokes *1) Drive (forehand & backhand) 2) Clear (forehand & backhand) 3) Drop 4) Smash	____	____	____
7. Wrist action *1) Proper timing-effective play	____	____	____
8. Basic Rules and Scoring *1) Singles and doubles	____	____	____
9. The "Doubles" Game *1) Formations 2) Strategy	____	____	____
10. Results *1) Badminton skill test results 2) General evaluation	____	____	____

* Points for evaluation

TOTAL SCORE _____

BADMINTON
Skill Analysis Score Sheet
(20 points)

Name _____   Date _____

Class _____   Evaluated By _____

POINT GUIDE

2 points -- Student appears competent
1 point -- Occasionally correct or minor errors
0 points -- Needs more attention before ready to
            play

	POINTS SCORED		
	0	1	2
1. Gripping the Racket	____	____	____
*1) Forehand/Backhand (thumb placement)			
2. Maintaining Good position	____	____	____
*1) Good footwork - stroke position			
2) The "ready position" - court coverage			
3. Overhead Shots	____	____	____
*1) Forehand(position/contact/ follow-through)			
2) Backhand(position/contact/ follow-through)			
4. Underhand Shots	____	____	____
*1) Position and best choices			
5. Good Serves	____	____	____
*1) Long serve technique			
2) Short serve technique			
6. The Basic Strokes	____	____	____
*1) Drive (forehand & backhand)			
2) Clear (forehand & backhand)			
3) Drop			
4) Smash			
7. Wrist action	____	____	____
*1) Proper timing-effective play			
8. Basic Rules and Scoring	____	____	____
*1) Singles and doubles			
9. The "Doubles" Game	____	____	____
*1) Formations			
2) Strategy			
10. Results	____	____	____
*1) Badminton skill test results			
2) General evaluation			

* Points for evaluation

TOTAL SCORE _____

CHAPTER 3

BOWLING

HISTORY

Bowling is one of the oldest and most widely played of the world's sports. Its history has been traced to Egypt and it has been played in dozens of forms, both indoors and outdoors, for more than seventy centuries. The earliest known example of bowling was discovered in the grave of an Egyptian child buried in 5200 B.C. Bowling implements found in the grave were similar to those used later in an English bowling game.

Although tenpins and the American Bowling Congress brought the world's heaviest concentration of organized, competitive bowling to the United States, some kind of bowling has existed at times in most areas of the world.

Bowling at pins probably originated in ancient Germany, not as a sport but as a religious ceremony. The game was called Kegling. It was used by religious leaders in the Middle Ages in Germany to determine if a person was leading a "good" life. A man would place his pin (kegel) at a distance and attempt to knock it down. A successful attempt would mean he was living a good life according to their religious principles.

Tenpins is an outgrowth of the European ninepin game that was brought to this country in the 1600's by Henrik Hudson and other early explorers who settled the northeastern seaboard. The tenth pin was added, according to popular legend, to circumvent a ruling in the 1840's by the Connecticut legislature which outlawed ninepins because of widespread gambling then rampant in the game.

Ula Maika, a game very similar to modern tenpins, flourished among the Polynesians in ancient times. The game involved rolling a stone 60 feet toward a target in a contest of accuracy.

Other bowling games which have flourished in various parts of the world include: lawn bowling, a still active English game which originated more than 800 years ago; other English games such as half bowls, skittles and ninepins; the Scotch favorite, curling-- "bowling on ice"--which was introduced in the 16th century; road bowling, an Irish game in which contestants roll stones from town to town; the Italian game of bocce, somewhat similar to lawn bowling.

Many of the early European games were played outdoors, some as lawn games and others using a narrow wooden board as a lane. These games often adjoined eating places or clubs and eventually either went indoors or were at least provided with a shelter at the players' end of the lane.

The early American bowling games were played outdoors, the most famous site being an area in New York City still known as Bowling Green. With the development of tenpins, the bowlers usually belonged to social clubs and carried on a lively rivalry in their games. The members of these clubs had much to do with the founding of ABC, American Bowling Congress, and provided the nucleus of the original membership.

BENEFITS

One of the reasons that bowling is such a popular game today is due to the fact that it does not require a high level of strength, power, speed, or endurance. The skills used in bowling are not too complicated for average performance and enjoyment. It can also be played in a relatively short period of time as compared to many other sports. Bowling is an activity that does not have to be highly competitive. A person can gain excellent social and psychological benefits simply by participation. It gives many people the opportunity to be around friends or family in a fun-filled atmosphere since the informal nature of the game allows for socializing and chit-chat between turns. League bowling also gives a person the unique opportunity to make new friends and gain greater social competence. It can also provide a good outlet for satisfying a desire to be more competitive in a sport.

TERMINOLOGY

ABC   American Bowling Congress (Men's organization)

AJBC   American Junior Bowling Congress (Boy's and Girls organization)

Alley   A bowling lane or a bowling center

All Events   The total of games bowled by an individual in one tournament, usually three games in the team event, three in doubles and three in singles. Sometimes the totals for the three events by the five members of one team.

Anchorman   Last bowler on a team. Usually the best bowler.

Approach   The area behind the foul line on which a player takes his steps prior to delivering the ball. At least 15' long.

Arrows   Sighting targets imbedded in the lane to help a player align the starting position on the approach with the ball path to the pocket.

Baby Split   The 2-7 or 3-10 split.

Backup   A ball that curves left to right for a right-hander and right to left for a left-hander.

Backswing   The path of the arm behind the body during the next to last step in the delivery.

Bedposts   The 7-10 split.

Blind   The score given for a missing bowler. The score is usually 90% of the person's average.

Blow   Failure to convert a spare. An error, miss.

Bridge   Distance between finger holes on the ball.

Brooklyn   A right-handed bowler hitting to the left of the head pin and a left-handed bowler hitting to the right of the head pin. Also called a crossover or Jersey.

Buck   A game under 200; i.e., A buck seventy-six is a 176 game.

Bucket   The 2-4-5-8 or 3-5-6-9 pin leaves.

Channel   Dropoff area on each side of the lane. Called the gutter.

Channel Ball   A ball rolled in the channel. A gutter ball.

Cherry   Knocking down the front pin of a spare and leaving the other pins standing. Also called a chop.

Chop   See Cherry.

Convert   When you successfully make your spare.

Count   The number of pins knocked down on the first ball.

Creeper   A ball rolled very slowly.

Crossover   See Brooklyn.

Curve   A ball that has a wide sweeping arc. The ball moves first toward the outside of the lane and then curves toward the inside.

Deuce   200 average or 200 game.

Dead Ball   A poorly rolled ball that has little or no spin or "action" and doesn't knock down as many pins as it should have. Also a ball delivered in an infraction of the rules, such as wrong lane or out of turn.

Dead Mark   A tenth frame strike or spare; no bonus is allowed.

Double   Two strikes in succession.

Double Pinochle Split   The 4-7-6-10.

Dutch 200   A game of exactly 200 made by alternating strikes and spares.

Error   Failure to convert a spare. Also called a blow, miss or open.

Fast Lane   A lane which holds down the hook. The lane is slippery and does not allow the ball the necessary coefficient of friction to track properly.

Fill Ball   Last ball strike in the tenth frame.

Foul   Touching or going beyond the foul line when delivering the ball.

Foul Line The line separating the approach and the lane.

Frame One-tenth of a game. Each large box on a scoresheet indicates a frame.

Graveyard A low scoring lane.

Grinder A powerful hook or curve ball.

Gutter See Channel.

Gutter Ball See Channel Ball.

Handicap A means of adjusting scores so as to place teams or individuals with varying degrees of skill on as equitable basis as possible for their competition against each other.

Head Pin The No. 1 Pin.

High Board An expanded or loose board in a lane which can cause a ball to veer from its path.

High Hit A ball hitting almost solidly on the head pin.

Holding Lane See fast lane.

Hook A left break ball for a right-hand bowler.

Kegler German word for bowler derived from the word kegel (pin).

Kickbacks Side partitions between lanes at the pit end.

King Pin The No. 5 pin.

Lane The sixty foot area between the foul line and the head pin.

Lead Off The first bowler in a team lineup.

Leave The pins that remain standing after the first ball delivery.

Light Hit A ball that barely hits the pocket.

Line A game of ten frames. Also refers to the path a ball travels.

Lofting Tossing the ball far out beyond the foul line. Normally caused by a late release.

Mark Getting a strike or spare.

Miss Failure to convert a spare leave. Also called a blow or error.

Mixer A ball which hits the pins lightly, causing the pins to ricochet, usually results in a strike.

Nose Hit A ball that hits full on the head pin. Also called a high hit.

Open A frame in which the player fails to strike or spare.

Perfect Game A 300 score. Strikes in all ten frames. Twelve consecutive strikes.

Pin The object which the bowler is trying to knock down.

Pin Bowler A bowler who aims (visually) at the pin when delivering the ball.

Pin Deck The area where the pins are placed.

Pitch The angle at which the finger holes are bored in a ball.

Pocket The area between the 1-3 pins for a right-hander and the area between the 1-2 pins for the left-hander.

Railroad Term associated with the 4-6 and 7-10 splits. Also called a double pinochle split.

Return The track or rails on which the ball rolls back to a player.

Sandbagging Deliberately holding down a league average in order to receive an advantage of a higher handicap in league or tournament play.

Scratch Bowler A bowler who has no handicap.

Series Usually three games or more in a league or tournament.

Sleeper A pin hidden behind another.

Sour Apple The 5-7 pin leave.

Span Distance between thumb and finger holes.

Spare Knocking down all ten pins with two balls in a frame.

Split Combinations of pins left standing after first delivery with a pin down immediately ahead or between them. The headpin must be down to receive a split.

Spot Bowler A bowler who uses the finders or spots as his/her primary target. Opposite of pin bowler.

Strike Knocking down all the pins with the first ball of a frame.

Strike Out To get three strikes in the tenth and final frame.

Tap A pin left standing on an apparent good strike hit.

Thin Hit See light hit.

Turkey Three consecutive strikes.

Washout The 1-2-4-10 leave for a right-hander; the 1-3-6-7 leave for a left hander.

Water Ball A ball delivered poorly.

WIBC Women's International Bowling Congress.

Working Ball A ball with much spin action which drives into the pocket. Also called a mixer.

RULES AND ETIQUETTE

Official bowling competition in the United States is governed by the American Bowling Congress (ABC). The following is a summary of some of the official rules and regulations as established by the ABC.

LANES AND EQUIPMENT

1. The bowling lane must be 60 feet from the foul line to the center of the 1-pin. The lane width must be a minimum of 41 inches and cannot exceed 42 inches. (See Figure 3.1).

2. A bowling ball cannot exceed 27 inches in diameter and weigh more than 16 pounds.

3. The height of the pins must be 15 inches.

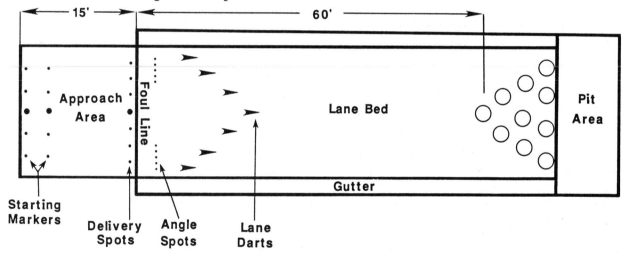

Figure 3.1 Lane Diagram

SCORING

1. The game of bowling shall consist of ten frames. Each player shall bowl two balls in each of the first nine frames except when a strike is made. A player who scores a strike in the tenth frame shall deliver three balls. The player receives a one ball bonus for a spare and a two ball bonus for a strike.

LEGAL DELIVERY

1. A ball is legally delivered when it leaves the bowler's possession and crosses the foul line into playing territory.

2. A bowling ball must be delivered entirely by manual means and shall not incorporate any device either in the ball or affixed to it which is either detached at time of delivery or is a moving part in the ball during delivery. Any person who has had his hand or major portion thereof amputated may use special equipment to aid in grasping and delivering the ball providing the special equipment is in lieu of the amputee's hand.

LEGAL PINFALL

Every ball delivered by the player shall count unless declared a dead ball. Pins must then be respotted.

1. Pins which are knocked down by another pin or pins rebounding in play from the side partition, rear cushion, or sweep bar when they are at rest on the pin deck prior to sweeping dead wood are counted as pins down.

2. If when rolling at a full setup or in order to make a spare, it is discovered immediately after the ball has been delivered that one or more pins are improperly set, although not missing, the ball and resulting pinfall shall be counted. It is each player's responsibility to determine if the setup is correct. The bowler shall insist that any pins incorrectly set be reported before delivering his ball, otherwise it is implied that the setup is satisfactory. No change in the position of any pins which are left standing can be made after the previous delivery in order to make a spare, unless the pin setter has moved or misplaced any pin after the previous delivery and prior to the bowling of the next ball.

3. Pins which are knocked down or displaced by a fair ball, and remain lying on the lane or in the gutters, or which lean so as to touch the kickbacks or side partitions are termed dead wood, counted as pins down, and must be removed before the next ball is bowled.

4. If a bowler knowingly makes a legal delivery while there is dead wood on the lane or in the gutters, and his ball comes in contact with such dead wood before leaving the lane surface, then the bowler shall receive a score of zero for that delivery.

ILLEGAL-PINFALL

When any of the following incidents occur the ball counts as a ball rolled, but pins knocked down shall not count:

1. When pins are knocked down or displaced by a ball which leaves the lane before reaching the pins.

2. When a ball rebounds from the rear cushion.

3. When pins come in contact with the body, arms, or legs of a human pinsetter and rebound.

4. A standing pin which falls when it is touched by mechanical pinsetting equipment, or when dead wood is removed, or is knocked down by a human

pinsetter, shall not count and must be replaced on the pinspot inscribed on the pin deck where it originally stood before delivery of the ball.

5. A pin which is bowled off the lane, rebounds, and remains standing on the lane must be counted as a pin standing.

6. If in delivering the ball a foul is committed, any pins knocked down by such delivery shall not be counted.

DEAD BALL

A ball shall be declared dead if any of the following occur, in which case the ball shall not count, the pins must be respotted after the cause for declaring such dead ball has been removed, and player shall be required to rebowl:

1. If, after the player delivers his ball and attention is immediately called to the fact that one or more pins were missing from the setup.

2. When a human pinsetter removes or interferes with any pin or pins before they stop rolling or before the ball reaches the pins.

3. When a player bowls on the wrong lane or out of turn.

4. When a player is interfered with by a pinsetter, another bowler, a spectator, or moving object as the ball is being delivered and before delivery is completed, player must then and there accept the resulting pinfall or demand that the pins be respotted.

5. When any pins at which he is bowling are moved or knocked down in any manner, as the player is delivering the ball and before the ball reaches the pins.

6. When a player's ball comes in contact with any foreign obstacle.

FOULS

1. If the bowler or any part of his body touches or goes past the foul line and touches any part of the bowling lane during or after the delivery, it is a foul. Touching a wall, post, or any other structure beyond the foul line also constitutes a foul.

2. A foul counts as a ball rolled, but any pins that are knocked down do not count. If the foul occurs on the first ball, the pins are reset and the bowler bowls his/her second ball. If all the pins are knocked down on the second ball, then the bowler scores a spare and not a strike.

3. If a bowler fouls on the second ball in a frame, then the score for that frame is based only on the first ball. If a foul occurs on both balls, then the score would be zero unless he/she was working on a strike or spare from the previous frame.

ETIQUETTE

Proper conduct, sportsmanship, consideration of others, and plain common sense are important to succeed and to enjoy bowling. The following rules of etiquette should be practiced by bowlers:

1. Be prepared to take your regular turn on the lanes.

2. Generally, the person on the right bowls first:
   --don't step on the approach until right of way is determined.
   --don't wait for bowlers several lanes away.
   --the spare bowler will go first.

3. Take your time, but don't waste time by pausing to wait until everyone else is off the approaches.

4. Stay on your own approach at all times. Step back off the approach after making each delivery.

5. Do not "double ball" (using two different balls during a game).

6. Do not use another player's equipment without permission.

7. Good bowling requires concentration. When a player is ready to bowl, give the bowler the courtesy of making the shot without interference. Save the kidding for the bench or the locker room.

8. Be ready to bowl, but wait until the pinsetting machine has completed its cycle and the sweep bar is raised before rolling the ball.

9. Respect the equipment. Getting the ball out on the lane is good, but lofting is bad for the lane, and it won't help your game. Wear regulation shoes so they don't ruin the approach and allow you to slide.

10. Play the game to win, but be gracious if you are on the short end of the score at the end of the game.

11. Control your emotions on the lanes. Kicking the ball rack or using foul language is always out of place.

12. Do not tell others about their errors, concentrate on your own game.

13. Observe common courtesy toward other bowlers at all times. This favor will also be returned to you, which helps makes bowling enjoyable for everyone.

EQUIPMENT

One of the reasons bowling is such a popular lifetime sport is because it does not require specialized expensive equipment to begin bowling. Bowling alleys provide balls and shoes for a minimal rental fee. Standards for lanes, pins, and balls are certified by the ABC, therefore, eliminating those decisions by the beginning bowler. As you become more skilled and begin to bowl on a regular basis, perhaps in a league, then personalized equipment can be purchased at a reasonable cost.

You don't need a uniform or any special clothing to bowl. Your main concern should be to dress for comfort, yet allow for freedom of movement. Bowling shoes are designed to assist you in your approach and delivery. For the right-handed bowler, the sole of the left shoe is leather to allow you to slide on the last step. The sole of the right shoe is made of rubber for better traction throughout the approach. Bowling alleys will usually have the correct sizes and types of shoes for right- or left-handed bowlers.

Selection of a <u>bowling ball</u> is very important. Men will usually select a ball weighing 15 or 16 pounds, whereas women often choose one that weighs between 12 and 14 pounds. Eight to 10 pound balls are available for young people and those with physical handicaps. The most important factor in choosing a ball is your ability to grip and swing it without excessive strain. Select a ball that fits your hand properly and one that you can deliver without dropping. The finger holes should not be so tight that the fingers stick, nor should they be so loose that it causes the ball to drop. If you are consistently dropping the ball at the foul line, then you probably have selected a ball that is too heavy.

All ABC-approved pins are 15 inches high. The pins are set up on the end of the lane, three feet from the front of the head pin (#1) to the pit area. They are spaced 12 inches apart. Pins are arranged in four rows and are numbered from left to right (Figure 3.2).

Bowling lane specifications are standardized by the ABC. The lane is divided into several areas. These areas and dimensions are shown in (Figure 3.1).

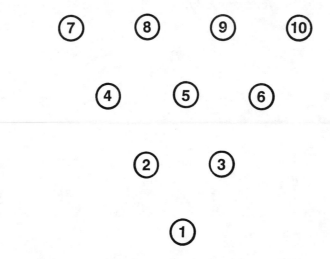

Figure 3.2 Pin Placement and Numbers

FUNDAMENTALS OF THE GAME

It appears to be so easy--simply rolling a large ball down a wooden lane to knock down a group of pins in a triangular formation. But bowling, as you soon learn, is a very deceptive game. It is basically a sport requiring finesse rather than power. Of course, many bowlers do send the ball down the alley with great speed and simply "shatter" the pins in all directions. However, the consistent scorers are the ones who are smooth and bowl with controlled speed.

As you observe bowlers, you will find that there is no perfect style or form. However, there are several basic fundamentals that you must learn to become successful. Once these fundamentals are learned only slight modifications will need to be made to help you improve.

BALL RETRIEVAL

The most important consideration in retrieving your ball is to avoid getting your hand or hands caught between two balls. Remove the ball with both hands. Place the hands on opposite sides of the ball, away from incoming balls. Avoid picking up the ball by inserting the fingers in the holes. The fingers should be inserted only after taking your bowling stance.

THE POSITION AND STANCE

In order to develop skill in bowling, you need to first establish a consistent starting position and a comfortable stance. To find a good starting position the bowler should stand slightly in front of the foul line facing the approach area. He should then take $4\frac{1}{2}$ steps forward and mark the spot. Starting from this spot the bowler should take several practice approaches toward the foul line and adjust the spot according to the results.

The right-handed bowler should be to the right of the center dot. The right foot should line up directly above the board that has the second dot to the right of the center. This places the bowler in line with the second arrow in the lane, the most common strike line. The left-handed bowler should be to the left of the center dot, lining up the left foot with the second dot to the left of center.

The stance should be comfortable and natural. This includes your body position and the position in which you hold the ball at the start of the approach. Stances often vary among bowlers (Figure 3.3), yet there are a few keys that should be observed.

1. Keep the shoulders square, level, and parallel to the foul line.
2. Keep both hands under the ball and keep the elbows in close to your sides.
3. The wrist should be firm and straight, not bent backward or cupped.
4. The knees should be bent slightly with the left foot slightly forward for a right-handed bowler; the right foot slightly forward for a left-handed bowler.
5. The initial movement should be the body weight transfer to the front foot (for the 4-step approach).

Figure 3.3 The Stance

THE GRIP

Beginning bowlers often have the problem of finding a ball of proper weight that fits their hand. As a simple rule, you need to bowl with the heaviest ball that you can deliver without undue effort. Make a trial swing with a ball and if you can control it throughout, then you can bowl with it. Equally as important as the ball weight is the size of the span. The span is the distance from the inside edge of the thumb hole to the inside edge of the finger holes. It's essential that the grip feel natural and comfortable. There should not be any strain on the thumb, fingers, or wrist. Most bowlers use one of three basic grips; conventional, fingertip, or semi-fingertip.

The conventional grip should be used by all beginning bowlers (Figure 3.4). To check for this grip you should insert the thumb all the way into the ball, then stretch the fingers out across the finger holes. The crease of the second joint should extend about one-fourth inch past the nearest edge of the finger holes. If the joints do not reach the edge, the span is too wide. If they go more than halfway past the center of the holes, the span is too narrow. This grip gives you a more secure feeling that you have complete control of the ball. Though it does not allow for good lifting action, it does provide you with the ability to hook the ball.

The fingertip and semi-fingertip grips are designed so that you can apply more hook lift with the fingers at the instant of release. The span is wider thus allowing the fingers a greater "pull," or "lift" on the finger holes. This puts more spin and thus a greater hook on the ball (See Figure 3.4).

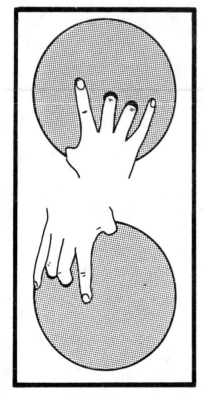 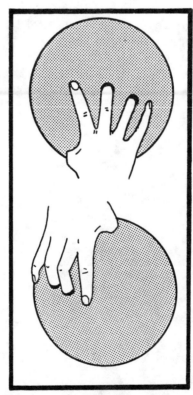 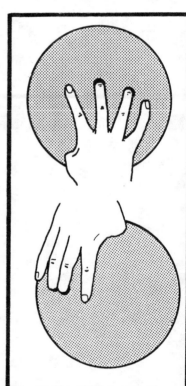

Conventional Grip   **Semifingertip Grip**   **Fingertip Grip**

Figure 3.4 The Grips

THE APPROACH

Your approach is how you advance toward the foul line to deliver the ball. There are three basic approaches: the three, four, and five step approaches. The three step approach is not recommended because it becomes too difficult to coordinate the pendulum swing in only three steps. The four step approach is easier to master and is strongly recommended. This approach allows for the most natural body movement, and thus tends to increase accuracy and reduce fatigue. The coordination of the foot and arm action in the delivery is one of the most important parts of the mechanics of bowling. The total movement begins with a short step with the rear foot (remember the weight is already on the front foot). Following this "shuffle step" the second and third steps are evenly spaced and progressively faster. The fourth step is more a slide with the toe pointing straight down the lane and finishing within 6 inches of the foul line.

The following mechanics should be learned and practiced until they become smooth and rhythmical:

1. Push Away--As the first step begins, the ball is pushed away from the body in a forward and downward motion.

2. Downswing--On the second step the free hand is released from the ball and is then used for balance. The ball should drop naturally to a position near the leg while the wrist remains firm and straight.

3. Backswing--On the third step the continuing pendulum motion of the ball should carry the ball straight backwards behind the body. The position of the ball at the completion of the backswing should not be higher than the hip. The body should be leaning forward and the knees slightly bent thus causing an increase in speed toward the foul line.

4. Forward Swing--On the fourth step (the "step-slide" with the front foot) the ball is brought forward with the continuous pendulum motion in a straight line toward the foul line. The ball and the foot should reach the foul line spot at the same time.

    --Remember at the completion of the swing, the weight should be on the front foot, the shoulders should be parallel to the foul line, the front foot should be pointed straight down the lane, the body should be leaning forward, and the eyes should focus on the spot or line you intend the ball to travel. (Figure 3.5)

The approach must be practiced until you can develop timing between the steps and the ball swing. It is a common problem in the early learning stages to have the slide foot arrive ahead of the ball. This often causes "dropping the ball" behind the foul line instead of delivering it out on the lane. The problem can be corrected through repeated practice geared toward a normal pendulum backswing, and good balance throughout the approach. Attempt to deliver the ball in perfect balance, as if you are posing for a picture.

The five step approach is very similar to the four step approach. The only real difference is that the first step is with the left foot for right-handed bowlers. The ball is not pushed away until the start of the forward movement of the second step as in the four-step approach.

Figure 3.5 The Approach

RELEASE AND FOLLOW-THROUGH

The ball is released by the thumb first from approximately a ten o'clock position. The wrist should remain firm as the thumb comes out and then the fingers lift the ball over the foul line. This lifting action gives the ball the rotation needed for a hook ball.

As the ball is released the body weight should be balanced over the front foot. The release hand and arm should continue upward in line with your target and should finish in front of the onside shoulder. Let your pose show you as balanced and relaxed with a bend at the knees and very little bend at the hips (Figure 3.6).

Figure 3.6 Follow-Through

DELIVERY STYLES

The delivery refers to the path the ball takes as it travels down the lane toward the pins. There are basically four styles of delivery: the straight ball, the hook, the curve, and the backup (Figure 3.7). Many beginning bowlers find it easier to roll the straight ball. This style, however, does not provide for good pin action, and because of the poor angle to the 1-3 pocket, is not a good strike ball. The hook ball is the most effective for producing strikes and is the style used by most good bowlers.

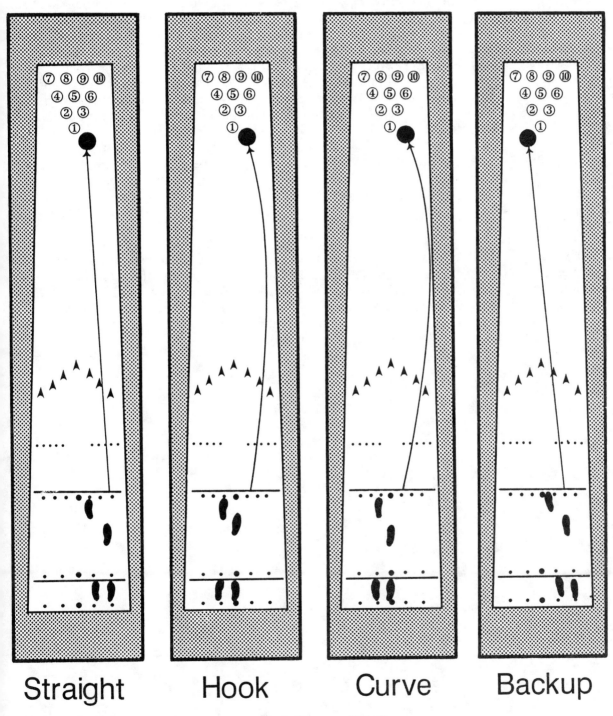

Figure 3.7 Types of Delivery

Straight Ball--It is delivered with the thumb in a 12 o'clock position and the fingers at the 6 o'clock position. Often bowlers with weak wrists believe they can support the ball better with this hand alignment. The most common approach for right-handed bowlers is from the right corner of the lane with the ball directed diagonally across the lane between the 1 and 3 pins. The path of the ball generally passes over the second arrow from the right (Figure 3.8).

Hook Ball--This is the best delivery to learn because it generates more pin action, thereby producing more strikes. Beginners often avoid this delivery, yet it's not really difficult to master. The ball should be held as though you were shaking hands. This places the thumb at approximately the 10 o'clock position and the ring finger at the 4 o'clock position. The hook action results from the lifting action of the fingers from their position beneath the ball. The wrist is kept straight and the fingers remain in the same position throughout the approach. The ball passes over the second arrow from the right, for right-handed bowlers, rolls straight down the lane and in the final 10-15 feet hooks into the 1-3 pocket (Figure 3.8).

Curve Ball--If the hand is pulled up sharply as the ball is released, the spin will be exaggerated and a hook ball will become a curve ball. This spinning motion provides for good pin action, but is more difficult to control. The ball is rolled in the same manner as the hook. The path usually carries it over the first arrow and then breaks towards the 1-3 pocket (Figure 3.8).

Backup Ball--This style is also known as the reverse hook. It is usually the result of either a faulty delivery or a natural tendency to roll a ball that curves the opposite direction. Often girls who have weak wrists will initially roll the backup ball as they begin bowling. For a right-handed bowler, the ball will move down the left hand side of the lane and curve into the 1-2 pocket. This style is not recommended and when continued it is almost always inconsistent (Figure 3.8).

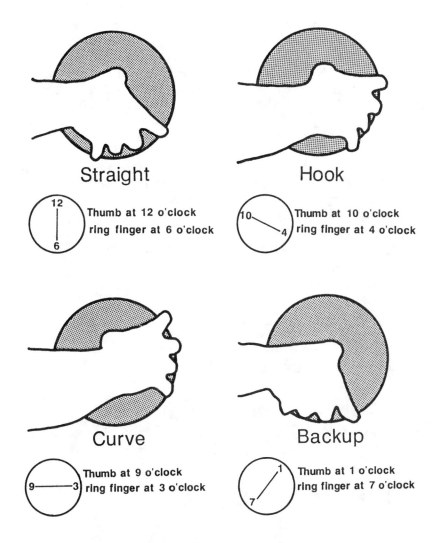

Figure 3.8 Hand Positions

Straight
Thumb at 12 o'clock
ring finger at 6 o'clock

Hook
Thumb at 10 o'clock
ring finger at 4 o'clock

Curve
Thumb at 9 o'clock
ring finger at 3 o'clock

Backup
Thumb at 1 o'clock
ring finger at 7 o'clock

AIMING

There are two targets to aim at in bowling, spots and pins. Most good bowlers roll for a spot in the lane. Beginners, however, will usually aim directly at the pins, especially if they are self-taught bowlers. A spot bowler uses the arrow as a guide to the 1-3 pocket. A hook bowler will generally use the second arrow from the gutter as the target spot. Straight bowlers use the same arrow but from more of an angle. Some bowlers prefer to use other spots as guides to aim for, yet they still must cross the second arrow to be on a strike course (Figure 3.7).

Pin bowling is simply aiming directly at the pins. This is more of an "instinctive" style of aiming and requires good concentration on the head pin throughout the approach.

Most beginners will achieve greater bowling success if they will practice the spot method of aiming. It must, however, be given a fair trial in order to master the technique. It is easier to consistently hit a target 16 feet away then one 60 feet away.

SPARE TECHNIQUES

The pins that remain standing after you have bowled your first ball are called spares. Your ability to convert spares (knock them down), and to continually improve at converting them, will be a key factor in how much you can improve your bowling average.

As a general rule for picking up spares, use the best angle and maximum use of the alley. With this in mind you would start on the side of the approach opposite the remaining pins. This would give you more lane width and a better angle. Always attempt to hit the pin that is nearest to you, aiming the ball so that it will directly strike as many pins as possible. Use the same delivery style on the second ball as you did on the first ball. The only changes you should make might be to adjust your starting position or your point of aim.

Remember there are very few spares that cannot be knocked down by a well-placed second ball. An average bowler can learn to convert them nearly 90 percent of the time. Take the time to figure out the best angle for converting different types of spares. Practice your spot bowling for spares and watch other bowlers' spare attempts to give you a better understanding of the pin action of various hits. Consider that a 180 or 190 score is within reason without making a single strike (Figure 3.9).

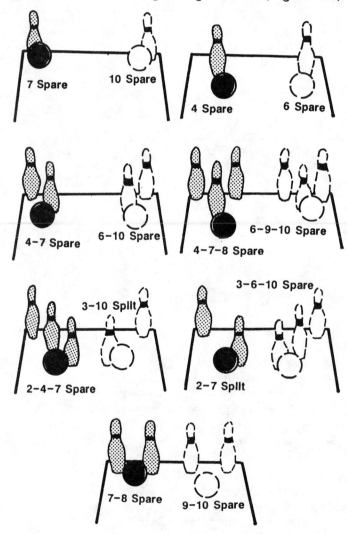

Figure 3.9 Converting Spares

SCORING

A game consists of ten frames. You roll two balls each frame unless you get a strike (X). In case of a strike, you would roll only one unless it occurs in the 10th frame. If you knock down all the pins with the two balls, you get credit for a spare (/). If you fail to knock down all the pins with the two balls you score it as a miss (-). Under certain circumstances you mark down a split (0). A split which is converted becomes a spare and is marked like this (∅).

Let's look at a game as it is scored frame by frame:

FIRST FRAME--You roll two balls and knock down a total of seven pins so you mark that number in the first frame and a (-) in the box to indicate the miss or error.

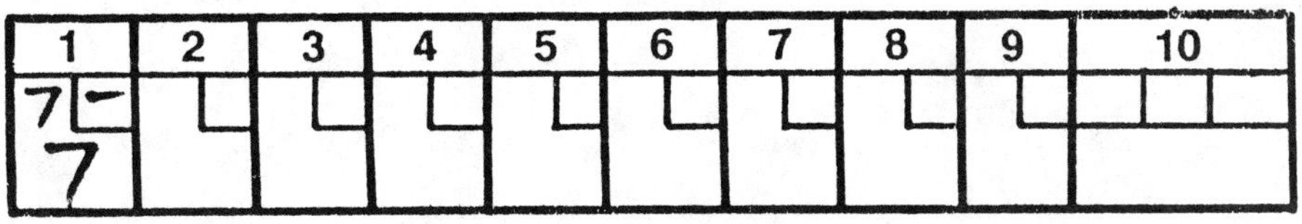

1	2	3	4	5	6	7	8	9	10
7 -									
7									

Figure 3.10

SECOND FRAME--On your first ball, you knock down all but the 7 and 10 pins. Circle the 8 to show the split. With your second ball you take out the 10 pin, giving you nine for the frame and a total of 16 for the first two frames. Put 1 in the box to show you knocked down one pin.

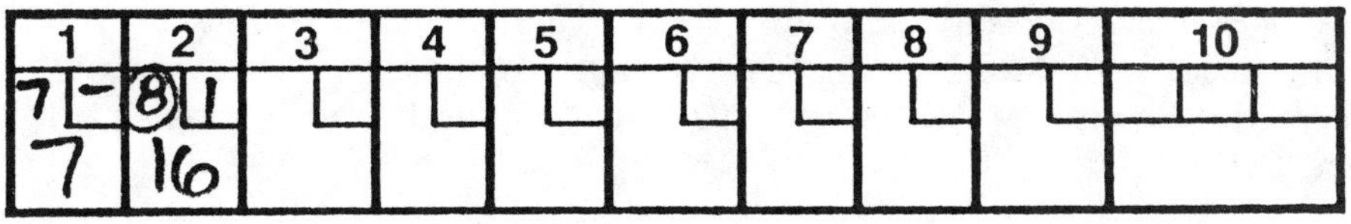

1	2	3	4	5	6	7	8	9	10
7 -	⑧ 1								
7	16								

Figure 3.11

THIRD FRAME--This time you make your spare. Your first ball leaves only the 5 and 8 pins and you knock both down with the second ball. Put a (/) in the box but do not mark any score for the third frame. Having spared, your first ball's total in the next frame will be added to your score for the first three frames.

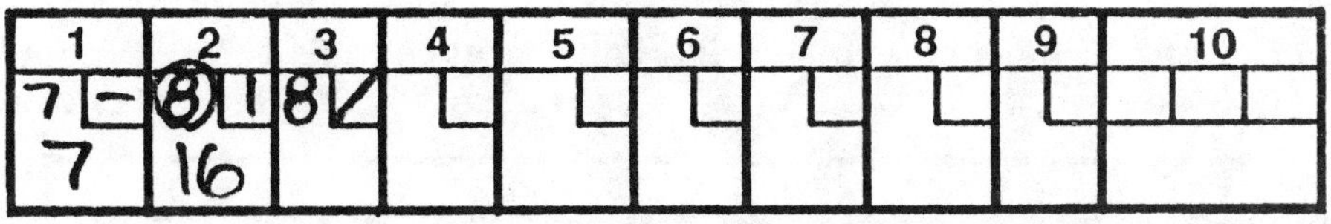

1	2	3	4	5	6	7	8	9	10
7 -	⑧ 1	8 /							
7	16								

Figure 3.12

FOURTH FRAME--You knock down seven pins with your first ball. Add 17 to your
second frame total (ten for the spare plus seven for the first ball in this frame). Your
second ball knocks down two more pins but leaves one standing, so add nine to your score
and put a 2 in the box.

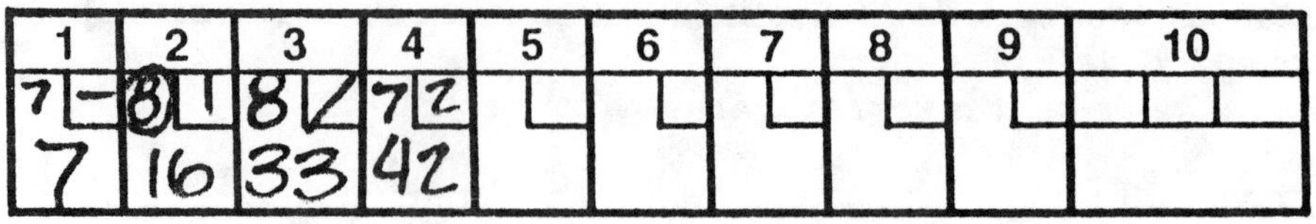

1	2	3	4	5	6	7	8	9	10
7 −	⑧ 1	8 /	7 2						
7	16	33	42						

Figure 3.13

FIFTH FRAME--You get your first strike here. Put the (X) in the box and wait for the
next two rolls before you compute your score.

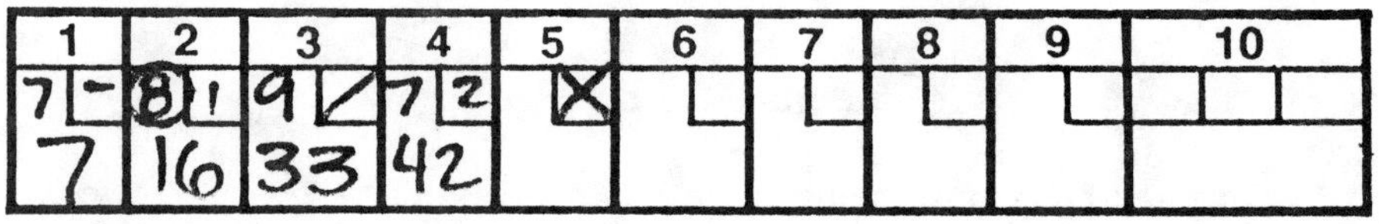

1	2	3	4	5	6	7	8	9	10
7 −	⑧ 1	9 /	7 2	X					
7	16	33	42						

Figure 3.14

SIXTH FRAME--Your first ball knocks down eight pins and leaves a 3-10 split. Circle 8
to show the split. Your second ball converts the split in a spare. Draw a (/) in the box to
indicate this conversion. Add 20 to your fourth frame total (ten plus eight plus two) for
your fifth frame total. Wait for your first ball in the seventh frame before computing
your sixth frame total.

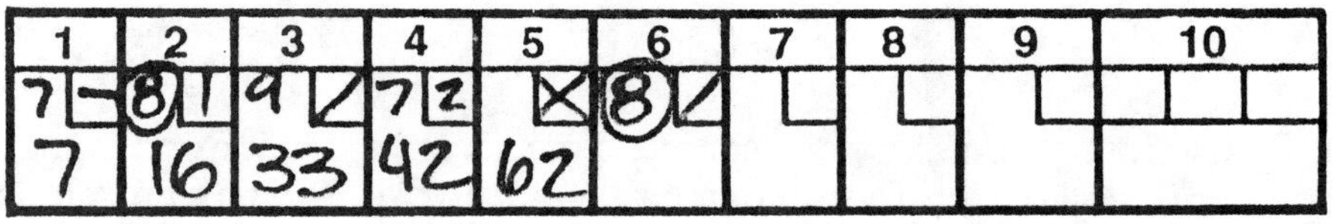

1	2	3	4	5	6	7	8	9	10
7 −	⑧ 1	9 /	7 2	X	⑧ /				
7	16	33	42	62					

Figure 3.15

SEVENTH FRAME--You score your second strike of the game. You put an (X) in the box
and wait for your next two balls before figuring your total for this frame. Your sixth
frame total can now be recorded. Add 20 (ten plus ten) to your fifth frame total.

1	2	3	4	5	6	7	8	9	10
7 −	⑧ 1	9 /	7 2	X	⑧ /	X			
7	16	33	42	62	82				

Figure 3.16

EIGHTH FRAME--On your first ball you take down nine pins, but fail to convert with the second ball. Mark the 9 and then put a (-) in the box to record the miss. Add 19 (ten plus nine) to the sixth frame total to get your seventh frame score. The nine pins are then added to the seventh frame total to complete scoring in the eighth frame.

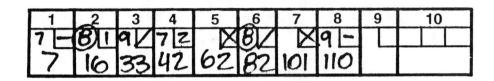

Figure 3.17

NINTH FRAME--You strike again. You put an (X) in the box and wait till you've rolled your next two balls before you can figure your ninth frame total.

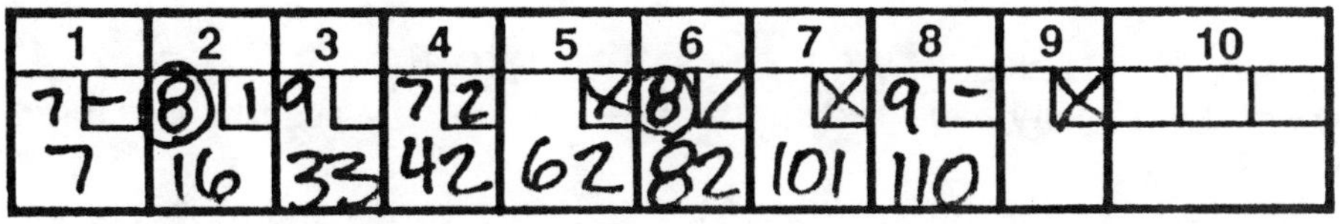

Figure 3.18

TENTH FRAME--You roll another strike which gives you two more rolls. With the first of the next two rolls, you knock down eight pins. This adds 28 to your eighth frame total (ten plus ten plus eight). With your next and final ball, you pick up the remaining two pins. This means you add 20 (ten plus eight plus two) for the tenth frame. Your total score for the game is 158.

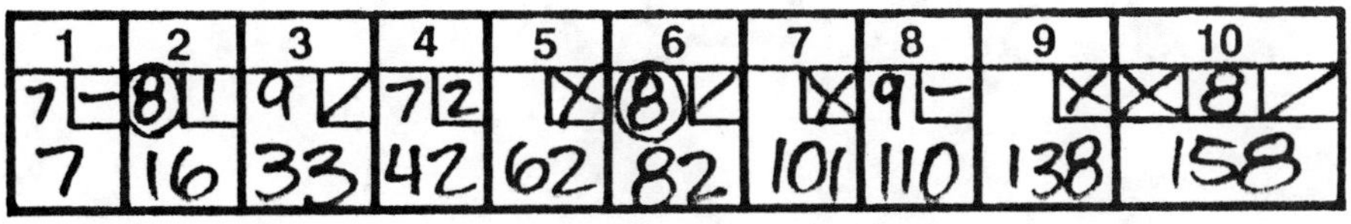

Figure 3.19

ERRORS AND CORRECTIONS

Illustrations of the <u>MOST COMMON</u> errors and how to correct them

<u>ERROR</u>
Dropping ball too soon

<u>ILLUSTRATION</u>

Figure 3.20

RESULTS AND CORRECTION

- Since you obviously have lost control of the ball the results will be very inconsistent.
- <u>Correct</u> this by checking to see if the ball fits your hand properly and is not too heavy. Dry your hands before lifting the ball and do not put your fingers in the holes too early. Put your weight on the forward foot; push the ball away on the first step.

<u>ERROR</u>
Lofting ball out on the lane

<u>ILLUSTRATION</u>

Figure 3.21

RESULTS AND CORRECTION

- This may be caused by the ball sticking to the fingers; or standing too erect upon delivery.
- This also results in poor control and often inadequate spin for good pin action.
- <u>Correct</u> this by checking the ball-hand fit. Practice a greater knee bend on the slide and release.

ERROR
Poor balance at the foul line

Figure 3.22

RESULTS AND CORRECTION

- This may be due to a lack of knee bend resulting in a forward lean or by turning the body sideways upon delivery.
- If you are not able to control your body, then the chances are good that you are not controlling the ball and hitting the spot in which you are aiming.
- Correct this by bending the knees and keeping the head and shoulders parallel to the foul line throughout the approach and release. Make sure that the toes slide straight toward the foul line on the last step.

ERROR
Poor Timing Between Swing and
Steps (no time for a backswing)

Figure 3.23

RESULTS AND CORRECTION

- The push-away may be too high and/or is started too late.
- The lack of good timing will likely cause a jerky, poorly coordinated release.
- Correct this by pushing the ball out and slightly down as opposed to lifting it on the first step. It is very important that the push away begins simultaneously with the first step.

ERROR
Ball skidding down the lane

Figure 3.24

RESULTS AND CORRECTION
- This usually occurs when the thumb and fingers release simultaneously and results with poor spin on the ball and therefore poor pin action.
- Practice the hook release with the thumb coming out first followed by the fingers. As the fingers release you should have a slight lifting action to put the proper spin in the ball.

OTHER PROBLEM AREAS

	ERROR	RESULT	CORRECTION
1.	Running during approach	The first step is probably too long. Poor timing and release.	Take a short shuffle step for the first step after push away. Allow the ball to make a pendulum swing.

	ERROR	RESULT	CORRECTION
2.	Ball goes in right gutter	No score. The following are the common causes of this error: 1. Wrap around backswing 2. Releasing too early 3. Poor timing 4. Dropping ball shoulder and/or dropping ball	Use the pendulum swing and follow through toward target. Keep the shoulders parallel to the foul line and point the front foot towards it. Check ball weight and fit.

ERROR	RESULT	CORRECTION
3. Ball goes in left gutter	No score. The following are the common causes of this error: 1. Wrap around backswing 2. Releasing late 3. Poor timing 4. Throwing across the body	Use the pendulum swing and make sure the elbow is near the body on the backswing. Keep the shoulders parallel to the foul line and point the foot towards it. Check follow-through.

ERROR	RESULT	CORRECTION
4. Rotating the wrist upon release	For a right-handed bowler the ball will break too far to the left	Keep the wrist and hand in the correct clock position on release and follow-through.

ERROR	RESULT	CORRECTION
5. Side arm throw	The ball is probably being held in the middle of the body. The resulting swing is either inside-out or outside-in. Poor accuracy is the usual result.	Position the ball in line with the right shoulder for a right-handed bowler. Push straight away, and walk and slide straight toward the target.

IMPROVEMENT DRILLS AND GAMES

1. Delivery Drill

   In this drill, you or your partner will simply chart the path that your ball travels down the alley. This will enable you to determine if you are achieving the desired curve, hook, or straight roll that you are attempting. Make a small diagram, as below, and chart each ball's course in relation to the head pin.

Figure 3.25

2.   Head Pin Drill
         You or your partner will mark the location
         of your ball as it reaches the head pin.
         If you knock the head pin down, then darken
         the circle, otherwise mark an "X" at the
         approximate location of your ball. This
         drill should help you determine adjust-
         ments or changes in delivery that will
         give you greater consistency. See the
         diagram for this drill. Charting the path
         of the ball could also be useful in this
         drill.

Figure 3.26

3.   7 Pin Drill
         This drill is identical to the head pin
         drill except you are attempting to pick
         up that spare by going for the 7 pin.
         Use an "X" and chart the path of your
         ball. See the diagram.

Figure 3.27

4.   Use the same drill for the 10 pin.

5.   Two-Four-Eight Game
         All the rules of bowling are followed except every player is automatically
         given a strike in the second, fourth, and eighth frames. You still bowl those
         frames but it's only for practice. This can be used as a fun tournament and
         modified very easily; i.e., 3-9, or 5-10 tournaments.

6.   No Tap
         This game improves scores and confidence. The regular rules are followed
         except that every time only one pin remains after the first ball, it is counted
         as a strike. The spare ball is only for practice. A modification of this would
         be to give "bonus" points for knocking down the remaining ball on the practice
         roll.

7.   Head Pin Tournament
         The object is to hit the head pin, No. 1 pin, with the first ball rolled. If the
         head pin is knocked down, 10 points are scored no matter how many other pins
         were knocked down. There are 10 frames and the best score is 100. If the
         head pin is not hit, the score is zero for that frame. If the head pin falls as a
         reaction from other pins, it does not count. You must observe carefully to
         determine if the head pin has been hit. You can modify this scoring, as in the
         No Tap game, by giving bonus points for additional pins knocked down on the
         second ball.

BOWLING SKILLS TEST

GENERAL INFORMATION

<u>Purpose</u>—To measure the student's ability to bowl by averaging three consecutive games. An activity specialist or a representative will administer and supervise the Bowling Skills Test on a scheduled day/time.

<u>Directions</u>
1) An Activity Specialist or representative will meet the students at the bowling alley on the appointed day and time.
2) The students must arrange their own transportation and arrive promptly.
3) The students are responsible for the cost of the three games.
4) The students must know how to keep score before coming to the skills test. If they do not know how to keep score, they will fail the Bowling Skills Test.

<u>Scoring</u>—Students must submit the bowling alley official score sheet to the Activity Specialist or the representative in order to receive credit.

BOWLING
Skills Test Score Sheet

_____ Male/Female Date _____ Instructor _____
circle

_____ Section _____ Time/Day _____

Description

nt will bowl three lines at specified bowling alley at his/her own expense.
verage of the three lines will count as the official score. The student will
signed to bowl with three other students.

Results

Score

_____

_____

_____

TOTAL _____   Three-Line Average _____   T-Score _____   Grade _____

BOWLING SKILLS TEST NORMS

	T-Score	Men	Women
	76	182	160
	74	180	158
	72	178	156
	70	172	152
	68	168	148
Advanced	66	164	144
	64	160	140
	62	156	136
	60	152	132
	58	148	128
Intermediate	56	144	124
	54	140	120
	52	136	116
	50	132	112
	48	130	110
Beginning	46	128	108
	44	126	106
	42	124	104
	40	122	102
	38	120	100
	36	118	98
	34	116	96
	32	114	94

BOWLING
Skills Test Score Sheet

_____ Male/Female Date _____ Instructor _____
                         circle

_____ Section _____ Time/Day _____

Description

ht will bowl three lines at specified bowling alley at his/her own expense.
verage of the three lines will count as the official score. The student will
signed to bowl with three other students.

Results

        Score

        _____

        _____

        _____

TOTAL _____   Three-Line Average _____   T-Score _____   Grade _____

BOWLING SKILLS TEST NORMS

	T-Score	Men	Women
	76	182	160
	74	180	158
	72	178	156
	70	172	152
	68	168	148
Advanced	66	164	144
	64	160	140
	62	156	136
	60	152	132
	58	148	128
Intermediate	56	144	124
	54	140	120
	52	136	116
	50	132	112
	48	130	110
Beginning	46	128	108
	44	126	106
	42	124	104
	40	122	102
	38	120	100
	36	118	98
	34	116	96
	32	114	94

BOWLING
Skill Analysis Score Sheet
(20 points)

Name _____ Date _____

Class _____ Evaluated By _____

POINT GUIDE

2 points -- Student appears competent
1 point -- Occasionally correct or minor errors
0 points -- Needs more attention before ready to
             play

	POINTS SCORED		
	0	1	2
1. Position and Stance	___	___	___
*1) Adjusting starting position			
2) Stance- comfortable/natural			
2. Gripping the ball	___	___	___
*1) Proper ball weight			
2) Conventional grip			
3. The Four Step Approach	___	___	___
*1) Push away -- 1st step			
2) Downswing -- 2nd step			
3) Backswing -- 3rd step			
4) Forward swing-4th step/slide			
4. Release and Follow-through	___	___	___
*1) Hand position and action			
2) "Pose" analysis			
5. Delivery Style	___	___	___
*1) Straight ball--thumb at 12:00			
2) Hook ball -- thumb at 10:00			
6. Aiming Technique	___	___	___
*1) Spot aiming			
2) Pin aiming (instinctive)			
7. Picking Up Spares	___	___	___
*1) Using the best angle			
2) "Hints" for consistency			
8. Score a Game	___	___	___
9. Rules and Etiquetté	___	___	___
*1) Legal/Illegal pinfalls			
2) Fouls			
3) Courtesy and consideration			
10. Results	___	___	___
*1) Bowling skill test results			
2) General evaluation			

* Points for evaluation

TOTAL SCORE _____

BOWLING
Skill Analysis Score Sheet
(20 points)

Name _____   Date _____

Class _____   Evaluated By _____
POINT GUIDE
2 points -- Student appears competent
1 point -- Occasionally correct or minor errors
0 points -- Needs more attention before ready to
            play

	POINTS SCORED		
	0	1	2
Position and Stance	___	___	___
*1) Adjusting starting position			
2) Stance- comfortable/natural			
Gripping the ball	___	___	___
*1) Proper ball weight			
2) Conventional grip			
The Four Step Approach	___	___	___
*1) Push away -- 1st step			
2) Downswing -- 2nd step			
3) Backswing -- 3rd step			
4) Forward swing-4th step/slide			
Release and Follow-through	___	___	___
*1) Hand position and action			
2) "Pose" analysis			
Delivery Style	___	___	___
*1) Straight ball--thumb at 12:00			
2) Hook ball -- thumb at 10:00			
Aiming Technique	___	___	___
*1) Spot aiming			
2) Pin aiming (instinctive)			
Picking Up Spares	___	___	___
*1) Using the best angle			
2) "Hints" for consistency			
Score a Game	___	___	___
Rules and Etiquetté	___	___	___
*1) Legal/Illegal pinfalls			
2) Fouls			
3) Courtesy and consideration			
10. Results	___	___	___
*1) Bowling skill test results			
2) General evaluation			

* Points for evaluation

TOTAL SCORE _____

CHAPTER 4

GOLF

HISTORY

The game of golf as it is played today had its beginning in the fields of Scotland. Records indicate that university students at St. Andrews in Fife played the game as early as 1415. The first championship competition was held at St. Andrews in 1754. This marked the historic beginning of the Royal and Ancient Golf Club of St. Andrews, the unquestioned "golfing Mecca" of the world. The rules that were established for this championship became the basic rules of golf.

Golf first came to the United States in the early 1800's. The first golf course was built in 1888 and was appropriately named the St. Andrews Golf Club of Yonkers, New York. John Reid was elected as the first president. This first U.S.A. course consisted of six holes through cow pastures and an apple grove. Since they had no lease on the land, they were soon forced to move. The first permanent course with a club house was established at the Shinnecock Hills Golf Course in Westchester County, New York.

The United States Golf Association was established in 1894. Two annual championships were to be conducted, one for amateurs and one open to everyone. These events have evolved to become two great American championships; the U.S. Open and the U.S. Amateur. By 1900 there were 1,000 golf courses in this country, and by 1920 American golfers were dominating competitive golf throughout the world. Bobby Jones, the amateur, and Walter Hagen, the professional, were two of the game's greatest players throughout the 1920's and 30's. Between them they won seven of nine British Open Championships from 1922 to 1930. In 1930 Jones won the "Grand Slam" of golf by winning the Open and Amateur Championships of both the United States and Great Britain.

Even though golf courses were being built throughout the United States, the game was considered to be a rich man's sport. Because of the "country club atmosphere" often associated with golf, many still view it as a game for the "well-to-do." This has greatly changed, however, from the early years and with the tremendous growth of public courses, there are over 10 million Americans playing the game today.

Many American golfers have been the dominate players since the 1940's. Recognized as golfing greats throughout the world such men as Byron Nelson, Ben Hogan, Arnold Palmer, Lee Trevino, Tom Watson, Jack Nicklaus, and many other Americans have won numerous championships. Because of the worldwide growth of golf in recent decades, many foreign players are currently challenging for the trophies. Gary Player of South Africa, Severiano Ballesteros of Spain, and Greg Norman of Australia have proven their right to rank with the world champions.

Women's golf has closely followed the development and growth of the men's game. Mildred "Babe" Didrickson Zaharias became one of the first golfing greats after achieving fame in other sports. She dominated amateur golf and then became the first star of the women's professional tour. Other women who have achieved golfing stardom include Louise Suggs, Patty Berg, Mickey Wright, JoAnne Carner, and Nancy Lopez. There are currently many foreign players on the women's professional tour that are challenging for the prizes.

BENEFITS

Golf is one of the most challenging games to ever touch American soil. The setting on a beautiful green carpeted course, the peace and quiet of the surroundings, and the basic simplicity of hitting a ball until it goes into a hole seem contradictory to fun and excitement. It is fun and exciting, however, especially when you feel the exhilaration of hitting the ball exactly the way you intended, or as you see your score drop from one round to the next. It is also humbling, frustrating, and embarrassing, often during the same round or even a single hole.

The psychological and social benefits are often the real values of golf. It offers a great way to release anxieties from the pressures of work. The beauty and serenity of the course is such a pleasant change from the hustle and bustle of the work place. Many golfers play with friends with whom their abilities are compatible, and the interaction and play is enjoyable and healthy. It is one of our lifetime sports, and it is common to see golfers in their 70's and even 80's still playing and enjoying the game.

Much of the physical benefit of golf comes from walking. Walking and carrying a bag for 18 holes can be a good muscular workout, especially if it's a hilly course. The aerobic benefits from golf would likely be minimal, but the value to the strength and endurance of the muscular structure could be worthwhile. Playing golf, and the drills associated with golf, can also improve body flexibility and coordination. One of the real paradoxes related to golf is that as the players get older and have a greater need for exercises such as walking, they are also more financially independent and are more likely to rent golf carts and ride the course, thus missing the physical benefits.

TERMINOLOGY

Ace   A hole in one from the tee into the cup.
Address   A player's position just before the swing, includes the grip, stance, and body position.
Approach Shot   A stroke played to the putting green.
Apron   The short grass area (fringe) that surrounds the putting surface.
Away   The player whose ball is farthest from the hole and is next to be played.
Backspin   A reverse spin put on the ball to make it stop on the green.
Ball Marker   A small coin or flat object used to spot a ball position on the green.
Birdie   A score of one stroke under par on any hole.
Bite   The action of the ball hitting the green with backspin on it.
Bogey   A score of one stroke over par on any hole.
Break   The slant or slope of the green.
Bunker   A depressed area covered with sand or grass placed there intentionally as a hazard. The term is used synonymously with "sand trap."
Caddie   A person who carries a player's clubs on the course, watches the golf balls, attends the flagsticks, and gives advice.
Casual Water   A temporary water accumulation not intended as a hazard.
Chip Shot   A short and often low trajectory shot played to the green.
Closed Stance   The rear foot is pulled back from the intended line of flight while at address.
Club Head (Face)   The hitting part of the club.
Divot   A piece of sod that is dug from the ground by the player's swing. It should be replaced and pressed down.
Dog Leg   A fairway that bends to the right or left.
Dormie   A player or team that is ahead in Match Play by as many holes as there are left to play.
Double Bogey   A score of two strokes over par on any hole.
Down   The number of strokes or holes a player or team is behind in a match.
Draw   A shot that curves slightly from right to left for a right-handed golfer.
Drive   A shot from the tee area. The first shot of a hole.
Driver   The #1 wood club.
Duffer   A poorly skilled golfer.
Eagle   A score of two strokes under par on any hole.
Explosion   A blast shot from a sandtrap.

Fade A shot which curves slightly from left to right for a right-handed golfer.

Fairway The closely mowed route between the tee and the putting green. The desired path to the green.

Fat Shot A shot in which the club hits the ground behind the ball first.

Flagstick The moveable pole to which the flag is attached and which indicates the position of the hole on the green.

Flat Swing A swing which is less upright than normal.

Flight The path of the ball in the air. Also the division of players ranked according to their ability for a tournament.

Follow-through The phase of the swing after the ball has been struck.

Fore A warning cry to anyone in the path of a ball.

Foursome Four players in a group, a typical playing format.

Gimmie A slang expression for a putt that is conceded, counts as one more stroke.

Grain The direction in which the grass on a green is growing. It can have an effect on both the break and the distance to "allow for" on a putt.

Green The putting surface in which the hole is cut and the flag placed.

Grip The handle of a club, also the player's grasp of a club.

Gross Score A player's actual score on a hole or for a round, with no handicap strokes deducted.

Handicap The rating of a player's ability relative to shooting par; used to equalize competition between players of unequal ability. Also a figure on the scorecard which ranks a hole as to its degree of difficulty in comparison to the other holes on that golf course.

Hazard A bunker (sand trap), creek, lake, or ditch which is played according to special rules.

Heel of Club The back part of the clubhead where the shaft is fastened.

Hole High A ball that is even with the hole, but is off to one side.

Hole Out To finish a hole by stroking the ball into the cup.

Honor The right to tee off first, earned by scoring the lowest on the preceding hole.

Hook A shot which curves from right to left for a right-handed golfer.

Irons The clubs with the metal heads that are much thinner than woods.

Lie The position in which the ball has stopped on the ground; also refers to the angle formed by the shaft and sole of a club.

Links Originally a seaside golf course, but now it's just another name for golf course.

Lip The edge of a hole.

Loft The degree of pitch that is built into the clubface.

L.P.G.A. Ladies Professional Golf Association

Match Play A type of golf competition where each hole is a separate contest. The winner is determined by the number of holes won instead of total score.

Medal Play A type of golf competition in which the winner is determined by the lowest score. (Stroke Play)

Mulligan In "sociable golf," the practice of allowing a second shot from the first tee if the first one is poorly hit. Each player is allowed one "mulligan."

Nassau A friendly wager round in which three points are awarded and bet on; one for each nine, and one for the eighteen.

Net Score A player's score after subtracting his handicap from his gross or actual score.

Obstruction Refers to artificial man-made objects such as: benches, shelters, ball washers, etc.

Par A numerical standard of scoring excellence for each hole; based on length, and allowing for two putts per hole.

Penalty Stroke A stroke added to your score for rules infractions and ball movement from problem areas.

PGA The Men's Professional Golf Association.

Pitch Shot A short lofted shot that is hit to a green.

Provisional Ball An extra ball that is hit when the player thinks his first ball may be out-of-bounds or lost.

Putter The club used on the green to roll the ball into the cup.

Rough The longer grass and other vegetation that borders the fairway and the green.

Sand Trap A bunker filled with sand, a hazard.

Scratch Player A player who shoots consistently around par and has a "0" handicap.

Shank A miss-hit which causes the ball to go sharply to the right for a right-handed player.

Skying Hitting the ball high into the air but only a short distance.

Slice A spinning shot that curves the ball from left to right for a right-handed player. The most common problem for male golfers.

Sole The bottom surface of a club.

Summer Rules The regular playing rules of golf that do not allow a player to improve the lie of his ball except under special conditions.

Tee The wooden or plastic peg put into the ground on which to place the ball for the first shot of a hole. Also refers to the hitting area to begin each hole.

Tee Markers The markers placed on the teeing ground to designate the area to begin each hole.

Toe The front tip of the clubhead.

Topped Shot A rolling shot that is caused by striking the top half of the ball.

Unplayable Lie A ball declared unplayable by a player, who must then take a penalty stroke for moving it.

U.S.G.A. United States Golf Association, the ruling body in American golf.

Waggle The back and forth preliminary motion during the address and before the swing.

Whiff To swing at the ball and miss it completely, counts as a stroke.

Winter Rules When the players are permitted to improve the lie of the ball on the fairway (usually a local golf rule).

Woods The clubs with wooden heads.

EQUIPMENT

Clubs--The golf clubs are the tools of the trade. Good clubs do not make a good golfer, but poor clubs can affect the performance of a player at any level of ability. The two kinds of clubs you need are woods and irons. The standard full set of clubs usually consists of four woods, eight irons, and two special clubs: the putter and the wedge. The clubs are engineered to give you approximately a 10-yard difference between clubs. Each club has sections called the grip, shaft, and head (Figure 4.1). In the early years of golf, each club was given a name; however, today they are identified by numbers. The number identifies the loft and length of the club. Unfortunately, someone numbered the clubs in reverse order of length. In a full set the woods are numbered 1, 2, 3, 4, 5, from the longest #1 to the shortest #5. The irons are numbered 2, 3, 4, 5, 6, 7, 8, 9, wedge, from the longest #2 iron to the shortest, the wedge. The lower the number, the less loft in the club face, and the longer the club in inches. Therefore the lower the number means the ball will have less arc in its flight, and therefore travel farther. Figure 4.2 illustrates an average range in clubs for men and women.

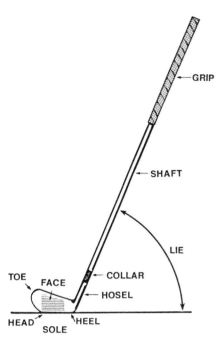

Figure 4.1 Parts of a Club

WOODS	MEN	WOMEN
1	200-220	180-195
3	180-200	160-175
4	170-190	150-165
5	160-180	140-155
IRONS	MEN	WOMEN
2	170-190	
3	160-180	140-160
4	150-170	130-150
5	140-160	120-140
6	130-150	110-130
7	120-140	100-120
8	110-130	90-110
9	100-120	80-100
PW	80-100	60-80

Range in yards.

Figure 4.2 Range

The Putter is a special club and is individualized for each golfer. They are made in many styles and lengths and golfers will often change putters while keeping the same set of clubs. It is designed to roll the ball into the cup after reaching the green. It is the most frequently used club in your set, often too frequently.

Buying a set of clubs, especially as a beginner, does not have to be an expensive venture. Although a full set of top-grade new clubs could cost from $500 to $700, a "starter set" may only cost around $50. The starter set usually has a combination of clubs consisting of the #1 and #3 woods, and the 3, 5, 7, and 9 irons, and a putter. These clubs will enable you to learn the game and improve your skill. If you become more serious about playing and continue to improve, then you should consider purchasing a full set of clubs. It would probably be wise to move up to a full matched set rather than trying to buy individual clubs to fill in with your starter set. Used clubs usually have a good resale value, so sell your first set and purchase a full set, new or used. Often your best dollar/quality value can be found in used top-grade equipment. Pro shops will occasionally have close-out sales on older models that will provide excellent quality clubs at discount prices.

Golf Balls--Balls come in a variety of prices and colors. The beginner should use inexpensive balls which have a lower compression, but have a more durable cover. Compression refers to the "squeezability" of balls, and the compression ratings range from 80 to 100. The higher compression balls are best suited for the hard swingers and the lower compression for the lighter ones. The best buys are often slightly used balls that are sold in pro shops for around 50¢ a ball.

The conventional ball is made by winding bands of rubber around a core and placing a cover over the ball. According to U.S.G.A. specifications, it must not be smaller than 1.68 inches in diameter and not weigh more than 1.62 ounces.

Golfbags--The type of bag that you should purchase will depend on how you plan to transport it around the golf course. A lighter, smaller bag would be easier to carry on your shoulder if you plan to walk most courses. Obviously, this would also be much more conducive to getting some exercise while you play. If you plan to ride in a golf cart or use a pull-cart, then a heavier bag with more storage areas could be used. Whichever type you choose, be sure it has these features: a wide, padded strap for carrying over your shoulder, pockets for balls, tees, etc., a larger pocket for a rain jacket or other apparel, an umbrella socket and strap, and holes in the bottom of the bag for drainage on rainy days.

Golf Shoes--Since the game is primarily a walking game, it is extremely important to find shoes that fit well and are durable. Golf shoes are especially designed with spikes in the soles and heels. This traction creates a much firmer foundation for the swing. It also allows for easier walking up and down hilly terrain. Many different types and styles of shoes are currently on the market. It would be wise to purchase a heavier leather pair for fall-winter play and a lighter style for summer. Tennis shoes or jogging type shoes can be worn and are fairly common on public courses. If, however, you are going to play at a private country club, then regular type golf shoes are a "must."

Golf rubbers or rubber shoes are important to have if you have a wet climate or if you are an all-weather golfer. Rubbers are inexpensive and can be worn over a pair of golf shoes.

Remember in an 18-hole round of golf you will walk from three to five miles. You should consider buying shoes slightly larger than your regular shoes, and then wear them around the yard some before you play in them. When purchasing your shoes, expect to get strictly what you pay for in quality.

RULES AND ETIQUETTE

Golf has had a set of rules since 1774, when the golfers of Edinburgh decided to play golfers from neighboring communities and were forced to develop some common rules to govern their play. Today the rules of golf are established by the U.S.G.A. These rules are in effect throughout the United States, but are modified on occasion by local rules. There are also rules of etiquette which should always be observed by all players. Often in friendly "sociable" games, the exact rules are not followed to the letter. In tournament type play, however, the rules are usually strictly enforced.

SOME BASIC RULES

One stroke penalties

A. Lost ball--If you lose a ball, you must go back to the original spot from which you hit that ball and hit another, adding a one stroke penalty. In order to save time, if you hit a ball into the rough or an area that looks as though there could be difficulty finding it, play a second ball from the same spot. This is called a "provisional" ball. If you find your first ball, then you play it and pick the provisional up.

B. Out-of-Bounds--The penalty is stroke and distance. You must play another ball from the same spot and add one penalty stroke, the same as for a lost ball.

C. Unplayable Lie--If your ball ends up in a situation that you choose not to attempt to play it, you have three options:

1. Move the ball two club lengths from the spot--in any direction except toward the hole you are playing, and drop it for a one stroke penalty.
2. You can go back to the original spot you played the ball, add a stroke, and hit again.
3. You can move back along the path of your ball, keeping the trouble spot between you and the green, drop the ball--add one stroke, and play from there.

D. Ball in a water hazard--If you hit into a creek or lake you are penalized one stroke. You may drop the ball anywhere from the "point of entry" along a line back towards the spot in which you hit the shot.

If the ball goes into a "lateral hazard," when the water is parallel to the direction of the hole you are playing, you may drop the ball two club lengths away from the point of entry, add a penalty stroke, and play from there.

E. Dropping the Ball--The correct way to drop the ball is to measure out the awarded distance, extend the arm to the side, and drop the ball. If it rolls into another bad situation, or closer to the hole, drop it again. After a second drop you are entitled to place it by hand.

Two stroke penalties

A. When on the putting green, there is a two stroke penalty for putting and striking the flagstick.
B. If you putt and hit someone else's ball, it is a two-stroke penalty.
C. Grounding club in a hazard--If your ball lies in a sand trap, you may not touch the sand with your club, except in the actual swing at the ball. If the ball is in any other type of hazard, such as the bank of a water hazard, the same rule applies.

SUMMARY OF OTHER RULES

A. The ball must be played as it lies. Exceptions are when local rules permit preferred lies, or "winter rules," in which case the ball may be moved with the club head provided it is not moved nearer the hole.
B. On the fairway, you may not improve the lie of the ball by moving, breaking, or bending the surrounding vegetation. You may, however, move loose, natural impediments out of the way.
C. When you are teeing your ball to begin the hole, the ball must be teed between the markers. It must be teed up within two club lengths behind the markers, and never in front of them.
D. After the tee shots, the player whose ball lies farthest from the hole plays first. This is true for the fairway and the green until all have holed out.
E. Every time you intentionally strike at the ball you must count a stroke, even if you "fan" it. On the tee, however, accidentally knocking the ball off the tee is not counted.
F. Touching the line of putt is not permitted, except in removing loose impediments, repairing ball marks, and touching with the putter while addressing the ball for the putt.
G. There are a number of reasons and situations for which a ball may be moved without penalty. Some of these are:

1. Casual water in the fairway or on the green. You are allowed to move your ball to a point of relief, no closer to the hole.

2. Equipment or ground under repair. If it interferes with the lie of the ball, your stance, or the path toward the green, then you are allowed a free drop, not nearer the hole.

3. If your ball lands on the wrong green, you must drop the ball off the green but not nearer the hole you are playing.

4. Newly planted trees which are usually staked and supported with wires. You should always drop away from staked trees. However, you must play out from under all other non-staked trees and bushes, unless you choose to take a stroke penalty for moving from an unplayable lie.

ETIQUETTE

Golf's unwritten rules are called "golf etiquette." It really means for each golfer to show consideration of the course and of other golfers. Most of the rules of etiquette are unwritten, but "all" are carefully observed by dedicated golfers.

On the Tee

A. The order of hitting off the first tee is by random choice. After the first hole, the lowest score hits first, second lowest hits second, etc., for the remainder of the round.

B. You should not move, talk, stand close to or directly behind a golfer who is addressing a ball.

C. You do not tee off until all players in the group ahead of you are out of range of one of your good shots.

D. After you hit, watch your ball carefully until it stops or disappears. Line the path of travel up with some landmark. This will provide tremendous benefit in finding an errant shot and save much time for you and your group.

In the Fairway

A. After you hit, pick up your equipment and move quickly toward your ball. Do not walk out in front of anyone who is about to hit. As you keep moving toward your ball, stop and wait for each person to hit as you approach them.

B. If a ball is lost, you should only take a few minutes looking for it, and then play another ball. If your group is playing slow and the group behind you is forced to wait on every shot, allow them to play through, providing there is a gap (room for them). Note: Help other members of your group find their lost balls.

C. Any time that you hit a ball that goes toward someone--yell "FORE!" This is a national warning to beware of an errant ball.

D. Be ready to hit when it's your turn, and then move smartly between shots.

E. If your ball lands on the wrong fairway, let the players coming up that fairway play their shots before you hit.

On the Green

A. The person closest to the hole in your group is obligated to "attend" the flag on that hole. The person farthest from the hole should putt first.

B. There should be no talking, fidgeting, or movement while someone is putting. You should never stand in their line, either behind them or in front past the hole. You should also avoid casting your shadow over another golfer's line of play.

C. Do not step on the line of any putt! As you walk across the green, walk around balls or carefully step over the paths or lines of putts.

D. When your ball is on the green, take your clubs past the back edge of the green toward the tee for the next hole. <u>Never</u> set clubs on the green or park carts near the edge.

E. Players will usually mark their balls on the green. You should always mark your ball if it's <u>on</u> or <u>near</u> the line of someone behind you. You mark the ball by placing a marker or a coin directly behind the ball and then removing the ball.

F. After everyone has holed out, replace the flagstick and move quickly off the green and on to the next tee. <u>DO NOT</u> record scores on the green. They can be recorded on the next tee.

Care of the Course

A. You should replace all <u>divots</u> and press them firmly into their original place. <u>Do not</u> take divots on practice swings.

B. Repair any ball mark your shot may have made in hitting the green. A small tool is available in pro shops for repairing marks and should be carried in your bag--or a tee can be used as a repair tool.

C. Walk very carefully on the green. You should especially avoid dragging your feet or stepping too close to the hole.

D. Keep manual carts off the apron area of the green and keep powered carts in their designated path.

E. Never bring carts or sets of clubs onto the tee--just a ball, tee, and the club you intend to use.

F. When you leave a bunker, smooth out the surface, leaving no footprints or indentations.

FUNDAMENTALS OF THE GAME

There are many "sayings" heard in the game of golf such as "Keep your head down," "Watch the ball," "Keep your arm straight," "Finish your swing," and one that often comes too late, "Look up and see a bad shot." These phrases all point to the basic fundamental of the game; a good sound swing results in good golf. The swing begins with the grip and stance, so let's start developing the good swing.

THE GRIP

The most commonly used grip for the golf swing is the <u>overlapping grip</u> (Figure 4.3). In this grip the target or forward hand is placed on the grip so that the club lies diagonally across the hand between the index finger and the palm. When gripping with the target hand, the back of the hand should be facing the target. The club face should be placed square to the target, with the thumb pointing down the grip. With the target hand on the club, you should be able to see only the first two knuckles of the hand. A good check point is to see if the "V" formed with the thumb and index finger is pointing toward the "away side" or right side of the face for a right-handed player.

The rear or away hand should then be placed over the thumb so that the palm is facing toward the target. The little finger will <u>overlap</u> the index finger of the target hand. The thumb and index finger of the away hand should be pointing downward with a slight pressure from the thumb pad toward the index finger. They <u>should not</u> be around the grip in a fist-type position. A firm but light touch is essential. Again the "V" formed between the thumb and the index finger of the away hand should be pointing the same as the "V" formed by the target hand, toward the "away side" of the face and neck.

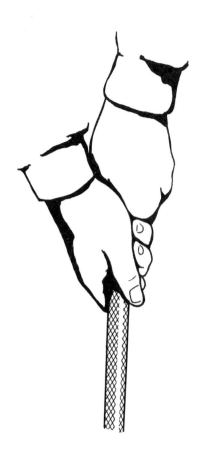

Figure 4.3 Overlapping Grip

Two other grips which are used much less frequently are the ten-finger grip and the interlocking grip. The ten-finger grip (Figure 4.4) is used most often by players with small weak hands or exceptionally long fingers. Some ladies prefer this grip, and many beginners use it initially. The interlocking grip (Figure 4.5) is where the little finger of the rear hand is interlocked with the index finger of the target hand instead of covered as in the overlapping grip. This grip is also used occasionally by ladies and men with small hands. These grips are least recommended because they encourage the development of a "dominant side" in the swing. Regardless of the grip used, the pressure points on the grip will be the same.

Figure 4.4 Tenfinger Grip

Figure 4.5 Interlocking Grip

POSITIONING FOR THE SWING

Body Position--The correct position for the golf swing involves the stance, address, and the actual swing. There are three basic stances: the square, the open, and the closed (Figure 4.6). The square stance will be used for most shots.

Square Stance   Open Stance   Closed Stance

Figure 4.6

Just prior to the golf swing the body is in the address position. This is the "set-up" position to begin the swing. Whether it is a full swing or shorter approach type swing, the routine for "setting up" or addressing the ball should be the same each time. It begins by placing the club face directly behind the ball and square to the target. From a position with the feet together, move the target foot forward several inches with the toes slightly opened outward. Move the rear foot until the feet are approximately shoulder-width apart. The rear foot should be square to the target line. The distance between the feet will vary according to each individual's anatomy. The target arm should be relatively straight from the shoulder to the clubhead. From this position you lower the body as though you were about to sit on a high stool, knees slightly flexed, keeping the back straight, you simply bend forward at the waist. As you assume this position you continue to maintain the soled, square position of the club face. The hands should be directly below the mouth and the weight should be on the inside halves of both feet. This may sound complicated but it will only take a few practices for this to become "old hat" (Figure 4.7).

For most shots the position of the ball will be in the middle of the stance. The most common exception will be the shot with a wood from the tee box. This shot is usually played with the ball lined up with the inside of the target heel.

Figure 4.7 Addressing the Ball

THE SWING

The "swing's the thing" in golf, and the grip and address position lead up to the backswing and downswing. In order to hit the ball straight, the club face must meet the ball in a square position toward the target. The backswing is started with a rotation of the shoulders and hips. With the target arm straight but not rigid and the rear arm relaxed, the club is rotated back in a plane that is similar to a ferris wheel that is tipped slightly backward. The center line of the body moves very little as the shoulders and hips rotate around. The clubhead is kept low to the ground as it moves away, and the wrists do not break until they "break naturally" or at approximately the halfway point of the backswing. The body weight shifts to the inside of the rear foot as the backswing progresses. The target heel should either remain on the ground or come up only slightly. At the top of the backswing the club shaft is at a 90° angle to the target arm and the club is virtually parallel to the ground. The wrists are straight, and the rear elbow is till close to the body. The target shoulder should be positioned under the chin. The head, as the hub of the rotation, has moved only slightly or not at all. From this "coiled" position you are now ready to smoothly uncoil and swing the clubhead through the ball (Figure 4.8).

Figure 4.8 Backswing

The downswing is started by the lower body with the legs driving laterally toward the target. A sequential movement pattern of legs, shoulders, arms, and hands brings the club in the desired plane and produces the clubhead acceleration in a smooth, rhythmic flow. As the weight is shifted from the rear to the target side, there should be a feeling of pulling from the target side. The wrists should remain cocked until they are approximately parallel to the ground.

Point of Impact--At impact the weight has shifted to the target foot as the legs and lower body have moved toward the target. The hands and clubface are square to the target, and the sequential movement of first the legs, then the shoulders and arms, is rotating the rear shoulder under the still-steady head (Figure 4.9). It is important to emphasize here that this must be a rhythmic, flowing motion that can become a consistent motor pattern. Think "swing to the target" and simply let the ball get caught in the middle. Any deviation from this sequence will often cause the club to change the swing plane and produce inconsistency or numerous other problems with the flight of the ball.

Figure 4.9 Point of Impact

Follow-Through--After impact the hips and arms continue to rotate and the front of your body (belt buckle) is facing the target as you complete the swing. The head turns only as a result of the momentum of the follow through. Both arms should be stretched out toward the target and then finish with the hands high above the head. Nearly all of the weight should be on the target foot, with only the toes of the rear foot touching. Sounds impossible, right! It's really not, but it will take many correct repetitions to firmly establish this swing pattern. The key is to make the swing consistent in order to strike the ball in the same way and in the desired direction. Remember, the golf downswing is initiated with a pulling motion with the target side, and is not a throwing or hitting motion with the rear arm. When using irons, the club contacts the ball with a descending blow through the ball and part of the ground resulting in a divot. With woods, the ball should be swept from ground or tee without a divot.

THE SHORT GAME

There comes a point on many holes when you do not need a full swing from any of your clubs. This is the short game and includes pitching, chipping, putting, and sand shots.

The pitch shot is most often executed with a #9 iron or a pitching wedge. This shot is used when you are approximately 40 to 80 yards from the green. The ball is lofted high and has very little roll when it lands on the green. The grip and swing mechanics are the same as the full swing. You simply shorten the swing according to the distance to the flag. The feet should be closer together and closer to the ball thus creating a more upright swing plane. The arc of the swing will still be that of a full swing.

The pitch-and-run shot is usually executed with a #6, #7, or #8 iron. If the ball is roughly between 20 and 40 yards from the flag and there are no obstacles, such as a sand trap, or elevated green, then this is an excellent approach shot. With the less-lofted clubs, the ball will be in the air approximately one-third of the distance, and the remaining two-thirds will be roll. For a beginner, as the full swing is developing, the pitch-and-run is an excellent adjustment shot when you are near the green. When properly executed, it can save you many strokes per round.

Regardless of the distance of the shot, it is important that you hit down and through the ball and don't try to lift or scoop it into the air. Each club is designed to give the ball the proper lift.

The chip shot is a short shot from near the edge of the green. A #5, #6, or #7 iron is commonly used, with the #5 being most preferred. This shot is used often when the ball is within 15 yards of the green. It is identical to the pitch-and-run, since you are trying to keep it low and roll it near the hole to avoid an extra putting stroke.

In pitching and chipping, the wrists should be kept firm as they pass through the shot. The back of the target hand should be swinging out to the flag. Most of the weight should be kept on the target foot throughout the swing to avoid excessive movement, and thus decrease the chance for errors during such a compact, finesse-type swing. The mechanics of these "short shots" are simpler, and there is less chance for error than with the full swing. They can be practiced more often than full swings, and they are truly "stroke savers" in golf (Figure 4.10).

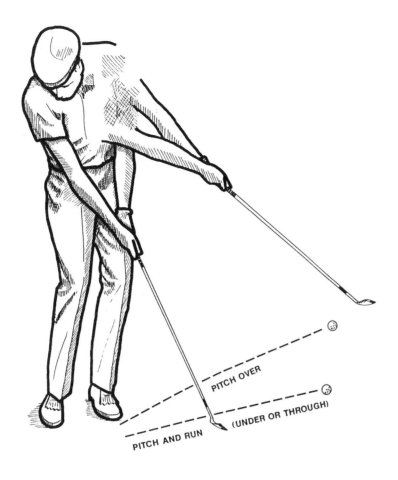

Figure 4.10 Pitching

Putting is the only stroke in golf in which the swing changes significantly. There are many styles of putting, making it the most unique and individualistic skill in golf. Up until now, the grip and stance were, more or less, standardized for the golf swing. Putting, however, allows for each golfer to experiment with their personal comfort, relaxation, and alignment. There are some basics which most good putters follow. The reverse overlap grip is the preferred grip style and is used by most professional golfers. Often beginning golfers find the grip difficult to adapt to initially, but as they practice, play, and develop their game, it becomes "second nature." It is formed by placing the palms of the hands facing each other on both sides of the shaft, with the palm of the rear hand facing the target. Grip the club with the target hand by placing the fingers around the shaft and the thumb on top of the shaft. Place the rear hand on the shaft below the target hand with the thumb on top also. Allow the index finger of the target hand to overlap fingers of the rear hand. Open and close the fingers to get the feel and sensitivity of both hands as "one" and the fingers controlling the grip.

The square stance with the feet approximately 12 inches apart is recommended. Your knees and elbows are bent, and the stance should allow for your eyes to be directly over the ball. The ball should be positioned between the center of your stance and the instep of the target foot, depending on your ability to feel relaxed and comfortable over the ball. The body weight is shifted in the direction corresponding to the ball placement and then the weight is stabilized throughout the stroke. There must be no body movement. The putter blade should be taken straight back in line with the direction required for a straight-through motion toward the hole (See Figures 4.11 and 4.12).

Figure 4.11 Putting Stance   Figure 4.12 Putting Stroke

Success in putting depends to a great extent upon the correct "reading" of the green and the sense of touch in applying the right amount of stroke motion needed to get the ball to the hole. Remember that the mechanics of the stroke are simple and the emphasis should be on a comfortable, relaxed position. To become a good putter, these guidelines should be followed: (1) Develop a sound, consistent, confident putting stroke, (2) Develop good judgment in "sizing up" putts, and (3) practice--practice--practice.

Sandshots--All golf courses are designed to penalize errant shots. These penalties may be in the form of "penalty strokes" for shots that go out-of-bounds or land in a water hazard, or they may result in types of shots that are challenging and more difficult. Most courses have numerous sand traps that lurk around the greens. Often if you miss the green, you will land in a trap and thus the trouble shot known as a sand shot needs to be learned. The most frequently used method from the sand is the explosion shot. A sand wedge should be used, and since the ball is in a "hazard," the club cannot touch the sand (be grounded) until the actual swing. Use a more open stance and position the ball toward the target foot. Work both feet into the sand for a solid base and then aim toward where the target foot is pointing instead of toward the flag. Using a 3/4 swing, take the club back more upright than the normal swing, thus causing the club plane to become more outside to inside on the downswing. Contact the sand slightly behind the ball and follow through, pulling down and through with the target side. The distance the ball travels will be in relation to the distance hit behind the ball. It's important to remember that the object is not to bury the club but to continue to swing smoothly through the sand and under the ball.

If the sand is hard or wet, it might be better to chip the ball onto the green. If there is only a slight "lip," or none at all on the trap, then putting the ball could be the most accurate shot.

STRATEGY AND DISCUSSION

To play golf and truly enjoy the game requires that we continually show signs of improvement. The best way to improve is to work toward a sound consistent golf swing that allows the club face to meet the ball solidly and keep it in the fairway and on the green. An educated guess would be that over 90 percent of all men golfers and over 50 percent of all women golfers swing across the ball. Women tend to be more relaxed and are more flexible and keep the club on the correct plane better than men.

Men are constantly striving to hit the ball hard and "over power" it, thus altering their downswing plane. When the upper body, shoulders, arms, wrists, and hands initiate the downswing, the club travels from outside the ball back to the inside causing the

118

common dreaded slice. This can be improved through correct practice--remember, the downswing begins with the target leg and hip as they move laterally toward the target.

As you begin to play the game, we would suggest that you use the clubs that are working the best for you. All golfers have more confidence in some clubs over others. For example, many would prefer hitting a #3 wood from the tee than a #1 wood (driver). Others would practically never use a #2 iron or #3 iron during a round of golf. Some of these clubs are more difficult to hit consistently than others; i.e., even though a driver might carry 15 or 20 yards further than a #3 wood, it is also more difficult to control. If the ball is out-of-bounds, in the woods, in the water, or other unplayable position, then 15 or 20 yards is insignificant. The place to develop skill and confidence with your tougher clubs is on the practice range and not on the course.

The short game in golf is where many strokes are saved or lost, depending on your skill. This part of the game should be practiced and developed because it is such a great equalizer. It doesn't require power, size, or strength, but it does require the finesse one gets through practicing for the feel for those touch shots. Anyone who takes a golf sabbatical and returns to play knows how difficult it is to keep the feel for the short game. The swing may still be sound but the finesse shots require practice and playing. The short shots do not require a different swing. There is only one golf swing. The mechanics are the same, you simply swing as hard as needed for the distance left to the flag. Look at where you want the ball to land on the green, and try to pitch the ball up to that spot. Every golfer, regardless of ability, can develop a good short game. The swing is simpler because it's not a full swing and, therefore, there is less chance for error. These shots can be easily practiced almost anywhere, including your front or backyard.

Putting is undoubtedly the simplest part of the game, if you learn to relax and become realistic about the results. You just cannot make every putt, no matter how much you "read" the green and study the shot. It is far easier, however, to develop putting skill than any other phase of golf, and this is a "stroke-saving" paradise. Relax and practice a sound, sensible putting stroke. The key is to avoid extra strokes. Learn to get down in two on those long putts, and to avoid three putting those medium and short-range ones. Mental concentration and emotional control are influential on the putting green. You will miss putts that you know you should easily make (which will be maddening), but you will also make some that will amaze you as to how the ball dropped in the cup. Your thoughts can often be your worst enemy. "If you think you cannot putt well, then you won't." Learn to size-up your putts and practice. The emphasis should be on a comfortable, relaxed, and "good feel" for the stance, grip and stroke.

Remember, there is only one way to gain skill, and that is through diligent practice. Your success in golf will be directly related to the amount of time devoted to worthwhile practice -- tempered, of course, by your inate abilities.

ERRORS AND CORRECTIONS

Illustrations of the **MOST COMMON** errors and how to correct them

ERROR
Rear hand is positioned too far
under shaft. V's are no longer
aligned to your "rear ear."

Figure 4.13

RESULTS AND CORRECTION
- The ball often is topped with overspin and fails to get into the air
- Hooks or pulls are common
- <u>Correct</u> this by checking the grip and align the V's of both hands toward the rear shoulder or ear. Make sure the palm of the rear hand is facing the target.

ERROR
Rearside dominance instead of
targetside in the set-up position.

ILLUSTRATION

Figure 4.14

RESULTS AND CORRECTION
- A slice or a pull is a typical result
- This set-up often leads to other problems, such as allowing the rear side to become the dominant force in the downswing
- <u>Correct</u> this by forming a straighter line from the target shoulder through the club shaft to the clubface. Drop the rear shoulder and allow the rear elbow and shoulder to become more relaxed.

ERROR
Bent target arm (lacks extension)

Figuer 4.15

RESULTS AND CORRECTION
- Hitting fat or topping are both common
- When the target arm bends, then it adds another mechanical adjustment that must be made on the downswing and this, especially for beginners, produces inconsistent results.
- <u>Correct</u> this by keeping the target arm firm (as though it were in a cast) from the set-up throughout the swing. Work on good flexibility and stretch and extend the target side, with the target shoulder coming under the chin.

ERROR
Downswing initiated with hands and/or arms

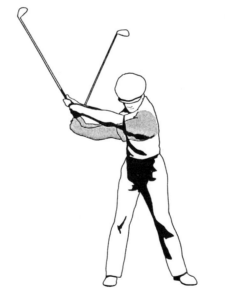

ILLUSTRATION

Figure 4.16

RESULTS AND CORRECTION
- Because of the reverse of the sequential swing pattern, the plane is changed from outside to inside--this <u>often</u> causes a slice or a pull and a loss of power.
- <u>Correct</u> this by initiating the downswing with the weight shift and lateral movement through the lower body toward the target.

At the end of swing, weight
remains on rear foot

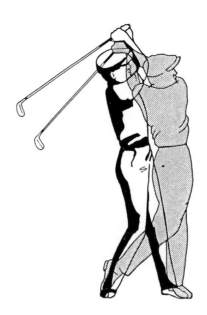

Figure 4.17

RESULTS AND CORRECTION

- This usually results in a slice or topped shot.
- Correct this by (1) initiating the downswing with the weight shift to the target foot; and (2) keeping the weight on the inside of the rear foot on the backswing and drive toward the target with the rear knee on the downswing.

OTHER PROBLEM AREAS

	ERROR	RESULT	CORRECTION
1.	Dipping head during backswing	Hitting fat	Keep the head steady throughout the swing.
2.	Breaking wrists too soon on downswing	Lack of distance Slice	Keep wrists firm through the ball. The downswing starts with the lower body -- through the shoulders - arms and finally the wrists break just before contact.
3.	Raising body during swing	Fat or whiffed (inconsistent)	Must maintain head position and basic posture throughout swing.
4.	Swaying of head and body on backswing	Slicing due to improper rotation Inconsistent pattern	Keep the weight on the inside of the rear foot on the backswing -- target shoulder should rotate under the chin as the head remains still.

5.	Lifting club primarily with the rear hand	Usually a slice or a pull	Practice a low, extended takeaway. Start the backswing with the target side pushing the clubhead away from the ball. The wrists should remain straight and only break naturally, high in the backswing.
6.	Taking a quick "peek"	Often a fat or topped "flubbed" shot	This often occurs as the beginning golfer gets near the green. Must concentrate on short shots to avoid this error. Pick a spot on the ball to insure that you watch it as you strike the ball.
7.	Letting legs get too involved in short game	Often a fat or topped "flubbed" shot	Most of the weight should remain on the target side throughout the swing when pitching and chipping. There should be very little below-the-waist motion.

IMPROVEMENT DRILLS AND GAMES

Golf places a premium on smooth, rhythmic, coordinated movements. The good swing demands a high degree of flexibility. It's therefore important to improve overall body flexibility through a variety of stretching exercises. Here are a few exercises that are good warm-ups prior to playing and also rehearse the actual body movements used in the swing:

The following group of exercise drills are virtually the same movements that are used in all parts of the golf swing. They should be practiced correctly.

1. Weight Transfer and Body Rotation I

    Place the club in position as in (Figure 4.18), with the feet approximately shoulder-width apart, and knees flexed. Keeping the head steady, twist the grip end of the club down toward the ground, using your target side, at the same time shifting your weight to the rear leg. Next, twist the head of the club down using your rear side and smoothly transferring your weight to the target leg. Perform the entire movement 8-10 times.

Figure 4.18

2. Weight Transfer and Body Rotation II

    Stand with the feet shoulder-width apart, knees flexed, gripping club as shown (Figure 4.19). Swing club back and high to the rear, shifting weight to the rear leg. Then swing back through the "contact area" and up to the target side, shifting the weight to the target leg. Continue to swing backward and forward, but place more emphasis on kicking your rear knee in on the forward swing. The head remains stationary throughout the motion.

Figure 4.19

3. Head Control Swing with Partner

Take your stance and golfing posture without a club, but allowing the arms to extend toward the ball position. Your partner stands opposite you and places the palm of his hand against your forehead (Figure 4.20). You then simulate the golf swing with particular concentration on the feel of the body rotation around a steady head. You continue the swing movement 10-12 times. (Your partner should allow only a slight natural movement of the head, and should observe to insure that your eyes are focused on the ball position throughout swing.)

Figure 4.20

4. Target Side Dominance Exercise

You assume the correct stance and posture, gripping the club with the target hand only. With the rear arm behind the back, practice the pendular swing, utilizing the target side as the primary mover (Figure 4.21). The club should be continuously pulled back and up, then down and through the hitting area by the target arm and side. During the downswing you should sense the target side pulling through toward the target, with the back of the target

125

hand leading the clubhead. Practice this movement in three sets of seven swings each set.

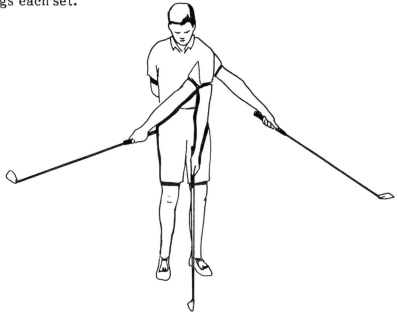

Figure 4.21

5-9. Golf Skills Test Items

Practice each item.

GOLF SKILLS TEST

GENERAL INFORMATION

The following test is designed for the beginning golfer; it may be modified for particular situations.* It is designed to objectively assess golfing ability for five types of shots.

The shots are the following:

1.   Chip shot -- 15 feet
2.   Pitch shot -- 25 yards
3.   Iron shot -- 30-60 yards
4.   Wood shot -- 50-125 yards
5.   Putt -- 15 feet

*Golf Skills Test was developed by Reggie Lipnick and Jerry Clark, 1985.

The maximum number of points is 100.

A = 70-100
B = 62-69
C = 52-61
D = 48-51
F = 0-47

Instructions for Skills Test:

1) Each student should be given adequate time for instruction and practice before the test is given. 2) Each student takes 12 balls for each test. The first two balls do not count for score. These first two balls are for practice so that the student will get the feel of the shot and have a chance to relax. 3) Other students who are watching should remain quiet.

CHIP SHOT

Purpose--To determine the student's ability to hit within a 10 foot radius of the cup from a distance of 15 feet from the green (Figure 4.22).

Equipment--1) One iron of choice. 2) 12 golf balls. 3) A green marked off as diagramed below with a flag in the center.

Procedure--The student stands anywhere around the green as long as he remains 15 feet from the edge. The student will hit 10 shots for scoring. The student may score a maximum of two points for each shot. If he/she hits the ball within a five foot radius of the cup, it counts two points. If he/she hits the ball between a five and 10 foot radius, it counts one point. The student may score a maximum of 20 points on this test.

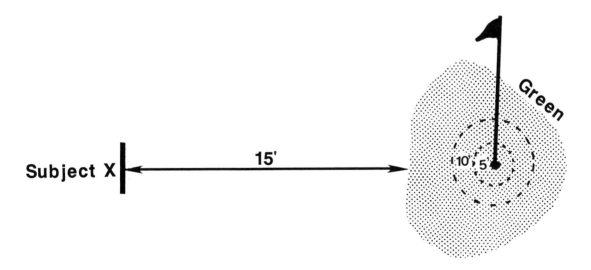

Figure 4.22 Chip Shot

PITCH SHOT

<u>Purpose</u>--To determine the student's ability to hit within a 30 foot radius of the cup from a distance of 25 yards from the green (Figure 4.23).

<u>Equipment/Facilities</u>--1) A no. 9 iron or wedge. 2) 12 golf balls. 3) A green with a flag in the center.

<u>Procedure</u>--The student will hit 10 shots for scoring. Each shot can score a maximum of two points. To score two points the ball must come to rest within a 15 foot radius of the cup. To score one point the ball must come to rest between a 15 and 30 foot radius. No credit is given for a shot that rolls all the way to either the 15 foot or 30 foot radius. The ball must have loft and carry over the restraining line in the air. A maximum 20 points can be scored on this test.

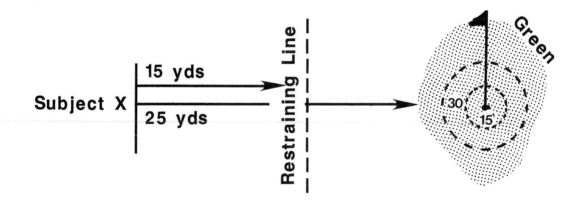

Figure 4.23 Pitch Shot

SHORT IRON SHOT

Purpose--To determine the student's ability to hit the ball in the air a specified distance and within a 50 yard wide fairway (Figure 4.24).

Equipment/Facilities--1) One 7, 8, or 9 iron. 2) 12 golf balls. 3) Area 50 yds. wide and 90 yds. long. 4) One green or marked off area with a flag in the center.

Procedure--The student will hit 10 shots for scoring. Each shot can score a maximum of two points. Credit is given the student in this test on where the ball first hits the ground. To gain two points the ball must carry 60 yards for men and 50 yards for women, and remain in a 50 yard fairway. To gain one point the ball must carry 40 yards for men and 30 yards for women, and remain in a 50 yard fairway. If the ball lands on one of the designated restraining lines, the higher value will count. No credit will be given if the ball carries out of bounds. The student can score a maximum of 20 points.

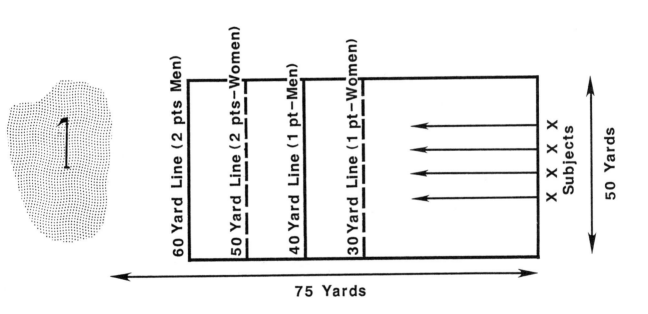

Figure 4.24 Short Iron Shot

WOOD SHOT

Purpose--To determine the student's ability to hit the ball in the air for a specified distance within a 75 yard wide fairway (Figure 4.25).

Equipment/Facilities--1) Wood. 2) 12 golf balls. 3) An area 150 yds. long and 75 yds. wide.

Procedure--The student will hit 10 shots for scoring. The student can score a maximum of two points on each shot. For two points the student must hit the ball within the 75 yard wide fairway and carry in the air, 125 yards for men and 75 yards for women. For one point the ball must stay within the 75 yard wide fairway and must carry in the air, 75 yards for men and 50 yards for women. If the ball lands on a restraining line, the higher value will be given. No credit will be given if the ball carries out of bounds. A student can score a maximum of 20 points on this test.

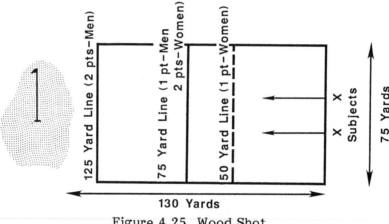

Figure 4.25 Wood Shot

PUTTING

Purpose--To determine the student's ability to putt the ball from a distance of 15 feet into a two foot area around a cup (Figure 4.26).

Equipment/Facilities--1) Putter. 2) Supply of golf balls. 3) Putting green or suitable carpet area.

Procedure--The student will putt 10 balls for scoring. The student can score a maximum of two points on each putt. To score two points the ball must land in the cup or stop within a one foot radius from the edge of the cup. One point is scored if the ball stops in the area between the one and two foot radius of the cup.

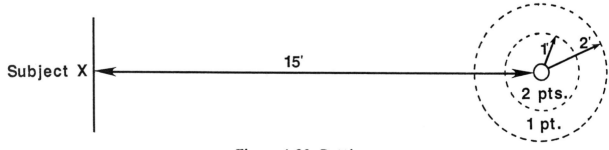

Figure 4.26 Putting

GOLF
Skill Test Score Sheet

NAME_____Male/Female Date_____Instructor_____
　　　　　　　　　　　　Circle
Class_____Section_____Day/Time_____

TEST ITEM	TRIALS	TOTAL SCORE	T-SCORE	RECORDER'S SIGNATURE
I.　Chip Shot	__ __ __ __ __ __ __ __ __ __	_____	_____	_____
II.　Pitch Shot	__ __ __ __ __ __ __ __ __ __	_____	_____	_____
III.　Iron Shot	__ __ __ __ __ __ __ __ __ __	_____	_____	_____
IV.　Wood Shot	__ __ __ __ __ __ __ __ __ __	_____	_____	_____
V.　Putt	__ __ __ __ __ __ __ __ __ __	_____	_____	_____

TOTALS _____　AVERAGE_____
　　　　　　　　　　　GRADE _____

GOLF SKILLS TEST NORMS

	Chip Shot Men	Chip Shot Women	Pitch Shot Men	Pitch Shot Women	Iron Shot Men	Iron Shot Women	Wood Shot Men	Wood Shot Women	Putt Men	Putt Women
	18	15	18	15	19	16	19	16	18	15
Adv.	17	14	17	14	18	15	18	15	16	14
	16	13	16	13	17	14	17	14	15	13
	15	12	15	12	16	13	16	13	14	12
Int.	14	11	14	11	15	12	15	12	13	11
	13	10	13	10	14	11	14	11	12	10
	11	9	11	9	12	10	12	10	10	9
	9	8	9	7	10	8	11	9	9	7
Beg.	8	6	7	5	8	6	9	7	8	6
	7	5	5	4	7	5	7	6	6	5
	6	4	4	2	5	4	6	4	5	3
	4		3			3	4			

GOLF
Skill Test Score Sheet

AME_____Male/Female Date_____Instructor_____
                    Circle
lass_____Section_____Day/Time_____

	TEST ITEM	TRIALS	TOTAL SCORE	T-SCORE	RECORDER'S SIGNATURE
.	Chip Shot	— — — — —			
		— — — — —	____	____	_____
I.	Pitch Shot	— — — — —			
		— — — — —	____	____	_____
II.	Iron Shot	— — — — —			
		— — — — —	____	____	_____
V.	Wood Shot	— — — — —			
		— — — — —	____	____	_____
.	Putt	— — — — —			
		— — — — —	____	____	_____

TOTALS _____ AVERAGE_____
GRADE _____

GOLF SKILLS TEST NORMS

	Chip Shot Men	Women	Pitch Shot Men	Women	Iron Shot Men	Women	Wood Shot Men	Women	Putt Men	Women
	18	15	18	15	19	16	19	16	18	15
dv.	17	14	17	14	18	15	18	15	16	14
	16	13	16	13	17	14	17	14	15	13
	15	12	15	12	16	13	16	13	14	12
nt.	14	11	14	11	15	12	15	12	13	11
	13	10	13	10	14	11	14	11	12	10
	11	9	11	9	12	10	12	10	10	9
	9	8	9	7	10	8	11	9	9	7
eg.	8	6	7	5	8	6	9	7	8	6
	7	5	5	4	7	5	7	6	6	5
	6	4	4	2	5	4	6	4	5	3
	4		3		3		4			

GOLF
Skill Analysis Score Sheet
(20 points)

ame _____ Date _____

lass _____ Evaluated By _____

	POINTS SCORED		
	0	1	2
Good Grip	____	____	____
*1) Overlapping or Interlocking			
2) "V"'s pointing to rear ear			
3) Firm but light touch			
Body Position	____	____	____
*1) Square stance			
2) Aligned toward target			
3) Sitting on a stool			
4) Hands below mouth			
5) Address the ball			
The Swing	____	____	____
*1) Backswing(shoulder under chin)			
2) Weight inside rear foot			
3) Back to target			
4) Downswing(started by legs)			
5) Weight shift to target side			
Point of Impact	____	____	____
*1) Hands & club face - alignment			
2) Head slightly behind ball			
3) Hit through the ball			
Follow Through	____	____	____
*1) Beltbuckle facing target			
2) Hands above head			
Putting	____	____	____
*1) Stance(good balance & alignment)			
2) Grip(reverse overlap)			
3) Stroke(body still - wrist firm)			
Short Game	____	____	____
*1) Chip shot(wt. on target foot)			
2) Pitch shot(mini-swing)			
Club Selection	____	____	____
*1) A general guide			
2) Your personal selections?			
Basic Rules & Etiquette	____	____	____
*1) The most common rules of golf			
2) Etiquette - know before playing!			
0. Results	____	____	____
*1) Golf skill test results			
2) General evaluation			

Points for evaluation

TOTAL SCORE _____

GOLF
Skill Analysis Score Sheet
(20 points)

ame _____   Date _____

lass _____   Evaluated By _____

POINT GUIDE

2 points -- Student appears competent
1 point   -- Occasionally correct or minor errors
0 points -- Needs more attention before ready to
              play

	POINTS SCORED		
	0	1	2
Good Grip	___	___	___
*1) Overlapping or Interlocking			
2) "V"'s pointing to rear ear			
3) Firm but light touch			
Body Position	___	___	___
*1) Square stance			
2) Aligned toward target			
3) Sitting on a stool			
4) Hands below mouth			
5) Address the ball			
The Swing	___	___	___
*1) Backswing(shoulder under chin)			
2) Weight inside rear foot			
3) Back to target			
4) Downswing(started by legs)			
5) Weight shift to target side			
Point of Impact	___	___	___
*1) Hands & club face - alignment			
2) Head slightly behind ball			
3) Hit through the ball			
Follow Through	___	___	___
*1) Beltbuckle facing target			
2) Hands above head			
Putting	___	___	___
*1) Stance(good balance & alignment)			
2) Grip(reverse overlap)			
3) Stroke(body still - wrist firm)			
Short Game	___	___	___
*1) Chip shot(wt. on target foot)			
2) Pitch shot(mini-swing)			
Club Selection	___	___	___
*1) A general guide			
2) Your personal selections?			
Basic Rules & Etiquette	___	___	___
*1) The most common rules of golf			
2) Etiquette - know before playing!			
0. Results	___	___	___
*1) Golf skill test results			
2) General evaluation			

Points for evaluation

TOTAL SCORE _____

CHAPTER 5

PICKLE-BALL

HISTORY

PICKLE-BALL--THE NEWEST GAME AROUND!

This is a new, fun game that has gained great popularity in only a few years (mid '0's). The game is easy to learn, regardless of age, sex, strength, or athletic skill. It's basically a "narrowed-down" version of tennis that is usually played indoors on a doubles badminton court. It has strokes and strategies that include forehand and backhand drives from the baseline for long rallies, overhead smashes, lobs, and fast and furious volleys at the net. A lightweight wooden paddle is used to stroke a plastic "whiffle ball" that's slightly larger than a tennis ball. Since the ball and paddle are lightweight and the court is small, many students who were not very successful in other racket sports have found pickle-ball easier to learn and thus more fun to play.

It has also enjoyed great popularity among the skilled athletes. Our experience has shown that many college athletes who begin playing pickle-ball in the off-season become virtually "addicted" to the sport. No one loves it more nor has better skill than the varsity tennis players. They adapt to it easily since the ground strokes and volleys are so similar to tennis strokes.

Pickle-ball originated in the summer of 1965 on Bainbridge Island, a short distance by boat from Seattle, Washington. The co-inventors were U.S. Congressman Joel Pritchard, William Bell, and Barney McCollum. They were motivated to provide a recreational type of sport in which the entire family could participate. The name pickle came from Pritchard's dog named Pickles, who would occasionally retrieve the ball during play. The game was initially played by families in their backyards, on driveways, or on residential dead-end streets. Since the mid-seventies, however, the recreational game has spread and grown into a net court sport with formalized rules. It is currently being played in thousands of educational institutions, parks and recreation centers, correctional facilities, health clubs, fitness centers, and on multi-purpose courts at family residences.

BENEFITS

There is some aerobic conditioning occurring when good players play singles and keep the ball in play. As a general rule, however, the greatest benefit comes in developing motor fitness qualities. As in tennis, hand-eye coordination, agility, and quick reactions are essential for a good level of play.

Pickle-ball has become one of our newest "lifetime sports" and one in which there need not be an expensive investment. By converting part of the driveway or patio into a temporary court, the game can be played at home with family or friends. This social value and convenience of play can provide active enjoyment for a lifetime right in your backyard.

TERMINOLOGY

Pickle-ball terminology has evolved from tennis and badminton. Since the basic skills and overall play is so similar to tennis, much of the language is identical. There are, however, some new terms that are unique to pickle-ball. To understand the game, it is important to become familiar with all of the language of pickle-ball.

Ace A serve that the receiver cannot even touch with the paddle. A "winner" for the server.

Angle Shot A shot that is hit sharply crosscourt.

Approach Shot A groundstroke hit by the player allowing him/her to move to the net position.

Back Court The area near the baseline.

Backspin Backward spin on the ball, with the top of the ball rotating away from its direction of flight. Slice, chop, or cut the ball.

Crosscourt Shot A shot in which the ball travels diagonally across the net from one corner to the other.

Deep A shot that lands within the court near the baseline.

Doubles This consists of two players on each team.

Down-the-Line A shot hit parallel to the sideline.

Drive A groundstroke that is hit hard enough to carry deep into the opponent's court.

Drop Shot A softly hit ball with backspin that clears the net and lands in the non-volley zone.

Error A point that is lost because of poor play and not caused by your opponent.

Even Court The right side of the court. When serving from the right side, an even number of points have been played.

Face Refers to the hitting side of the paddle.

Fault A serve that does not land within the proper service court. Results in a loss of serve.

Foot Fault An illegal serve, usually caused by the server's failure to keep one foot behind the baseline.

Game When one side has a score of eleven. Winner must be ahead by two points.

Groundstroke A forehand or backhand stroke hit after the ball has bounced.

Half-Volley The ball is hit or blocked immediately after it bounces.

Head The part of the paddle used to hit the ball.

Let A point that must be replayed.

Let Serve When the ball hits the top of the net on the serve and lands within the proper service court.

Lob A high arching shot that carries over the net player and lands deep in the court.

Mixed Doubles Male and female partners composing one team.

Net Game Involves getting to the net position to use volleys and smashes to win points.

No Man's Land Between midcourt and the baseline. In this area, balls that are hit near the feet are difficult to return with any control.

Non-Volley Zone They are marked by lines seven feet on either side of the net. The player cannot volley while inside this area, nor can the follow-through of a stroke carry him/her into the area.

Odd Court The left side of the court. When serving from the left side, an odd number of points have been played.

Out A ball which lands outside the playing court.

Smash An overhead stroke used to put the ball away.

Pace Refers to the speed of the ball. Good pace means good speed.

Passing Shot A ball hit past the opponent on either side.

Poach Strategy used in doubles when the net player moves across to cut off and volley a ball that would normally be played by his/her partner.

Put Away A shot that is hit too good for opponents to return it.

Rally Keeping the ball in play after the serve. Often refers to numerous groundstrokes hit in succession without a miss.

Rush the Net Moving quickly to the net position as soon as the ball has bounced and been returned. This strategy is the key to winning in pickle-ball.

Serve The underhand stroke that puts the ball in play.

Singles This consists of one player on each team.

Top Spin Forward rotation of the ball caused by striking the ball with the paddle moving upward. This is often desirable, especially for more advanced players, since it allows you to hit the ball higher and harder and still keep it in bounds.

Volley A ball hit before it bounces.

EQUIPMENT

Court--The size of the court is 20' x 44' for both doubles and singles. This is identical to a badminton doubles court. The badminton court service lines are also used, except for the singles side lines and the doubles service backline which are disregarded for pickle-ball. The badminton short service line serves as both the short service line and the non-volley zone line in pickle-ball (See Figure 5.1). These court dimensions have greatly enhanced the rapid spread of the game, since many educational and recreational facilities already have permanently marked badminton courts.

Unlike the badminton net, the pickle-ball net should be at 36" on the ends and 34" in the center. Although special heavy duty pickle-ball nets are available, badminton nets have proven to be quite adequate.

Paddles--The paddles are lightweight and wooden and are made in three slightly different styles by the lone manufacturer, Pickle-Ball, Inc. of Seattle, Washington. The paddle length cannot exceed $15\frac{1}{2}$ inches, and the maximum width of the head is 8 inches.

Balls--The plastic balls are three inches in diameter and can either be purchased from the pickle-ball company or from other stores, but without the pickle-ball inscription on them.

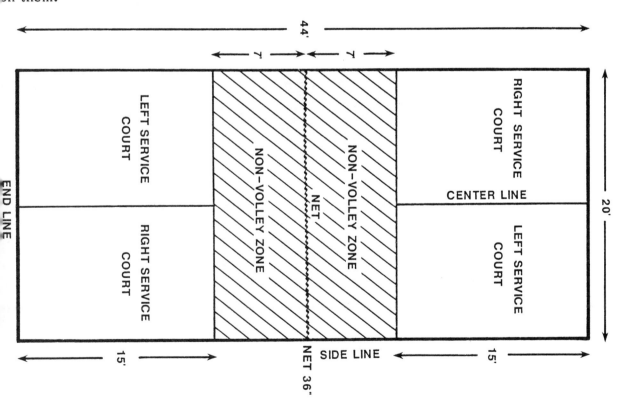

Figure 5.1 Pickle-Ball Court

RULES AND ETIQUETTE

RULES

Pickle-ball rules are similar to those for badminton. To begin a game, a coin toss or a rally until a fault occurs, determines which team has the option of serving or receiving first.

Serving--A player must keep one foot behind the back line when serving. The serve must be underhand with the paddle passing below the waist. The ball must be struck in the air and not bounced and hit. The serve is made diagonally cross court and must land within the service court. Only one service attempt is allowed, unless the ball touches the net and then lands within the service court. This constitutes a "let" serve and the server has one more serve.

At the start of each new game in doubles, the team serving first is allowed only one fault before the serve goes to the other team. For the remainder of the game, both team members will serve before the serve goes out. When a team wins the serve, the player in the righthand court will always serve first. When the serving team makes a fault, the players stay on their same side of the court, and the other team member serves. The server will alternate sides and serve as long as his/her team is scoring. This is the only time throughout the game that team members change sides of the court to begin a point.

Volley--As in tennis, this means hitting the ball in the air before it bounces. All volleying in pickle-ball must be done from behind the non-volley zone line (Figure 5.2). It is also a fault if the player steps on or over the line on his/her follow-through. If a player sees that the ball will bounce in the non-volley zone, he/she can move into the zone before it bounces but must let it bounce before returning it.

Figure 5.2 Non-Volley Zones

Double-Bounce Rule--The first stroke in a rally by each team or player must come after the ball bounces. The player receiving the serve must obviously let the serve bounce, and then on the return shot the server or serving team must also let the ball bounce before they can return it. After two bounces have occurred, the ball can then be either volleyed or played off the bounce.

Faults--

1. Hitting the ball out of bounds.
2. Hitting the ball into the net; not clearing it.
3. Volleying the ball while in the non-volley zone.
4. Volleying the ball before it has bounced once on each side of the net.

Scoring--As in badminton, a team can score only when serving. The player who is serving continues to serve until he/she or their team commits a fault. The game ends at 11 points, except that a team must win by two points.

ETIQUETTE

Good etiquette in pickle-ball is the same as for many other racket sports. It involves using good manners, courtesy and an avoidance of unnecessary distractions. Here are some guidelines that especially apply to pickle-ball:

1. Avoid walking across the court or behind the court while a point is being played. Wait until play stops and then move quickly to your court or destination.
2. The server should keep the score and announce it after each point occurs. The server's score should be called first. This helps to prevent disagreements and interruptions in the game.
3. Avoid hitting serves and other shots back that are obviously out. This is distracting and it often causes delays for chasing down the ball.
4. Give your opponent the benefit of the doubt on close line calls. If you are not sure whether it was in or out, always call it in.
5. When the ball strays onto another court, wait until play stops, and then reply "thank you," or "ball, thank you." Don't run and chase a ball across or behind a court while play is in progress.
6. Avoid smashing a ball into your opponent at the net. A smash at the opponent's feet or a volley directly at the opponent is often good strategy, but avoid a hard shot that could cause injury.
7. When you retrieve the ball for your opponent, either toss the ball to him with your hand or stroke it directly toward him with the paddle. Avoid hitting the ball extremely hard or haphazardly in a rush of anger or disgust. Such a retrieval is very discourteous and causes unnecessary delays for "chasing the ball."

FUNDAMENTALS OF THE GAME

The basic types of pickle-ball strokes, with the exception of the serve, are essentially the same as tennis:

Forehand drives	Lobs	Overheads
Backhand drives	Volleys	

Good tennis strokes produce good pickle-ball strokes. The major differences in the shots for the two games are as follows:

1. Spin is more effective in tennis than pickle-ball.
2. Because the pickle-ball is so lightweight, more wrist action can be used to return shots.

3. The pickle-ball serve is underhanded and tennis is overhanded.
4. Depending on the court surface, the pickle-ball often does not bounce as high as a tennis ball, thus requiring more knee bend for strokes.

THE SERVE

The serve in pickle-ball is an underhanded motion in which the paddle must pass below the waist, and the ball must be struck before it touches the floor. The body position is similar to pitching a softball with the weight on the rear foot, then shifting forward to the front foot. As the weight shifts forward, the ball is dropped forward of the body and the paddle is brought forward to strike the ball at approximately knee height. When the ball is struck, one foot can be inside the court but the rear foot must be behind the baseline.

The server should use the basic forehand grip. For the drive serve, the ball is struck with the wrist cocked and then allowing the paddle to "break into" the ball for the desired speed and trajectory. The ball action resembles a forehand or backhand drive shot (Figure 5.3).

The lob serve can be used as a change-of-pace but should be hit deep enough to prevent an easy put-away return. This serve is hit with an upward motion following a pendulum arc of the arm and paddle. The ball flight is similar to the lob in tennis or pickle-ball (Figure 5.4).

GRIPS AND FUNDAMENTAL STROKES

The basic skill techniques are not different from those of tennis. For grips and fundamental stroke skills, the reader's attention is directed to the chapter on tennis. For the backhand shot, it is not as essential to rotate the grip since the pickle-ball is much lighter and can be returned with arm action that is less firm than for tennis.

Figure 5.3 Drive Serve

Figure 5.4 Lob Serve

PICKLE-BALL STRATEGY

The most effective way in singles or doubles to win rallies is to gain the advantageous position at the net, just behind the non-volley zone line. From this position, the player or players can hit deep or angled volleys that are difficult for the opponent to return with good shots (Figure 5.5).

Figure 5.5 Volley Position

Singles--Unlike tennis, the receiver has the advantage in pickle-ball. Because of the double-bounce rule, the server must let the returned ball bounce before making a stroke. This allows the receiver to return the serve and then move to the net position to volley the return shot. The receiver should return the serve with a shot that carries deep into the opponent's court, preferably to the backhand side. This allows the receiver more time to reach the net and it forces a long return by the server, which gives the receiver more time to react and volley. Conversely, the server in singles must try to either serve the ball deep enough to make it more difficult for the receiver to move to the net position, or serve a hard, well-placed ball that forces a weak return. If the serve is deep enough, the receiver may not have time to hit the return and rush the net, thus allowing the server to hit the ball, after the bounce, and move to the net.

When your opponent has the net position, you should mix forehand and backhand drive shots low and away from the net player. Try to make the volleyer hit the ball upward, which would allow you to return with an offensive shot. Occasionally a lob to the opponent's backhand court will force an error or weak return.

Doubles--The game was invented with "doubles play" as the primary style. As previously mentioned, the best offensive position for both partners is at the net. When both teams are at the net, the fast-paced volleying displays some exciting action that is unrivaled in most games. As in singles, the receiving team has the advantage for first taking the net position. The double-bounce rule rule forces both partners of the serving team to stay deep until the serve is returned and bounces. The non-receiving member of the receiving team should start play at the net position since the ball will have already bounced twice before he/she has a stroke opportunity. The receiving partner should hit a deep return and quickly move to the net position in the front center of the service court. From the net both partners should hit sharp-angled volleys and/or short drop shots to win the rally. The best strategy for the serving team is to either hit the serve deep enough to prevent the receiver from reaching the net, or hit a serve with good pace and placement that forces a poor return. If the receiver is unable to come to the net then the serving team should hit the return, after the bounce, back to the same open side and both take the net. If the service return is short, the serving team should attempt low down-the-line or down-the-middle ground strokes that would be difficult to return with an effective offensive shot.

Occasionally, when the receiving team has the net position, a well-placed lob will force the defensive player away from the net and give you an opportunity to move up. A drop shot that bounces in the non-volley zone, can be used to surprise the opponents and ideally force them to hit the ball upward to clear the net. A rising ball provides an excellent opening for an offensive volley or smash return.

When both partners are side-by-side in doubles, a lob should be played by the partner who has the forehand shot. A drive between the partners should also be played by the forehand whenever possible. If one partner is forced wide of the court to return a shot, the partner should move in that direction to help maintain the best court coverage.

ERRORS AND CORRECTIONS

Illustrations of the <u>MOST COMMON</u> errors and how to correct them.

ERROR (GROUNDSTROKES)

Face of paddle "open" or tilted up as ball is struck. Often a "wristy" stroke.

Figure 5.6

RESULTS AND CORRECTION
- This will cause you to consistently hit too long and/or an undesirable high shot over the net.
- Work on the "basics" for the tennis forehand and backhand. The paddle should start each swing perpendicular to the court and finish at about head height and still be perpendicular. Start the paddle low on the backswing and try to reduce the wrist action in the stroke.

ERROR (GROUNDSTROKES)

Dropping the head of the paddle to hit low shots.

ILLUSTRATION

Figure 5.7

RESULTS AND CORRECTION
- This usually causes a "wristy" return that is too high, too slow, and difficult to accurately place.
- Stroke all forehand and backhand shots the same way; simply <u>bend your knees</u> more for low balls. Adjust your body to the height of the ball and keep the paddle even with the wrist.

ERROR (GROUNDSTROKES)
Not transferring weight to front foot and not contacting ball even with or forward or the front leg.

Figure 5.8

RESULTS AND CORRECTION
- Shot will often not clear the net or if it does, there is little pace on the ball.
- Again, the basic forehand and backhand tennis technique should be reviewed and practiced. The player should attempt to step forward into each stroke. Contact the ball even with the front leg on the forehand and slightly forward of the front leg on the backhand.

ERROR (BACKHAND)
Consistently weak backhand returns.

Figure 5.9

RESULTS AND CORRECTION
- Usually results in an easy volley or ground stroke return by your opponent.
- Change to a backhand grip and try to swing firmly from low to high. Start with the paddle back below the hip and keep the wrist behind the paddle face as contact is made. Finish with the paddle at head height and past the direction the ball was hit.

ERROR (SERVES)
Serves that land short
consistently.

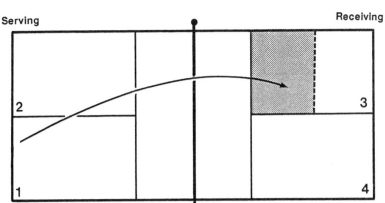

Figure 5.10

RESULTS AND CORRECTION
- This "sets up" your opponent for an easy return and allows him/her to take the net position.
- Practice serving deep to your opponent. This is not a difficult stroke, and practice will usually solve the problem. Try dropping the ball more in front of the body and delaying the wrist break slightly longer. At contact, however, forcefully snap through the ball.

OTHER PROBLEM AREAS

ERROR	RESULT	CORRECTION
1. Poor control over ball direction on serves.	Numerous missed serves landing to the right or left of the service court.	Practice stepping in the desired direction of the serve, and continuing the follow-through in the same direction. Imagine you are pitching a softball to a spot on the court and serve with the same motion.
2. Poor body position "set-up" for ground-strokes, resulting in ball getting "even with" or behind the body.	Causes you to use more wrist action and/or step backward to return shot. Usually results in short returns or shots that do not clear the net.	It is essential that you assume a "ready position" after each stroke. As soon as the ball is struck by the opponent, you should be moving quickly and simultaneously taking the paddle back for the stroke. If you wait until you have set up to take the paddle back, you will consistently use too much wrist action in the stroke.

ERROR	RESULT	CORRECTION
3. Volleys that are hit too softly with no pace.	Instead of putting pressure on your opponent, this allows him/her to take the offensive and hit a good return.	Try to meet the ball in front of the body. Hit it in the center of the paddle and use very little wrist action.
4. Not watching the ball all the way to your paddle.	Results in numerous miss-hit shots, especially on volleys, lobs, and overhead smash returns.	One of the most obvious characteristics when watching good tennis players, is how well they watch the ball and concentrate on each shot. You should practice following the ball from your opponent's paddle to yours for each stroke.

IMPROVEMENT DRILLS AND GAMES

-5. For beginning pickle-ball drills, see TENNIS drills #1-5 for forehand and backhand. Use the checkpoints for the forehand and backhand strokes.

6. Off-the-Wall Drill (Forehand)
   -- From a position approximately 15 feet from a solid wall--attempt to keep the ball in play by hitting forehand strokes. Hit the ball slightly higher on the wall, 5-8 feet, than you would normally hit from that distance to clear the net. This would facilitate the ball rebounding far enough back and would better similate ground strokes from the baseline.
   -- You should emphasize "good form" on each stroke.
   -- You should become fully aware of the importance of quick preparation, body position, and paddle preparation, for each stroke.
   -- Begin with 10 shots off the wall--try to increase by five each new practice session.
   -- NOTE--Do not attempt to return to a "ready position" after each stroke. Keep the non-paddle side to the wall due to the quickness of the ball return.
   -- Use the same drill for the backhand stroke. NOTE--Keep the paddle side toward the wall.

7-11. Practice pickle-ball skills test items: forehand--backhand--serve--volley--lob.
   -- Try to score a minimum of 80% on each item.

12. Rally Drill (Singles)
   -- Two students--one near each baseline with a box of pickle-balls nearby each.
   -- Begin rally with a serve and then attempt to keep the ball in play with forehand and backhand ground strokes.
   -- Try to hit the ball deep in the court so that both can rally near the baseline.
   -- NOTE--Do not try to hit winners--Concentrate on good technique and shot preparation.

13. Rally-Volley Drill (Doubles)
   -- Four students--two on one side in volley position--six-ten inches behind the non-volley zone line. Two on opposite side near the baseline.
   -- One box of balls behind the baseline players.
   -- One baseline player puts the ball in play with a drive serve--volleyers then stroke the ball firm and deep back to baseline area.
   -- Both baseline players try to hit ground strokes toward either of the volleyers.
   -- Change positions after 10 minutes.

14. Volley Game
   -- Game is played on one side of the court; center line is the boundary.
   -- Two students on opposite sides of the net at the volley position.
   -- The ball is then volleyed or half-volleyed until a fault occurs. If the ball lands in the non-volley zone, it can be played as a ground stroke after the bounce, otherwise the stroke must be a volley or half-volley.
   -- A point is scored on each fault regardless of serve.
   -- The player committing the fault serves first BUT a point cannot be scored on a serve--only after the rally has begun.
   -- Game is 11 points. Must win by two points.

PICKLE-BALL SKILLS TEST

GENERAL INFORMATION

The following test is designed for the beginning pickle-ball player. It is designed to objectively assess ability in four areas

        1. Serve
        2. Forehand/ Backhand Drives
        3. Lob
        4. Volley

I. SERVE

Purpose--To measure the player's ability to serve deep and accurately into the opposite court.

Directions--The student starts behind the baseline but is allowed to step into court as he serves. He will serve 10 times underhanded from the side of his choice. The student should attempt to serve deep into the opposite court for the maximum point value (Figure 5.11). Two practice serves are allowed. Maximum score 50.

Scoring--Score each serve by the numerical value of the area in which it first lands. Balls landing on the line will score the higher value. The final score is the sum of 10 serves.

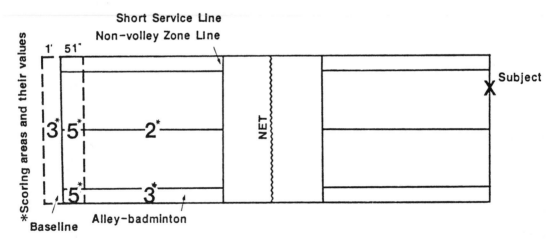

Figure 5.11 Serve

II. FOREHAND AND BACKHAND DRIVES

Purpose--To measure the player's ability to hit a forehand and backhand shot with power and accuracy into the opponent's court.

Pickle-ball Skills Test developed by Jerry Clark, 1986.

Directions

1. The student will stand at the baseline of the pickle-ball court and will be tossed 10 balls to the forehand and 10 to the backhand.
2. The tester will toss the balls underhanded.
3. The student will attempt to hit the balls over the net and under a rope $3\frac{1}{2}$ feet above the net, back into the opponent's court.

Scoring

1. Each ball passing between the net and the rope and into the opponent's court will count five points.
2. A ball passing over the rope and landing in the opponent's court will count two points.
3. Any shot that does not land in the opponent's court will score a "0."
4. Maximum score is 100; forehand 50, backhand 50.

III. LOB

Purpose--To measure the player's ability to hit a high shot over the opponent at the net and deep into his/her court.

Directions

1. The subject will attempt 10 lobs from the side of his choice (forehand or backhand).
2. The lob must pass over a rope which is 10 feet above the court at the net.
3. The tester will toss the balls underhanded, and place the balls so that they land in the back one-third of the court.

Scoring

1. The score is determined by the numerical value of the area in which it lands.
2. It is scored as "0" if it does not pass over the rope.
3. The maximum score is 50.

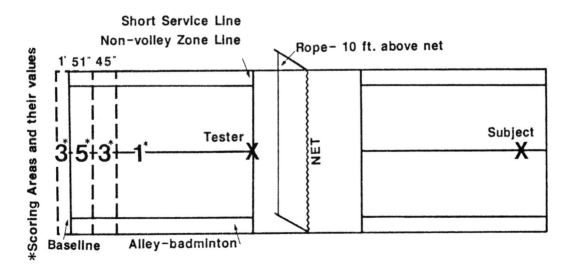

Figure 5.12 Lob

IV. VOLLEY

Purpose--To measure the player's ability to volley balls back into the opponent's court from the net position.

Directions--The student will stand behind the pickle-ball volley line and attempt to return ground strokes with a volley that passes between the net and a rope 3' above the net. The tester, standing on the baseline, will hit 10 ground strokes toward the student. The tester will drop the ball and hit it on the bounce. If the student cannot reach a ball, it will be replayed without scoring. (Balls should be hit toward student without regard to forehand or backhand.)

Scoring--Each ball hit back into the opponent's court will score according to the area in which it lands (Figure 5.13). If the student steps on or over the non-volley line, or if the ball goes over the rope or fails to go over the net, the shot is scored "0." The maximum score is 50.

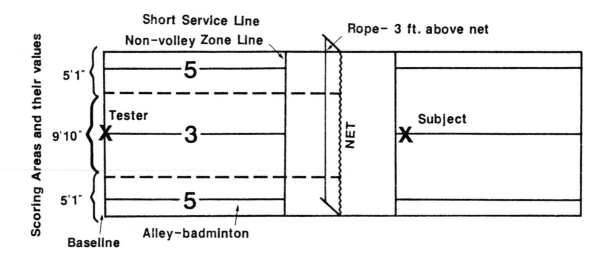

Figure 5.13 Volley

Figure 5.14

ACROSS CLUES

2. a winner
5. a high arching shot
9. when the score is tied
10. hitting off of a bounce
12. hitting your partner's shot
13. 11 points with a 2 point lead
14. a put-away shot
15. the left court
16. hit off of a bounce to the end of the opposite court
18. put the ball in play at the beginning of a point
19. replayed point
20. four players

DOWN CLUES

1. illegal serve or return
3. the right court
4. a shot from one corner to the opposite diagonal corner
6. non-paddle side of the body
7. area in front of the baseline
8. a stroke on the paddle side of the body
11. a hit with no bounce
14. two players
17. continuation of play after the serve

WORD LIST:

ACE	EVEN	ODD
ALL	FAULT	POACH
BACKHAND	FOREHAND	RALLY
BACKCOURT	GAME	SERVE
CROSSCOURT	GROUNDSTROKE	SINGLES
DOUBLES	LET	SMASH
DRIVE	LOB	VOLLEY

ANSWERS: PICKLE-BALL

Figure 5.15

Puzzle contributed by Dr. Kathy Black, Central State University, Edmond, Oklahoma.

PICKLE-BALL
Skills Test Score Sheet

NAME_____ Male/Female Date_____ Instructor_____
                                    Circle
Class_____ Section_____ Day/Time_____

	TEST ITEM	TRIALS	TOTAL SCORE	T-SCORE	RECORDER'S SIGNATURE
I.	Serve	— — — — —			
		— — — — — —	_____	_____	_____
II.	Forehand	— — — — —			
		— — — — — —	_____	_____	_____
III.	Backhand	— — — — —			
		— — — — — —	_____	_____	_____
IV.	Lob	— — — — —			
		— — — — — —	_____	_____	_____
V.	Volley	— — — — —			
		— — — — — —	_____	_____	_____

TOTALS _____   AVERAGE _____
                  GRADE _____

PICKLE-BALL SKILLS TEST NORMS

	Serve		Forehand		Backhand		Lob		Volley	
	Men	Women	Men	Women	Men	Women	Men	Women	Men	Women
	44	37	48	44	46	42	41	38	46	44
	42	35	46	41	44	40	39	35	45	42
Adv.	40	33	44	40	42	38	38	34	43	40
	38	31	42	38	40	36	36	32	41	38
	36	29	41	37	39	34	35	30	38	35
	34	27	40	35	38	32	34	29	36	33
Int.	32	25	38	33	36	30	32	27	34	31
	28	22	36	31	34	28	30	25	32	29
	24	19	34	29	32	27	28	23	31	28
	22	17	32	27	30	25	27	21	30	27
Beg.	20	15	30	25	28	23	25	19	29	26
			20	25	19					
	18	14	25	16	23	15	21	16	27	23
	16	12	20	12	18	10	18	12	25	21
	11	9					14	10		

PICKLE-BALL
Skills Test Score Sheet

NAME_____ Male/Female Date_____ Instructor_____

                                     Circle

Class_____ Section_____ Day/Time_____

TEST ITEM	TRIALS	TOTAL SCORE	T-SCORE	RECORDER'S SIGNATURE
I. Serve	— — — — — — — — — —	___	___	___
II. Forehand	— — — — — — — — — —	___	___	___
III. Backhand	— — — — — — — — — —	___	___	___
IV. Lob	— — — — — — — — — —	___	___	___
V. Volley	— — — — — — — — — —	___	___	___

                           TOTALS _____   AVERAGE _____
                                                    GRADE _____

PICKLE-BALL SKILLS TEST NORMS

	Serve		Forehand		Backhand		Lob		Volley	
	Men	Women	Men	Women	Men	Women	Men	Women	Men	Women
	44	37	48	44	46	42	41	38	46	44
	42	35	46	41	44	40	39	35	45	42
Adv.	40	33	44	40	42	38	38	34	43	40
	38	31	42	38	40	36	36	32	41	38
	36	29	41	37	39	34	35	30	38	35
	34	27	40	35	38	32	34	29	36	33
Int.	32	25	38	33	36	30	32	27	34	31
	28	22	36	31	34	28	30	25	32	29
	24	19	34	29	32	27	28	23	31	28
	22	17	32	27	30	25	27	21	30	27
Beg.	20	15	30	25	28	23	25	19	29	26
			20	25	19					
	18	14	25	16	23	15	21	16	27	23
	16	12	20	12	18	10	18	12	25	21
	11	9					14	10		

PICKLE-BALL
Skill Analysis Score Sheet
(20 points)

Name _____   Date _____

Class _____   Evaluated By _____

POINT GUIDE
2 points -- Student appears competent
1 point -- Occasionally correct or minor errors
0 point -- Needs more attention before ready to
            play

	POINTS SCORED		
	0	1	2
1. Gripping the Paddle *1) (continental - (tennis)	___	___	___
2. Basic Strokes (tennis skills) *1) Forehand drives 2) Backhand drives 3) <u>Body position - contact point - follow-through</u>	___	___	___
3. The Volleys and Lobs *1) Volleys-:"The Real Game" 2) Lobs - for change of pace	___	___	___
4. Serving the Ball *1) Underhanded motion 2) Drive serve (most effective) 3) Lob serve	___	___	___
5. Skill Comparison (pickle-ball - tennis)	___	___	___
6. Singles Strategy *1) Serving 2) Net control	___	___	___
7. Doubles Strategy *1) Receiving team - control net	___	___	___
8. Understanding the <u>Non-Volley Zone</u> and <u>Double-Bounce Rule</u>	___	___	___
9. Rules and Etiquette *1) Faults 2) Scoring 3) Serving 4) Courtesy and good manners	___	___	___
10. Results *1) Pickle-ball skill test results 2) General evaluation	___	___	___

*Points for evaluation

TOTAL SCORE _____

PICKLE-BALL
Skill Analysis Score Sheet
(20 points)

Name _____ Date _____

Class _____ Evaluated By _____

POINT GUIDE
2 points -- Student appears competent
1 point -- Occasionally correct or minor errors
0 point -- Needs more attention before ready to
              play

	POINTS SCORED		
	0	1	2
1. Gripping the Paddle	____	____	____
*1) (continental - (tennis)			
2. Basic Strokes (tennis skills)	____	____	____
*1) Forehand drives			
2) Backhand drives			
3) Body position - contact point - follow-through			
3. The Volleys and Lobs	____	____	____
*1) Volleys-:"The Real Game"			
2) Lobs - for change of pace			
4. Serving the Ball	____	____	____
*1) Underhanded motion			
2) Drive serve (most effective)			
3) Lob serve			
5. Skill Comparison (pickle-ball - tennis)	____	____	____
6. Singles Strategy	____	____	____
*1) Serving			
2) Net control			
7. Doubles Strategy	____	____	____
*1) Receiving team - control net			
8. Understanding the Non-Volley Zone and Double-Bounce Rule	____	____	____
9. Rules and Etiquette	____	____	____
*1) Faults			
2) Scoring			
3) Serving			
4) Courtesy and good manners			
10. Results	____	____	____
*1) Pickle-ball skill test results			
2) General evaluation			

*Points for evaluation

TOTAL SCORE _____

CHAPTER 6

RACKETBALL

HISTORY

The games of handball and paddleball are credited with the evolvement of the racketball game. Handball gave to the sport the court and a foundation for the rules. Similarly, paddleball introduce a solid wooden paddle with a safety wrist thong to be worn during play. The most recent game, racketball, uses a stringed short tennis racket with a wrist thong. All three sports use balls different in size, texture, color and amount of rebound.

Ireland is credited with first developing and holding the first handball championship, while the United States is credited with the sports of paddleball and racketball.

The two major racketball organizations are the International Racketball Association (IRA) and the National Racketball Club (NRC). The former is amateur and the latter is professional. Today, approximately 10 million persons are involved in the sport.

BENEFITS

Aerobic Fitness--With equally skillful players, racketball is rated high in its ability to maintain the cardiorespiratory system.

Motor Fitness--Quick movements and good eye-hand coordination is required.

Social--Racketball supports the 1970-80's fitness boom. It is an excellent socializing activity. There are three types of games in racketball; they are: singles (two players), cut-throat (three players), and doubles (four players).

The game can be played satisfactorily by a wide range of skill levels. Because of the fitness and skill values, the sport can be termed a "lifetime" sport. It utilizes strategy and experience to offset any speed, power or endurance losses as one ages. Another important consideration is that the standard equipment required to play is inexpensive.

TERMINOLOGY

Ace A legal serve untouched by the receiver's racket.

Apex The highest point a ball reaches in a bounce.

Advantage Position The position from which the kill and pass shots are best executed. (Center Court)

Around the Wall Shot A defensive shot that before touching the floor, hits a side wall, the front wall, and then the other side wall.

Avoidable Hinder A player's interference with his/her opponent's play that could have been prevented or avoided.

Backhand A stroke hit across the body beginning on the side opposite the racket hand.

Backhand Corner The corner where the back wall and side wall join on the same side as the player's backhand.

Backwall Shot A shot taken on a ball rebounding off the back wall.

Backswing The action of bringing the racket back behind the body from the ready position in preparation for a forward swing.

Blocking Moving your body into a position to obstruct your opponent's ability to see or hit the ball.

Ceiling Ball A ball that strikes the ceiling first, then the front wall, and then rebounds deep into the back court.

Center Court Control Maintaining position in center court, forcing your opponent to return the ball from deep court.

Closed Face Position where racket face is not parallel to front wall; the top of the head is tilted forward.

Front Court The court area in front of the service line.

Middle or Center Court The court area from the service line to the receiver's line.

Back Court The court area from the receiving line to the back wall.

Court Hinder Artificial interference caused by some court structure such as a door.

Cross-Court Pass Shot A ball hit from one side of the court to the other side of the court.

Crotch Shot A ball that hits the juncture of any two playing surfaces.

Cutthroat A game involving three players with each player playing against the other two.

Dead Ball A ball that is no longer in play.

Defensive Shot A shot used in an attempt to keep the ball in play and move the opponent out of the center court position.

Dig To barely retrieve a low shot before it hits the floor a second time.

Doubles A game where two teams composed of two players each compete.

Down-the-Wall Shot A shot hit near a side wall that hits the front wall directly and then rebounds back along the same side wall.

Drive Shot (Serve) A shot hit very hard that strikes the front wall and rebounds in a straight line.

Drop Shot A shot hit with such little force that it rebounds only a few feet from the front wall.

Fault An illegal serve or other infraction of the rules while serving (two faults results in a side out).

Follow-Through The continuation of the swing after the ball has been hit.

Foot Fault An illegal position in which the server's feet or foot are outside the service zone during the serve.

Forehand A shot hit from dominant side of the body.

Forehand Corner The corner where the side wall and back wall join on the same side as the player's forehand.

Front Wall-Side Wall Kill A kill shot that first hits the front wall, then strikes a side wall before bouncing.

Game When a player or team scores 21 points.

Garbage Serve (Half Lob) A serve hit softly to the front wall that rebounds to the receiver at about shoulder height.

Hand-Out Loss of serve by partner in doubles team. In singles referred to as a side out.

Hinder An unintentional interference or screen of a ball that prevents your opponent from having a fair chance to return the ball (the point is replayed without penalty).

Kill Shot An offensive shot that hits the front wall so low that it is practically impossible to return.

Lob Shot (Serve) Soft high-trajectory shot that lands deep in the back court, preferably a corner.

Long Serve A serve that hits the front wall and rebounds to the back wall without hitting the floor.

Match The winning of two out of three games.

Non-Front Serve Any serve that hits any surface before striking the front wall. This is a double fault and results in a side out.

Offensive Shot An aggressive shot (usually kill or pass) designed to either end the rally or put your opponent in a poor court position.

Open Face Position where racket face is not parallel to the front wall; the top of the head is tilted backwards.

Overhead Shot Kill shots, passing shots, etc. hit above shoulder height.

Pass Shot A ball hit either down-the-line or cross-court that the opponent will either miss or have to move out of position to reach.

Pinch Shot A kill shot that hits the side wall--front wall or the front wall-side wall.

Rally An exchange of shots that is continued until play ends.

Ready Position Stance taken by a player while waiting for a serve or a shot.

Roll-Out A shot where the ball rolls out on the floor after it rebounds off the front wall--a sure point since it is impossible to retrieve.

Screen Interference with the opponent's view of the ball.

Serve Method of putting ball into play.

Service Box Designated rectangular area at the end of the service zone--used in doubles for non-serving member to wait until serve has been made.

Service Line The front line of the service zone--fifteen feet from the front wall. It is used in calling foot faults.

Service Zone The court area bounded by the service line, the short service line, and the sidewalls.

Setup A shot that is easily returned--a plum ball.

Short Line The back line of the service zone--midpoint of the court.

Short Serve Serve that fails to carry beyond the short service line. This constitutes a service fault.

Side-by-Side Player positioning in Doubles where each partner covers one vertical half of the court.

Side-Out Loss of serve.

Singles A game in which one player opposes another player.

Skip Ball A ball that hits the floor before reaching the front wall.

Straddle Ball A ball that passes between the legs of a player who has just returned a shot.

Three-Wall Serve An illegal serve that strikes three walls before hitting the floor--counts as one service fault.

Throat The portion of the racket between the strings and the grip.

Time-Out A legal break in play (30 seconds) called for by one player or team.

Unavoidable Hinder An interference of normal play brought about unintentionally or uncontrollably by the players, court, equipment, or other hindrance.

Volley Playing the ball in the air before it bounces. Also called a fly shot.

Wallpaper Shot Shot hit close to the side wall making it difficult to return.

Z-Serve A serve that hits the front wall, a side wall, and then bounces before hitting the opposite side wall.

Z-Shot A shot that hits the front wall, a side wall, and then the other side wall before hitting the floor.

EQUIPMENT

Recommended equipment includes a racket, ball, shoes, and an eyeguard. Additional equipment includes sweat bands and a glove.

Guidelines for selecting a racketball racket are similar to selecting a tennis racket. The key is to select a comfortable racket. Also, every racket must have a safety thong. It is a band of rope, leather or nylon extending from the end of the handle. According to the rules, the thong must be securely wrapped around the wrist during play to keep the racket from flying away from the player.

The Racket--The racket should have a maximum head length of 11 inches and a width of 9 inches computed from the outer edge of the racket head rims. The handle may not exceed 7 inches and total length and width of racket may not exceed 27 inches.

Rackets are available in a variety of models. Rackets are made of metal, wood, fiberglass, or graphite. The beginner will often choose a metal racket and progress to a fiberglass, while the advanced player would choose a graphite racket which is designed for precision play. The grip is made of leather or rubber. Leather is slightly more expensive, but lasts longer. Rubber, on the other hand, is cheaper and easily replaced. Gloves can be worn to cut down on hand slippage and perspiration. The racket string is either gut or nylon. Nylon is durable, inexpensive, and resists corrosion caused from perspiration. Gut is more expensive, stronger and sensitive to perspiration.

Balls for racketball are about the same size as a tennis ball. They are manufactured by many companies in a variety of colors. You should select a non-carbon black ball which has good "liveliness."

Regular tennis shoes are acceptable to use in playing racketball. There are official racketball shoes available which are specifically designed for the sport.

Eyeguards are regarded as essential equipment because of the danger and prominence of eye injuries. The closeness of play required in the racketball court make eyeguards a wise decision.

With equally skillful players, racketball can have a high aerobic exercise value. Therefore, the physical workout is good and perspiration can become profuse. Sweat bands keep moisture from the eyes and/or hands.

Gloves are becoming very popular among players who find perspiration a problem. Although not necessary, gloves help contribute to a good grip and alleviate blisters.

RULES AND ETIQUETTE

THE GAME

Types of Games - Racketball may be played by two, three, or four players. When played by two, it is called "singles," by three, "cut throat," and when played by four, "doubles."

Objective - The objective is to win each rally by serving or returning the ball so the opponent is unable to keep the ball in play. A rally is over when a side makes an error, or is unable to return the ball before it touches the floor twice.

COURTS AND EQUIPMENT

Courts--The specifications for the standard four-wall racketball court are:

Dimension--The dimensions shall be 20 feet wide, 20 feet high, and 40 feet long, with back wall at least 12 feet high.

Lines and Zones--Racketball courts shall be divided and marked on the floors with $1\frac{1}{2}$ inch wide red or white lines as follows:

A. Short Line. The short line is midway between and is parallel with the front and back walls dividing the court into equal front and back courts.
B. Service Line. The service line is parallel with and located 5 feet in front of the short line.
C. Service Zone. The service zone is the space between the outer edges of the short and service lines.
D. Service Boxes. A service box is located at each end of the service zone by lines 18 inches from and parallel with each side wall.

E. Receiving Lines. Five feet back of the short line, vertical lines shall be marked on each side wall extending 3 inches from the floor. See Return of Serve.

The Racket--Rackets must conform to the following guidelines:

A. The racket must include a thong that must be securely wrapped on the player's wrist.
B. The racket frame may be made of any material, as long as it conforms to the specifications for length and width.
C. The strings of the racket should be gut, monofilament or nylon. Metal or steel strings are permitted only if they do not mark or deface the ball.

SCORING

Points are scored only by the serving side when it serves an ace or wins a rally. When the serving side loses a rally, it loses the serve. Losing the serve is called an "out" in singles, and a "handout" in doubles.

Game--A game is won by the side first scoring 21 points.

Match--A match is won by one side winning the first and second games.

PLAY REGULATIONS

Serve, Generally

A. Order--The player or side winning the toss becomes the first server and starts the first game, and third game, if any.
B. Start--Games are started from any place in the service zone. No part of either foot may extend beyond either line of the service zone. Stepping on the line (but not beyond it) is permitted. Server must remain in the service zone until the served ball passes short line. Violations are called "foot faults."
C. Manner--A serve is commenced by bouncing the ball to the floor in the service zone, and on the first bounce the ball is struck by the server's racket so that it hits the front wall and on the rebound hits the floor back of the short line, either with or without touching one of the side walls.
D. Readiness--Serves shall not be made until the receiving side is ready.

Serve, in Doubles

A. Server--At the beginning of each game in doubles the group shall decide the order of service, which order shall be followed throughout the game. Only the first server serves the first time up and continues to serve first throughout the game. When the first server is out - the side is out. Thereafter both players on each side shall serve until a hand-out occurs. It is not necessary for the server to alternate serves to their opponents.
B. Partner's Position--On each serve, the server's partner shall stand erect with his back to the side wall and with both feet on the floor within the service box until the served ball passes the short line. Violations are called "foot faults."

Defective Serves

There are three types of defective serves that result in penalties, as follows:

A. Dead Ball Serve--A dead ball serve results in no penalty and the server is given another serve without canceling a prior illegal serve.
B. Fault Serve--Two fault serves result in a hand-out.
C. Out Serves--An out serve results in a hand-out.

Dead Ball Serves

Dead ball serves do not cancel any previous illegal serve. They occur when an otherwise legal serve:

A. Hits Partner--Hits the server's partner on the fly on the rebound from the front wall while the server's partner is in the service box. Any serve that touches the floor before hitting the partner in the box is a short.
B. Screen Balls--Passes too close to the server or the server's partner to obstruct the view of the returning side. Any serve passing behind the server's partner and the side wall is an automatic screen.
C. Court Hinders--Hits any part of the court that under local rules is a dead ball.

Fault Serves

The following serves are faults and any two in succession result in a hand-out:

A. Foot Faults--A foot fault results:
    1. When the server leaves the service zone before the served ball passes the short line.
    2. When the server's partner leaves the service box before the served ball passes the short line.
B. Short Serve--A short serve is a served ball that first hits the front wall and on the rebound hits the floor in front of the back edge of the short line either with or without touching one side wall.
C. Three-Wall Serve--A two-sided serve is any ball served that first hits the front wall and on the rebound hits two side walls on the fly.
D. Ceiling Serve--A ceiling serve is any served ball that touches the ceiling after hitting the front wall either with or without touching the floor.
E. Long Serve--A long serve is any served ball that first hits the front wall and rebounds to the back wall before touching the floor.
F. Out-of-Court Serve--Any ball going out of the court on the serve.

Out Serves

Any one of the following serves results in a handout:

A. Serving Time--The server is required to put the ball into play within 10 seconds after the referee calls the score.
B. Missed Ball--Any attempt to strike the ball on the first bounce that results either in a total miss or in touching any part of the server's body other than his racket.
C. Non-Front Serve--Any served ball that strikes the server's partner, or the ceiling, floor or side wall, before striking the front wall.

D. Touched Serve--Any served ball that on the rebound from the front wall touches the server, or touches the server's partner while any part of his body is out of the service box, or the server's partner intentionally catches the served ball on the fly.

E. Out-of-Order Serve--In doubles, when either partner serves out-of-order. Any points which may have been scored during an out-of-order serve will be automatically void with the score reverting to the score prior to the out-of-order serve.

F. Crotch Serve--If the served ball hits the crotch in the front wall, it is considered the same as hitting the floor and is an out. A crotch serve into the back wall is good and in play. A served ball hitting the front wall-side wall crotch is an out serve.

Return of Serve

A. Receiving Position--The receiver or receivers must stand at least 5 feet back of the short line, as indicated by the 3-inch vertical line on each side wall, and cannot enter into this safety zone until the ball has been served and passes the back service line (short line). At that point the receiver may enter the safety zone to return serve, however, neither his racket nor his body may infringe on the imaginary plane marked by the short line. A violation of this plane would result in a point for the server.

B. Defective Serve--To eliminate any misunderstanding the receiving side should not catch or touch a defectively served ball until called by the referee or it has touched the floor for the second time.

C. Fly Return--In making a fly return, no part of the receiver's body or racket may enter into the serve zone. A violation by a receiver results in a point for the server.

D. Legal Return--After the ball is legally served, one of the players on the receiving side must strike the ball with his racket either on the fly or after the first bounce and before the ball touches the floor the second time. The ball must return to the front wall either directly or after touching one or both side walls, the back wall or the ceiling, or any combination of those surfaces. A returned ball may not touch the floor before touching the front wall. It is legal to return the ball by striking the ball into the back wall first, then hitting the front wall on the fly or after hitting the side wall or ceiling.

E. Failure to Return--The failure to return a serve results in a point for the server.

Changes of Serve

Hand-Out--A server is entitled to continue serving until:

A. Serve--He makes an out serve. See Out Serves.
B. Fault Serves--He makes two fault serves in succession. See Fault Serves.
C. Hits Partner--He hits his partner with an attempted return before the ball touches the floor a second time.
D. Return Failure--He or his partner fails to keep the ball in play by returning it as required by return of serve. See Return of Serve.
E. Avoidable Hinder--He or his partner commits an avoidable hinder. See Available Hinder.
F. Side-Out--In singles, retiring the server retires the side. In doubles, the side is retired when both partners have been put out except on the first serve.

G.　Effect--When the server or the side loses the serve, the server or serving side shall become the receiver; and the receiving side, the server; and so alternately in all subsequent services of the game.

Rallies

Each legal return after the serve is called a rally. Play during rallies shall be according to the following rules:

A.　One or Both Hands--Only the head of the racket may be used at any time to return the ball. The ball must be hit with the racket in one or both hands. The use of any portion of the body is an out.

B.　One Touch--In attempting returns, the ball may be touched only once by one player on the returning side. In doubles both partners may swing at, but only one may hit the ball. Each violation of (a) or (b) results in a hand-out.

C.　Return Attempts

1.　In singles, if a player swings at but misses the ball in play, the player may repeat his attempts to return the ball until it touches the floor for the second time.

2.　In doubles, if one player swings at but misses the ball, both he and his partner may make further attempts to return the ball until it touches the floor the second time. Both partners on a side are entitled to return the ball.

3.　In singles or doubles, if a player swings at but misses the ball in play, and in his, or his partner's attempt again to play the ball there is an unintentional interference by an opponent it shall be a hinder.

D.　Touching Ball--Except as provided under Dead Ball Hinders, any touching of the ball before it touches the floor the second time by a player other than the one making a return is a point or out against the offending player. See Dead Ball Hinder.

E.　Out-of-Court Ball

1.　After Return--Any ball returned to the front wall which on the rebound or on the first bounce goes into the gallery or through any opening in a side wall shall be declared dead and the serve replayed.

2.　No Return--Any ball not returned to the front wall, but which caroms off a player's racket into the gallery or into any opening in a side wall either with or without touching the ceiling, side or back wall, shall be an out or point against the players failing to make the return.

F.　Dry Ball--During the game and particularly on service every effort should be made to keep the ball dry. Deliberately wetting shall result in an out.

G.　Broken Ball--If there is any suspicion that a ball has broken on the serve or during a rally, play shall continue until the end of the rally.

H.　Play Stoppage--If a player loses control of his racket, time should not be called until after the point has been decided, providing the racket does not strike an opponent or interfere with ensuing play.

Dead Ball Hinders

Hinders are of two types - "dead ball" and "avoidable." Dead ball hinders as described in this rule result in the point being played.

A. Situations--The following are dead ball hinders:

1. Hitting Opponent--Any returned ball that touches an opponent on the fly before it returns to the front wall.
2. Body Contact--Any body contact with an opponent that interferes with seeing or returning the ball.
3. Screen Ball--Any ball rebounding from the front wall close to the body of a player on the side which just returned the ball, to interfere with or prevent the returning side from seeing the ball.
4. Straddle Ball--A ball passing between the legs of a player on the side which just returned the ball, if there is no fair chance to see or return the ball.
5. Back Swing Hinder--If there is body contact on the back swing, the player must call it immediately. This is the only hinder call a player can make.
6. Other Interference--Any other unintentional interference which prevents an opponent from having a fair chance to see or return the ball.

B. In Doubles--In doubles, both players on a side are entitled to a fair and unobstructed chance at the ball and either one is entitled to a hinder even though it naturally would be his partner's ball and even though his partner may have attempted to play the ball or that he may already have missed it. It is not a hinder when one player hinders his partner.

Avoidable Hinders

An avoidable hinder results in an out or a point depending upon whether the offender was serving or receiving.

A. Failure to Move--Does not move sufficiently to allow opponent his shot.
B. Blocking--Moves into a position affecting a block on the opponent about to return the ball, or, in doubles, one partner moves in front of an opponent as his partner is returning the ball.
C. Moving into Ball--Moves in the way and is struck by the ball just played by his opponent.
D. Pushing--Deliberately pushes or shoves opponent during a rally.

Time-Outs

During a game each player in singles, or each side in doubles, either while serving or receiving may request a "time-out" for a towel, wiping glasses, change or adjustment. Each "time-out" shall not exceed 30 seconds. No player may call a time-out once the ball is in play.

One-Wall and Three-Wall

Basically, racketball rules for one-wall, three-wall, and four-wall are the same with the following exceptions:

A. One-Wall:
1. Court Size--Wall shall be 20 ft. in width and 16 ft. high, floor 20 ft. in width and 34 ft. from the wall to the back edge of the long line. There

should be a minimum of 3 feet beyond the long line and 6 feet outside each side line and behind the long line to permit movement area for the players.

2. Short Line--Back edge 16 feet from the wall. Service Markers--lines at least 6 inches long parallel to and midway between the long and short lines, extending in from the side lines. The imaginary extension and joining of these lines indicates the service line. Lines are 1½ inches in width. Service Zone--floor area inside and including the short, side and service lines. Receiving Zone--floor area in back of short line bounded by and including the long and side lines.

B. Three-Wall:

1. Serve--A serve that goes beyond the side walls on the fly is player or side-out. A serve that goes beyond the long line on a fly but within the side walls is the same as a "short."

ETIQUETTE

To ensure safety, always stop your swing if there is any possibility of hitting your opponent. Avoid overswinging since this can also cause injuries. Try not to crowd or push your opponent. The closer you get, the greater the chances are of getting hit with the ball or the racket.

A. Always wait until your opponent is ready before serving.
B. Call out the score before each serve. This will help you avoid confusion and disagreements.
C. Always control your temper. Outbursts of anger often lead to strained relationships with opponents and/or broken rackets.
D. Be honest on your calls and shots. If your shot skips before hitting the front wall and your opponent doesn't see it, call it against yourself.
E. Give your opponent a fair chance to return a shot. You should not intentionally block his/her view.
F. Call all hinders, but be gracious on "winners" that you had no chance of returning.

FUNDAMENTALS OF THE GAME

The object of the game is to hit a small rubber ball against the front wall of the racketball court in such a way as to make it difficult for the opponent to return the shot before it touches the floor twice. This sounds simple enough, so what's so hard about the game? Well, it's actually not a hard game to learn, but when you first step into the court and someone hits a hard shot angling off the front wall--get set! You may feel like an awkward baby deer as you try to get your feet and body going in the right direction just to have a swing at the ball. You will quickly improve, however, and with a little correct practice be playing one of the most popular indoor games in the USA.

FOREHAND STROKE

The forehand stroke is the most fundamental stroke in racketball. It is a very natural stroke to the player's strong side and enables him to put the ball away or to get the ball past the opponent.

Grip--The racket handle should be gripped so the "V" made by the thumb and forefinger is located directly on top of the handle. This grip is known as the "handshake" grip and can best be practiced by holding the racket perpendicular to the floor and simply shaking hands with the handle. There should be a slight separation between the forefinger and middle finger, the "trigger finger" concept, which allows for better control of the racket face. The handle should be controlled by the fingers and therefore should not be placed too deeply in the palm of the hand.

Body Position--As you anticipate the approaching ball to the forehand side, you should begin adjusting for the forehand stroke. You should turn and be facing the side wall with the nonhitting shoulder pointing towards the front wall. The knees should be slightly bent and the weight on the balls of the feet. As the ball approaches, the weight should shift to the back foot and the racket taken back until it is pointing towards the back wall. The wrist should be fully cocked and the racket held at approximately head height.

Contact Point--The shoulders and front arm should rotate in a circular motion around the front and side walls as the forward swing begins. The racket is brought forward with a slight downward arch, and the body weight is shifted from the back to the front foot as the point of contact is reached. The wrist remains in a cocked position with the racket pointing backwards. Just prior to the point of contact the wrist is extended and flexed toward the front wall. As the ball is met slightly behind the front foot, your head should be down and your eyes on the ball as they have been throughout the stroke (Figure 6.1).

Follow-Through--As the wrist is snapped through the ball, the front arm continues to rotate and pulls the body through the completed stroke. The weight has shifted to the front foot and the racket moves forward as though it were following the shot. As the stroke ends, the back foot should be moved forward to quickly resume a balanced "ready" position.

Figure 6.1 Forehand Stroke

BACKHAND STROKE

Beginning racketball players are usually comfortable with the forehand stroke, but they often feel awkward and weak with the backhand stroke. For the backhand shot, the ball comes to the player's non-racket arm side and the stroke and contact phase is virtually the same as for the forehand stroke.

Grip--There is no predetermined grip for each player. Some will make greater adjustments than others, and some will make no adjustment at all from the forehand to the backhand stroke. However, if time permits, it is important to make a grip adjustment to keep the racket face square at impact with the ball. The hand should be rotated counterclockwise slightly so the "V" of the thumb and forefinger is on the left top ridge of the racket handle.

Body Position--The body position is the same as for the forehand stroke except that the racket shoulder is pointing to the front wall. At the top of the backswing, the racket should be pointed toward the back wall at shoulder height. The arm should be bent at the elbow.

Contact Point--As the ball approaches the point of contact, you should shift forward into the ball and begin rotating the shoulders and upper body. As you uncurl your arm at the point of release, simply fling your wrist as in throwing a frisbee. The contact point is a few inches in front of the forward foot and as low as possible. The racket should be moving parallel to the floor as contact is made and the head should be down with the eyes concentrating on the ball (Figure 6.2).

Follow-Through--Same as the forehand stroke.

Figure 6.2 Backhand Stroke

SERVE

The serve initiates the action in each point during a match. A well-hit serve may easily win you a point or it may result in a weak return, giving you the opportunity for an easy put away. There are three basic types of serves: drive serve, lob serve, and the "Z" or cross-court serve.

Drive Serve--This is the most common serve in racketball today. It is hit hard and low off the front wall and angles to a corner of the back court.

Body Position--The beginning racketball player should stand with both feet perpendicular to the desired line of flight. (The basic forehand stroke should be used for the drive serve.)

Contact--Ball contact should be made at a point between the ankle and the knee, usually not more than 1 foot above the floor. To be most effective, you should find a spot on the front wall for which to aim and then align the feet accordingly.

Follow-Through--(See forehand stroke)
Make sure your weight shifts forward as you rotate the upper part of your body. With the ball drop you should force yourself to move forward to make good contact.

The Lob Serve--A high arc serve that forces the opponent to return from deep in the court.
The server uses a forehand stroke but uses an upward arc which causes the ball to hit 12-15 feet upon the front wall. The ball should then bounce high near midcourt and land, on the second bounce, in the court but near one of the back corners. The stroke is much softer than a kill or passing shot.

Body Position--You should stand about 5 feet from the side wall with an open stance. (Front foot moved back beyond parallel to the intended line of flight.)

Contact Point--The ball should be dropped forward of the front foot (4-8 in.) and hit with an upward arc of the racket.

Follow-Through--Same as forehand stroke except in an upward direction toward the desired spot on the front wall.

The "Z" Serve--A very effective change of pace serve that can confuse the receiver because of the changes in direction taken by the ball.
The ball is hit to either corner of the front wall between waist and head level. It is designed to stroke the front wall, the side wall, and then travel diagonally across the back court.

Body Position--Same as drive serve and forehand stroke.

Contact Point--Same as drive serve and forehand stroke.

Follow-Through--Same as drive serve and forehand stroke.

Summary of Serves--When you are practicing your serves, you should experiment with serving from various areas within the service box, different spots that you can hit on the front wall, and varying degrees of force from your stroke (Figure 6.3).

Figure 6.3 Serving

PASSING SHOTS

It is the basic forehand or backhand stroke and can be either an offensive or defensive shot. It is the next best option to the kill shot or it may be used when your opponent is out of position. As the name implies, you are trying to hit the ball away from your opponent, either down the wall or cross-court. The object of the shot is to get the ball by the opponent with a shot that is hard and fast so that it is unlikely that he/she can play it off the back wall (Figure 6.4).

The techniques used for the passing shots are the same as those for the forehand and backhand strokes.

Body Position--Align the feet for the desired direction of the shot.

Contact Point--Contact the ball about knee level with ball in same position as forehand and backhand strokes.

Follow-Through--Same as forehand and backhand strokes. The ball should strike the front wall about 3 feet above the floor.

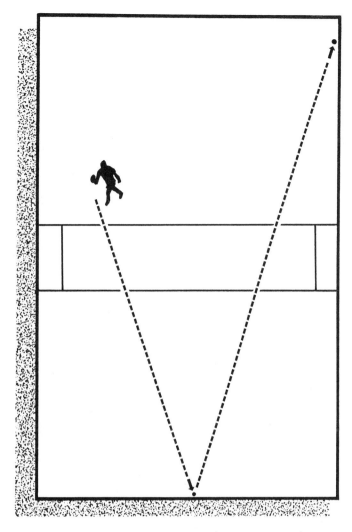

Figure 6.4 Passing Shot (Cross-Court)

KILL SHOTS

The kill shot is the primary offensive shot that every racketball player should continue to develop. The well-executed shot should hit the front wall as low as possible to allow a rebound of only a few steps off the floor. The technique is the same as the forehand and backhand strokes with slight variations.

Body Position--The feet should be aligned perpendicular to the desired line of flight. Feet should be in position to allow for exaggerated hip and knee flexion to allow player to hit the ball as close to the floor as possible.

Contact Point--The ball should be struck from a point whereby the ball is no higher than 12 inches above the floor. Racket should be moving parallel to floor when contact is made.

Follow-Through--The movement of the racket parallel to floor should produce a horizontal trajectory. Racket should continue towards the desired impact target on the front wall as the weight is shifted to the front foot (Figures 6.5 and 6.6).

Figure 6.5 Forehand Kill Shot   Figure 6.6 Backhand Kill Shot

VARIATIONS

Straight Kill--Low hard kill which is hit to rebound directly off the front wall and away from the opponent.

Pinch Kill--Shot is hit to side wall before hitting front wall. It should be hit to wall on the side the opponent has position to allow for the rebound to the opposite side.

Front-Wall/Side-Wall Kill--Shot is most effective if opponent is deep in the back court. Pinch shot that hits front wall first must then hit the side wall. It is not as effective as the pinch kill because it tends to rebound toward the middle of the court.

Overhead Kill--Executed with an overhead forehand similar to ceiling shot technique. It is, however, aimed low to hit either the front-wall/side-wall or vice versa. Shot should be used more as an element of surprise to catch the opponent off guard as he is playing too deep in court to react to low rebound.

DEFENSIVE SHOTS

Ceiling Shot--Basically, the ceiling shot is a defensive shot but can also be used offensively if the opponent is playing too far forward in the court. The ball should hit the ceiling first, 3-5 feet from the front wall, then rebound off the front wall, hit the floor, and bounce deep into either back corner of the court.

The ceiling shot can be executed with either the forehand or backhand overhead stroke. The forehand motion is more common and therefore more quickly mastered. The forehand or backhand grip is used for the shots.

Body Position--The movement of the body is almost identical to the overarm throwing motion or overhead smash in tennis. The arm motion should be directly over the shoulder of the striking arm. The feet should be planted and weight shifting to the front foot as the ball is hit. (It is very important to get in position to hit the ball with full arm extension.)

Contact Point--The ball should be struck with the arm at full extension and with a snap of the wrist that will propel the ball at the desired point on the ceiling. The ball should be slightly in front of your striking shoulder as it is contacted. The backhand ceiling shot should be contacted above the waist but below the top of your head.

Follow-Through--The racket should briefly follow the ball path as the weight is transferred forward, and then it continues down and around the body. You should quickly assume a strategic court position for the next shot (Figures 6.7 and 6.8).

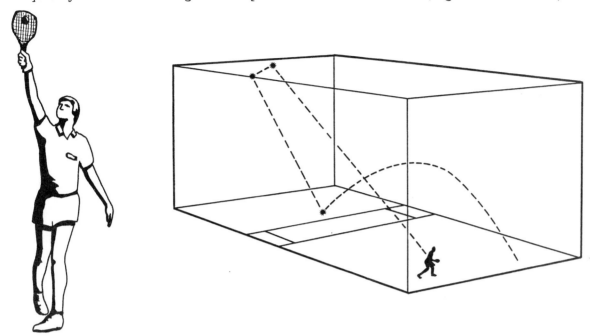

Figure 6.7 Stroke

Figure 6.8 Ceiling Shot Ball Pattern

The backhand ceiling shot is simply a high backhand shot that is aimed at a point on the ceiling instead of the front wall.

Lob Shot--This shot is not used as much as the ceiling shot but can still be effective for those having difficulty with the ceiling shot. The ball is hit with an underarm pattern, slightly open racket face, and little power for more precision and results. (See Lob Serve.)

"Z" Shot--This shot is executed as a side arm or overhead stroke and is used primarily in moving your opponent to the back court. It is executed like the Z serve but with a more overhead motion. It is desirable to have the ball hit the side wall first in the back corner. This will cause it to come off almost parallel to the back wall and make it difficult to return. The shot requires a fair amount of power to be effective.

Back-Wall Techniques--Almost any type of shot can be used when returning the ball off the back wall. However, if the ball is hit in such a way that allows you to use an offensive shot, then the kill or passing shots are most effective.
A ball which hits the floor and then the back wall will generally rebound farther out than a ball which hits the back wall on the fly. The beginning player will often underjudge the distance the ball will bounce off the back wall. It is very important to keep your eye on the ball and learn to judge the rebound distances in order to be in good position for a forehand or backhand stroke.

ERRORS AND CORRECTIONS

Illustrations of the <u>MOST COMMON</u> errors and how to correct them.

<u>ERROR (FOREHAND AND BACKHAND)</u>   <u>ILLUSTRATION</u>
Improper point of contact

Figure 6.9

<u>RESULTS AND CORRECTION</u>
-     poor control of ball direction. Often a loss of power resulting in a weak shot.
-     Re-examine the following: Are you meeting the ball slightly in front of the <u>front foot</u> for your backhand, and even with, or slightly behind it on your forehand strokes? Is your weight on the front foot as you strike the ball?

<u>ERROR</u>   <u>ILLUSTRATION</u>
Racket face is not square on impact
(usually angles upward)

Figure 6.10

<u>RESULTS AND CORRECTION</u>
-     Ball hits too high on the front wall, setting opponent up for an easy shot.
-     The wrist should be in a cocked position as the stroke is made. If the wrist is straight, then the tendency is to swing in an arc and hit the ball upward.

ERROR
Not bending your knees according to the height of the ball

Figure 6.11

RESULTS AND CORRECTION
- Inconsistency with many shots. Shots either hitting too high on the front wall, or hitting the floor first.
- You should stroke the ball in nearly the same way on each shot, and simply adjust your body position by bending your knees to allow for the ball position.

ERROR (SERVING)
Drive serves not going to the desired corner

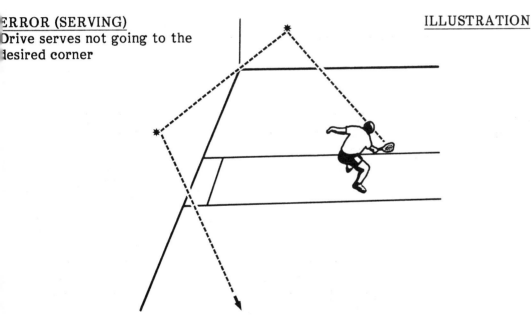

Figure 6.12

RESULTS AND CORRECTION
- Instead of being an offensive weapon, they quickly put you on the defensive because of their poor placement.
- Change the spot on the front wall in which you are aiming your serve. Practice and experiment with various wall spots from various service positions until you find a groove for hitting to the corners consistently.

ERROR (BACKHAND)
Lack of power on
backhand shots

Figure 6.13

RESULTS AND CORRECTION
- Consistent weak returns and inability to hit shots with good placement and power.
- Remember to stroke ball with the same motion as throwing a "frisbee." Keep the wrist cocked and at impact, release through the ball...in front of your front foot.

OTHER PROBLEM AREAS

ERROR/SERVING	RESULT	CORRECTION
1. Serves often short	Opponent can easily step forward to make return	Must either hit to a spot higher on the wall or use more power. A combination of the two might be the best correction.
2. Poor ball drop for serve--too high or too close to body	A poorly placed serve--either too short, too long, or in the middle of the court	Practice dropping the ball for a forehand stroke and meeting the ball in a low power position.

ERROR/FOREHAND BACKHAND	RESULT	CORRECTION
3. Weak wrist--too much wrist action	Very little control over shot placement. Shots will often go high and from wall to wall.	Keep the wrist firm and cocked prior to contact. Meet the ball with a hard wrist break and let the racket follow through toward the desired target area.

ERROR/LOB SHOTS	RESULT	CORRECTION
. Lob shots rebounding too far off the back wall	Provides an easy set-up for your opponent to "put-away"	The lob shot is a "touch" shot that requires much practice. Practice both the lob serve and the shot to improve skill.
ERROR/BACKWALL SHOTS	RESULT	CORRECTION
. Misjudging the bounce of the ball off the back wall	Poor position for shot which results in a miss or a weak return	Initially you should move forward several feet in front of the point to which you think the ball will bounce. As above, this shot requires much practice with balls of different speed and spin.
ERROR/CEILING SHOTS	RESULT	CORRECTION
. Ceiling shots miss the ceiling or do not hit the front wall after hitting the ceiling	Ineffective shot or fault if it fails to hit the front wall	Remember that the point of contact is almost directly overhead. You should aim for a spot on the ceiling.

IMPROVEMENT DRILLS AND GAMES

1. **Drop Drill**--(Forehand and Backhand Drives)
   --Standing three feet behind the short service line and three-four feet from the side wall, gently bounce the ball off the side wall and execute a proper forehand drive--Hit 10 drives and attempt to keep them below an eight-foot line on the front wall--Move to the other side of the court and repeat the drill using the proper backhand drive. (Practice strokes until you can hit eight out of 10 with each stroke.)

2. **Partner Drill**--(Forehand and Backhand)
   --The receiving position will be five-six feet behind the short service line--A partner will drop and hit the ball off the front wall to your forehand. Attempt to return eight of 10 shots to the front wall below the eight-foot line--Repeat the same drill to your backhand.

3. **Rally Drill**--(Forehand and Backhand) (See Skills Test)
   --Standing behind the short service line, begin a rally off the front wall to the forehand side only--Attempt to keep the ball in play for 20 seconds (to be in play, each shot must be successful according to the rules)--Repeat same rally using the backhand as the only stroke.
   --Attempt to keep ball in play using both forehand and backhand shots--depending on which side the ball returns. (Remember, it is very important to quickly assume a "ready position" after each stroke since you will not be certain as to the side the ball will return.)

4. **Cross-Court Partner Drill**
   --With both players standing near the short service line, hit cross court in an inverted "V" fashion to one's forehand and the other's backhand. Switch sides to work on both shots.

5. **Wall Bounce For Kill Shots** (See Skills Test)
   --Using the same procedure as the Drop Drill, attempt to hit six out of 10 Kill shots below a line three feet above the floor--Move to the other side of the court for backhand kill shots. (Remember to bend your knees and let the ball drop near or below one foot before striking it.)
   --After successfully completion of the above, attempt to hit kill shots below a two-foot line.

6. **Partner Drill For Kill Shots**
   --A partner will bounce and hit the ball off the front wall, 10 to forehand and 10 to backhand, for kill shot practice. Try to hit six out of 10 below a three-foot line on the front wall.

7. **Drive Serve Drill**--(Spot)
   --Practice hitting a spot on the front wall that causes the ball to bounce slightly past the short service line into the back corner. Practice to the opponent's backhand and forehand sides but with greater emphasis on the backhand side. Attempt to hit seven out of 10 serves that angle directly into the corner. (Experiment with various service positions, spots on the front wall, and force on the ball.)

3. Lob Serve Drill (See Skills Test)
   --Practice hitting the lob serve to each corner of the court so that it "dies" as it reaches the corner. (See Drive Serve Drill)

4. Backwall Drill--(Forehand and Backhand)
   --Stand approximately five feet from the back wall and six feet from the forehand side wall--facing the side wall. Toss the ball at medium speed off the back wall at waist level. The ball should rebound off the back wall and bounce slightly in front of you and to the side. As the ball moves away from you, move quickly to assume a stroke position. When the ball is approximately at knee level, strike it with a forehand stroke. Attempt to hit a down-the-wall or a cross-court passing shot. Hit five out of 10 that hit the front wall below the six-foot line.
   --Change sides of the court and repeat the drill using the backhand stroke.

RACKETBALL SKILLS TEST

GENERAL INFORMATION

Each student is tested individually. They will be evaluated on four test items, which appear in the order they are administered:

1. Lob Serve
2. Ceiling Shot
3. Kill Shot
4. Wall Volley

LOB SERVE

Purpose--to measure the student's ability to lob a serve with height and accuracy.

Directions

1) The student may stand anywhere within the boundaries of the service court area.

2) While facing the front wall, the student is given a total of 10 lob serves (five right; five left). The first five serves must hit the floor beyond the short service line on the right side of the white line marked on the wall (see Figure 6.14).

3) To begin the lob serve, the student drops the ball on the floor and hits it into the front wall above the dashed line (see Figure 6.14).

4) A score of "0" is recorded if:
   a. the ball first hits anything other than the front wall (e.g., side wall, ceiling or floor).
   b. the student drops the ball, swings and entirely misses it.
   c. the ball hits anything other than the floor (e.g., side wall, ceiling or back wall) after properly hitting the front wall. (EXCEPTION: the ball may hit the side wall as long as it does so between the dashed line on the side wall and the back wall and then hits the floor before hitting the back wall.)

Scoring

1) Points are awarded where the ball first hits the floor beyond the short service line after the ball has properly hit the front wall.

2) The score is determined by the point value assigned to an area marked on the floor.

3) The maximum score is 50 points.

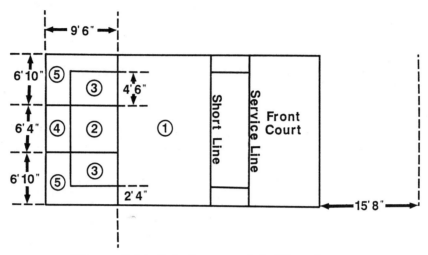

Figure 6.14 Lob Serve and Ceiling Shot

II. CEILING SHOT

Purpose--To measure the student's ability to hit a ceiling shot with height and accuracy.

Directions

1) The student may stand anywhere behind the short service line.

2) The student is given a total of 10 shots (five right; five left). The first five ceiling shots must hit the floor in the scoring area on the right-hand side of the white line marked on the wall (see Figure 6.14). Repeat the procedures on the left side of the court. After hitting the front wall, the ball's first bounce on the floor does not have to be beyond the short service line.

3) To begin the ceiling shot, the student drops the ball on the floor and hits it into the front wall. He/she may hit it anywhere on the front wall. After the ball hits the front wall it must bounce once and then the student, using the stroke of his/her choice, must hit the ball into the ceiling. After hitting the ceiling the ball must go directly into the front wall and then bounce two times on the floor.

4) A "0" is recorded if:
   a. on the rebound from the front wall the student swings and misses the ceiling shot.
   b. the ball rebounds from the front wall, back to the student and bounces more than once.

c. the student does not hit the front wall rebound directly into the ceiling.

d. the ball does not go directly from the ceiling into the front wall.

e. after hitting the front wall the ball does not go directly to the floor. (EXCEPTION: The ball may hit the side wall after hitting the front wall if it does so between the dashed line on the side wall and the back wall and is on the second bounce.

Scoring

1) The point values are the same as for the Lob Serve, except that in the ceiling shot the points where the ball hits on its _second_ floor bounce is the score.

2) A "0" is recorded if:
   a. the subject catches the ball before it makes a second bounce.
   b. the ball hits the back wall before it makes a second bounce.
   c. the second bounce does not hit behind the short service line.

3) Maximum score is 50 points.

III. KILL SHOT

Purpose--To measure the student's ability to accurately execute a forehand and backhand kill shot.

Directions

1) The student may stand anywhere behind the short service line.

2) The student will be allowed a total of 10 kill shots (five forehand; five backhand). The first five must be taken on the forehand side, while the last five must be taken on the backhand side.

3) To begin the kill shot, the student faces the side wall and gently tosses the ball against the side wall. After hitting the side wall the ball must bounce on time on the floor. The student is required to hit it into the front wall.

4) A "0" is recorded if:
   a. after the ball bounces the subject swings and misses.
   b. the subject does not attempt to hit the ball after it bounces.
   c. after the ball bounces the student hits it against anything before it hits the front wall (e.g., floor, side wall, or ceiling).

5) It does not matter how hard the student hits the ball or where the ball rebounds after hitting the front wall.

6) Maximum score is 50 points.

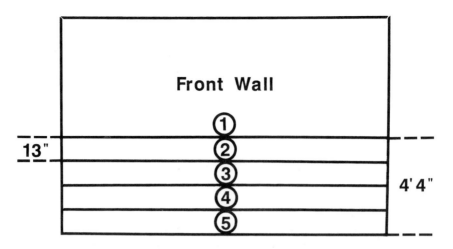

Figure 6.15 Kill Shot

IV. <u>WALL VOLLEY</u>

<u>Purpose</u>--to measure the player's ability to continuously volley a ball with speed and agility.

<u>Directions</u>

1) The object of the test is to determine the number of times the student can legally volley a ball to the front wall in 30 seconds.

2) To start the wall volley, the subject drops the ball on the floor and hits it into the front wall using either a forehand or backhand stroke. On this first shot the ball must hit the front wall first.

   After the first shot the ball may hit the side wall, back wall or ceiling before hitting the front wall. However, it may not hit the floor before hitting the front wall.

3) After one bounce on the floor or while the ball is airborne, the student may hit the ball. If, however, the ball bounces more than once before the student hits it, "0" points are scored. The student should continue volleying until time has expired.

4) For the volley to count toward the total score, the student must hit the ball behind the short service line. The student may, however, cross the short service line to recover a bad shot. When the student crosses the short service line and volleys the ball, it will not count toward the total score.

5) If the ball dies on the floor and the student does have to cross the short service line to retrieve it, he should pick the ball up and run behind the short service line to continue the test.

<u>Scoring</u>--One point is scored for each legal volley hit behind the short service line to the front wall. The score is the best of two trials.

RACKETBALL
Skills Test Score Sheet

_____ Male/Female Date _____ Instructor_____
                     circle
_____ Section_____ Day/Time_____

ST ITEM		TRIALS	TOTAL SCORE	T-SCORE	RECORDER'S SIGNATURE
b	Right:	__ __ __ __ __		_____	_____
	Left:	__ __ __ __ __			
iling Shot	Right:	__ __ __ __ __		_____	_____
	Left:	__ __ __ __ __			
11 Shot	Forehand:	__ __ __ __ __		_____	_____
	Backhand:	__ __ __ __ __			
ll Volley		_____ _____ _____		_____	_____

TOTAL ____   AVERAGE _____

GRADE _____

RACKETBALL SKILLS TEST NORMS

T-Score	Lob Men	Lob Women	Ceiling Shot Men	Ceiling Shot Women	Kill Shot Men	Kill Shot Women	Wall Volley Men	Wall Volley Women
76	46	44	36	33	45	44		
74	44	42	34	32	43	42		
72	42	40	33	30	41	40		
70	40	38	31	28	39	38		
68	39	36	30	26	37	36	32	
66	37	34	28	24	35	34	30	28
64	35	32	26	23	33	32	28	26
62	33	31	24	22	31	30	26	24
60	31	29	22	21	29	28	24	22
58	29	27	21	20	27	26	22	20
56	27	25	20	19	26	24	20	18
54	25	23	18	16	25	22	19	17
52	23	21	17	14	23	20	17	14
50	21	19	16	13	21	18	15	12
48	19	17	14	12	19	16	14	11
46	17	15	13	10	17	14	13	10
44	15	13	12	9	15	12	12	9
42	13	11	10	8	13	10	11	8
40	11	9	9	7	11	8	10	7
38	9	7	7	5	9	6	9	6
36	7	5	6	4	7	4	8	5
34	5	3	5	3	5	3	7	4
32			3	2	3	2		
28			2	1	2	1		
26								
24								

(left margin labels: ed, ediate, ing)

RACKETBALL
Skills Test Score Sheet

_____ Male/Female Date _____ Instructor _____
                                 circle
_____ Section _____ Day/Time _____

ST ITEM		TRIALS	TOTAL SCORE	T-SCORE	RECORDER'S SIGNATURE
b	Right:	__ __ __ __ __			
	Left:	__ __ __ __ __	____	_____	_____
iling Shot	Right:	__ __ __ __ __			
	Left:	__ __ __ __ __	____	_____	_____
ll Shot	Forehand:	__ __ __ __ __			
	Backhand:	__ __ __ __ __	____	_____	_____
all Volley		_____	_____	_____	_____

TOTAL ____   AVERAGE _____

GRADE _____

RACKETBALL SKILLS TEST NORMS

	Lob		Ceiling Shot		Kill Shot		Wall Volley	
T-Score	Men	Women	Men	Women	Men	Women	Men	Women
76	46	44	36	33	45	44		
74	44	42	34	32	43	42		
72	42	40	33	30	41	40		
70	40	38	31	28	39	38		
68	39	36	30	26	37	36	32	
66	37	34	28	24	35	34	30	28
64	35	32	26	23	33	32	28	26
62	33	31	24	22	31	30	26	24
60	31	29	22	21	29	28	24	22
58	29	27	21	20	27	26	22	20
56	27	25	20	19	26	24	20	18
54	25	23	18	16	25	22	19	17
52	23	21	17	14	23	20	17	14
50	21	19	16	13	21	18	15	12
48	19	17	14	12	19	16	14	11
46	17	15	13	10	17	14	13	10
44	15	13	12	9	15	12	12	9
42	13	11	10	8	13	10	11	8
40	11	9	9	7	11	8	10	7
38	9	7	7	5	9	6	9	6
36	7	5	6	4	7	4	8	5
34	5	3	5	3	5	3	7	4
32			3	2	3	2		
28			2	1	2	1		
26								
24								

ed

ediate

ing

RACKETBALL
Skill Analysis Score Sheet
(20 points)

Name _____   Date _____

Class _____   Evaluated By _____

POINT GUIDE

2 points -- Student appears competent
1 point -- Occasionally correct or minor errors
0 points -- Needs more attention before ready to play

	POINTS SCORED		
	0	1	2
The Forehand	___	___	___
*1) Grip			
2) Body position			
3) Contact and follow-through			
The Backhand Stroke	___	___	___
*1) Grip			
2) Body position			
3) Contact and follow-through			
Serving	___	___	___
*1) Drive serve			
2) Lob serve			
3) Other serves ("Z" serve)			
Offensive Shots	___	___	___
*1) Passing shots			
2) Kill shots			
Defensive Shots	___	___	___
*1) Ceiling shot			
2) Lob shot			
Back-wall Techniques	___	___	___
*1) Good position - the key			
Rules and Scoring	___	___	___
*1) Serving-receiving			
Safety and Etiquette	___	___	___
*1) Don't swing if too close			
2) Doubles -- crowded area			
3) Honest calls -- honor hinders			
Hinders (Unique in Racketball)	___	___	___
*1) "Dead Ball"			
2) Avoidable			
Results	___	___	___
*1) Racketball skill test results			
2) General evaluation			

*Points for evaluation

TOTAL SCORE _____

195

RACKETBALL
Skill Analysis Score Sheet
(20 points)

ame _____   Date _____

lass _____ Evaluated By _____

POINT GUIDE

2 points -- Student appears competent
1 point -- Occasionally correct or minor errors
0 points -- Needs more attention before ready to
            play

	POINTS SCORED		
	0	1	2
. The Forehand	____	____	____
*1) Grip			
2) Body position			
3) Contact and follow-through			
. The Backhand Stroke	____	____	____
*1) Grip			
2) Body position			
3) Contact and follow-through			
. Serving	____	____	____
*1) Drive serve			
2) Lob serve			
3) Other serves ("Z" serve)			
. Offensive Shots	____	____	____
*1) Passing shots			
2) Kill shots			
. Defensive Shots	____	____	____
*1) Ceiling shot			
2) Lob shot			
. Back-wall Techniques	____	____	____
*1) Good position - the key			
. Rules and Scoring	____	____	____
*1) Serving-receiving			
. Safety and Etiquette	____	____	____
*1) Don't swing if too close			
2) Doubles -- crowded area			
3) Honest calls -- honor hinders			
. Hinders (Unique in Racket-ball)	____	____	____
*1) "Dead Ball"			
2) Avoidable			
0. Results	____	____	____
*1) Racketball skill test results			
2) General evaluation			

Points for evaluation

TOTAL SCORE _____

CHAPTER 7

TENNIS

HISTORY

Considerable evidence indicates the modern games of tennis and handball are outgrowths of the game of Irish handball. A type of handball is probably the oldest of all ball games because it dates back to Greeks and Romans.

The early game was very popular in England and France in the 16th and 17th centuries. It was played by kings, aristocrats, and noblemen. The game became popular with commoners, too. In fact, kings expressed concern that tennis was being practiced more than archery which was used for military purpose.

The name "tennis" was given to the game after English visitors mistook it for the French term "tenez". When used by French officials, it meant "Ready" or "Resume Play," which is similar to the English term "Play Ball." The name "tennis" has been accepted universally.

Gambling and professionalism almost destroyed the sport in the 18th century. Major Walter Clopton Wingfield, a British army officer stationed in Bermuda, first patented the game of lawn tennis and is recognized as its founder. He introduced the game at a lawn party in 1873. He patented the game under the name "Sphairistike," which means "ball game." It was viewed like other lawn games (e.g. croquet) and was appropriate for feminine play.

Mary Ewing Outerbridge of Staten Island, New York, vacationed in Bermuda in 1874. She saw and played the game. She purchased rackets and balls and brought them to Staten Island where she introduced the game.

By 1880 some version of tennis was being played in many parts of the United States. Mary's brother, E. O. Outerbridge, called a meeting in New York in 1881 to standardize rules. The group adopted the exact rules as had been adopted by the All England Lawn Tennis Club, known today as Wimbledon. The United States Lawn Tennis Association (USLTA) was founded. In 1976 the "Lawn" was omitted, and the organization is now simply the United States Tennis Association (USTA).

BENEFITS

Aerobic Fitness--In general, little aerobic fitness can be achieved through playing tennis. A highly skilled person playing singles against an equally skillful person can maintain some endurance and conditioning benefit, however, not enough to use tennis as a sole program of endurance and conditioning. It is recommended a person become involved in a regular total fitness conditioning program and play tennis for its other values.

Motor Fitness--Good hand-eye coordination is vital in attaining any degree of success in tennis. Quick movements and good motor abilities contribute to a good game.

Social--Perhaps tennis's greatest value is social in nature. Individuals of all ages can enjoy tennis year round for a lifetime. Tennis can be played in a variety of settings that include family fun, recreational or highly competitive.

TERMINOLOGY

ad   short for advantage

ad in   advantage of one point in favor of server after a deuce game

ad out   advantage of one point in favor of receiver after a deuce game

aerobics   activities which involve a continuous pattern of movement such as runing, swimming, cycling, et

all-court game   strategy in singles play which combines baseline and net play

approach   a stroke used in advancing toward the net when the opponent's ball has been hit somewhere ne
the service line;

backhand drive   a groundstroke which is hit from the left side of the body for right-handed players, and fro
the right side for left-handed players

baseline   end boundary line of a tennis court

baseline game   strategy used in singles play where player hits groundstrokes from the end boundary line

carciovascular endurance   ability to sustain an activity over an extended period of time

cavus foot   a high-arched foot

center line   the perpendicular line from the net dividing the court into two equal halves or service areas

center of percussion   area of tennis racquet where ball contact causes the least amount of vibration; or creat
the greatest rebound; also known as the "sweet spot"

concentric contraction   results from an exercise which is performed in the opposite direction as the force
gravity

conditioning   a program of strength and power development, stretching/flexibility, and cardiovascular endu
ance designed for performing at optimal efficiency

contact phase   phase in stroke execution where racquet meets ball

continental grip   an alternate method of holding the racquet in which the hand is placed midway between th
Eastern forehand and Eastern backhand grip

Davis Cup   competition held between men's teams with a nation vs. nation format

deuce   a tie game with both players having scored three points

drop shot   ta "touch shot" in which the ball is placed in the opponent's forecourt near the net

Eastern grip   hand placement on the racquet used for the groundstrokes and serve

eccentric contraction   results from an exercise which is performed in the same direction as the force of gravi

exercise heart rate   the rate at which the heart should beat during an aerobic activity;   based upon ag
maximum heart rate, and desired intensity

Federation Cup   competition held between women's teams with a nation vs. nation format

flexibility   the range of motion about a joint

follow-through   continuation or finish of a stroke following contact

forehand drive   a groundstroke which is hit from the right side of the body for a right-handed player, and fro
the left side for a left-handed player

ame   player who first reaches four points and has a margin of at least two points

and slam   a name give for winning the four major tennis championships of Wimbledon, U. S. Open, French Open, and Australian Open

oundstroke   either the forehand or backhand drive where the ball bounces one time before being hit

alf-volley   a stroke in which contact is made with the ball immediately after it has bounced

itial reaction   the first movement in response to the oncoming ball

st   the form over which the upper part of the shoe is pulled during the manufacturing process

t   a ball that touches the net but lands in the proper court on a serve

b   a high arched "touch" shot which can be used as an offensive or defensive shot

atch   a maximum of three or five sets for men, and three sets for women

aximum heart rate   an estimate of the highest heart rate which can be achieved in an all-out exercise effort; based on age

ational rating scale   a classification of individuals according to skill level for the purpose of competition

o man's land   an imaginary area just behind the service line

ne up, one back   a strategy in doubles play where one partner plays the net position while the other partner plays the baseline position

verhead   an offensive shot hit from a position above the head and directed downward forcefully into the opponent's court

verspin   rotation on a ball resutling from it being lifted upward and forward

assing shot   a ball which is out of the opponent's reach when he/she is at the net

es planus foot   low arched foot

ower   the rate at which work is done

reparation phase   in which the racquet is placed in proper position to execute the stroke

ally   hitting the ball back and forth across the net

eady position   a balanced and stable position of the body in preparation for reacting to the ball

eceiver   the player opposing the server

ectus foot   a "normal" arched foot

eturn of serve   the act of returning a ball to the opponent's court following his/her serve

erve   stroke which begins play in a point or game

erve and volley game   strategy in singles play in which player approaches the net immediately after serving the ball

erver   the player who first delivers the ball in a game

ervice line   the boundary line at the back of the service court

set player who first wins six games and who wins by at least a margin of two games
sideline the line which runs from the net to the baseline and marks the outer edge of the playing court
slice rotation on a ball in reverse of the topspin; also known as a backspin rotation on the ball
split-step a slight jump landing on the balls of the feet when advancing toward the net
static stretch a slow stretching exercise through a range of motion with a hold position at the end
strategy a plan of attack for placing your opponent in a position of disadvantage
strength the force a muscle exerts against a resistance in one maximal effort
sweet spot *see* center of percussion

tie-break game in operation when the score reaches six games all in any set
topspin an exaggerated overspin
two-back strategy in doubles play where both partners play the baseline position
two-handed backhand an alternate backhand stroke in which two hands are placed together on the racque
two-up strategy in doubles play where both partners play the net position

USLTA United States Lawn Tennis Association, later to become the USTA
USTA United States Tennis Association, the governing body for tennis in the United States

volley a stroke, other than the serve, in which the ball is hit before it touches the ground

Wightman Cup annual competition between womens' teams from the United States and England
Wimbledon Championships considered to be the most prestigious of the four major tennis tournaments; hel
    annually in England
wind-up phase phase of a serve characterized by a wide circular motion of the arms in preparation for ba
    contact

EQUIPMENT

The consumer is flooded with different shapes, sizes and brands of tennis rackets. Basically, there is no perfect racket. Each person must choose the racket best suited to his personal tastes, physical characteristics, level of skill and type of game played. Because rackets are becoming so expensive ($30-$250+), it is recommended the consumer ask to use a demonstration racket or borrow from someone before purchasing.

The essential factors to consider when purchasing a tennis racket are:

Racket Size--Standard, mid-sized, and over-sized. The mid-sized and over-sized racket have become very popular. It would be difficult to find someone playing in a tennis tournament today with a standard size racket. The reason being the hitting area is 10-20 percent greater with mid- and oversized rackets. The stigma that these rackets are for older people has passed. Beginners should strongly consider a larger faced racket to learn the game.

Racket Material--Much research has taken place to develop a quality racket material. Many different materials have been used with varying degrees of success. These materials help ball control, flexibility, weight and stiffness. Wood continues to be popular, but aluminum, steel, fiberglass, and graphite have gained popularity.

Racket Weight--The weight depends on the strength of the individual. Select a racket that is heavy enough, but not too heavy. One that is too heavy will tire you and cause a loss of control. A general guide is:

Light Weight: 12-13 oz. for girls and women
Medium Weight: 13-1/2 to 13-3/4 ozs. for boys and most men
Heavy Weight: 14-15 ozs. for some large men

Racket Grip--The size of grip depends on the size of hand. Be certain to avoid a grip that is too large. Too large a grip will also tire you and cause a loss of control. Try several sizes and pick the one that feels the best. A general guide is:

4-1/4" - 4-1/2" - children and women
4-1/2" - 4-5/8" - boys and some women
4-1/2" - 5" - men

String--Choices of string are nylon or gut. Nylon is relatively immune to moisture, inexpensive and durable. For beginners and novice players nylon is preferred because it is serviceable.

Gut is impervious to moisture, expensive and wears out rather quickly. It is preferred by more advanced and tournament players because of its resiliency and playability."

Nylon is strung at 50-60 pounds of tension while gut is strung 55-70 pounds of tension. Generally, the tighter the string, the less control the player has. More advanced players use tighter strings.

Balls--Other equipment essential for play include balls. They are made of wool felt and natural synthetics or rubber. The rubber is molded into two cups cemented together and covered with felt. The hollow inside of the ball is inflated with compressed air.

For beginners or novice players balls marked "Heavy Duty" by the manufacturer are recommended. Remember to discard balls that are worn. When the fuzzy outer covering has been worn away, buy new balls.

Attire--Another important consideration in playing tennis is attire. Traditionally, the attire for the tennis player has been white clothing with women generally wearing short skirts. Today, dramatic changes have taken place in both the style and color. Some highly traditional tournaments and clubs, like Wimbledon, still cling to the traditional attire. The Tulsa Tribune reported that 18-year old Steffi Graf, finalist in the 1987 Wimbledon tournament, was told "to leave a practice court for breaking one of the strictest rules of the All England Lawn Tennis Club." Because she was wearing blue shorts officials told Graf, "She would have to change into an outfit in keeping with the regulation that tennis outfits are predominantly white."

Another important consideration is shoes. Any tennis shoe may be worn on hard top courts but low top "sneaker" type shoes are recommended. A smooth rubber sole must be worn on clay top courts or the surface will soon be badly cut up.

Care of Equipment--A racket press is recommended for a wooden racket, although warping is not the problem it has been in the past. Strips of tape placed along the top edge of the racket help to protect exposed string as well as wood when it comes in contact with the court.

Court Surfaces--The type of court surface varies. Different types cause the ball to bounce in different ways, thus varying the style of play. Common types of courts and play used are:

> Grass Surface--The ball plays fairly fast, has a low bounce and skids along the surface.

> Clay Surface--The ball has a slow rebound, but tends to slide on the surface.

> Wood--The ball is very fast and skids along the surface. Usually wood surfaces are indoors and glare from lights poses an added challenge.

> Asphalt--The ball has a moderate to high bounce. On hot days, the surface becomes soft and the bounce is reduced.

> Concrete--The ball has a normal and uniform bounce and travels fast.

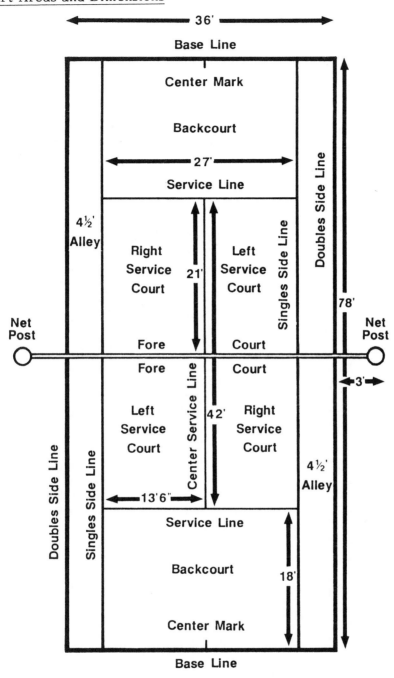

Tennis Court

Figure 7.1 Court Areas and Dimensions

RULES AND ETIQUETTE

RULES

Choice of Service or Side--The choice of sides and the right to be server or receiver in the first game is decided by toss. Generally one player in the first game spins his racket and the other player calls one of the options presented by the markings on the racket (e.g. "M" or "W", "number" or "no number"). The player winning the toss may choose, or require the opponent to choose one of the following:

A. The right to be server or receiver, in which case the other player chooses the side; or

B. The side, in which case the other player chooses the right to be server or receiver.

Changing Sides--Players change sides after the games played in each set total an odd number which means after the first game and every two games thereafter.

Good Return--It is a good return if:

A. The ball lands on the line.

B. The ball touches the net, provided it passes over it and lands in the proper court (except on a serve, see Let).

C. The player reaches over the net to hit a ball that has blown or rebounded back to the other side of its own accord, provided the player does not touch the net with the racket, body, or clothing.

D. The player's racket passes over the net after the ball has been returned, provided the net is not touched.

E. The player returns a ball which has hit a ball lying in the court. (A player may request a ball lying in the opponent's court to be removed, but not while the ball is in play.)

F. The ball is returned outside the post, either above or below the level of the net, provided it lands in the proper court, even though it touches the post.

A Player Loses a Point When:

A. Player serves a double fault.

B. Player fails to return the ball before it bounces twice, or if he does not return it into his opponent's court.

C. Player returns the ball so that it hits the ground, a permanent fixture (e.g. fence), or other object outside any of the lines which bound his opponent's court.

D. Player volleys the ball and fails to make a good return even when standing outside the court.

E. Player touches the ball in play with the racket more than once when making a stroke. (In doubles, the ball may be returned by only one partner.)

F. The racket or anything worn or carried touches the net or the ground within the opponent's court.

G. Player volleys the ball before it has passed the net.

H. The ball in play touches the player or anything worn or carried except the racket.

I. Player throws the racket at the ball and hits it.

J. Player deliberately commits any act which hinders the opponent in making a stroke.

Faults

The serve is a fault if:

A.   The server fails to hit the ball into the proper court.
B.   The server misses the ball in attempting to strike it (Note: The ball may be tossed several times without penalty.)
C.   The ball served touches a permanent fixture (other than the net) or the server's partner before it hits the ground.
D.   A footfault is committed.

A footfault is called if:

A.   The server changes his position by walking or running before he hits the ball. A server may jump at the serve, and one or both feet may be over the baseline, provided he does not touch the court or line before contacting the ball.
B.   The server touches the baseline or the court area within the baseline before he hits the ball.
C.   The server serves from outside the area between the sideline and the center mark.

Lets--A let is a served ball which touches the net, strap or band and is otherwise good. In this instance, the server is allowed one more serve. If a let is called when play is interrupted or if the serve is delivered before the receiver is ready, the server is allowed two serves.

Order of Service in Doubles--The order of serving is decided at the beginning of each set. The pair who serve in the first game of each set decide which partner shall do so. The other partner serves the third game. The opposing pair shall decide who shall serve the second game of the set. The partner then serves the fourth game. This order is followed throughout the set so that each player will serve every fourth game. If a player serves out of turn, the correct player must serve as soon as the mistake is discovered. All points earned are counted. If a game is completed with the wrong player serving, the order remains as altered.

Order of Receiving in Doubles--The order of receiving is determined at the beginning of each set. The receiving pair decide who is to receive the first point, and that player continues to receive the serves directed to that particular service court throughout the set. (In other words, he receives every other point in every other game.) The other partner does the same to the serves directed to the other service court.

If a player receives out of turn, he remains in that position until the game in which it is discovered is completed. The partners then resume their original position.

SCORING IN TENNIS

The Scoring of a Game--The server's score is always called first. Point values are:

0 points	-	"Love"
1st point	-	15
2nd point	-	30
3rd point	-	40
4th point	-	game

"Deuce" means that each side has won three points. One side must now win two consecutive points to win the game. The first point after deuce is called "advantage." A score of "Advantage in" means the server is ahead one point. If the receiver wins the first point after deuce, the score is called "advantage (ad) out" (Figure 7.2).

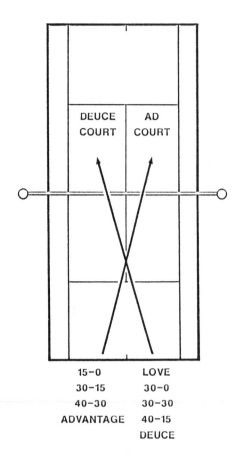

Figure 7.2 Scoring

The Scoring of a Set--Traditionally, the side first winning six games wins the set, if ahead by at least two games (e.g. 6-4). If the score is 5-5 (5-all), play continues until someone gets two games ahead, such as 7-5 or 8-6. An average set takes about 30 minutes to complete.

A match is composed of two out of three sets for men and women, except for professional tennis where the men usually play three out of five sets.

Tie Break Scoring--To help eliminate extended sets (20-18), etc. The U.S.T.A. has authorized a best of twelve point tie-break system that can be used when the score reaches 6-6 in any set. (A best of nine point system may also be used.) The new "sudden death" system is played as follows:

In singles, the player who first wins seven points wins the game and the set provided he is ahead by two points. If the score is tied at six-all, then one of the players must win two consecutive points to win. The player whose turn it is to serve is the server for the first point; his opponent serves the next two points; and thereafter each serves two points until the end of the set. The same order follows in doubles except that each of the (three) players serve twice after the first server serves only once.

From the first point, each service is started alternately from the right and left courts, beginning from the right court. In singles and doubles, players change ends after six points have been played and at the conclusion of the tie-break game. The team that served first in the tie-break game will be service receivers in the first game of the next set.

No-ad scoring--The Vass "no-ad" scoring is used to help speed up the game. It is sometimes used with young players or in the event a tournament has been delayed by weather or has a large number of entrants. It is commonly used in college and university varsity tennis matches. Sometimes no-ad scoring is used in the initial rounds of a tournament and conventional scoring is then employed from the quarter- or semi-finals on up.

In "no-ad" scoring, a player needs only four points (1-2-3-game) to win a game. If the score reaches 3-all, a sudden death is played and the next point decides the game. At 3-all or deuce, the receiver has the option to choose to which court the serve is to be delivered.

A pro-set is a shorter match which consists of a player winning at least 8 games and is ahead by at least two games. This is a good procedure for class tournaments when time is a factor or for beginners who tend to tire easily.

ETIQUETTE

Since its origin tennis has been referred to as the sport of kings, aristocrats and a gentleman's game. This is reflected in the various ways a player is expected to conduct himself during the match, otherwise known as etiquette. In short, etiquette demonstrates respect for your opponent and other players. It says to others, "I'm a good sport."

Unfortunately, there are many expert tennis players seen and written about in the media that do not exemplify these rules of etiquette. Their outrageous behavior is a disservice to the historical roots of the game.

Several rules of etiquette to follow while participating in a game are:

1. Introduce yourself.
2. Keep the warm-up time to a minimum. (10 minutes maximum).
3. Call out the score before each serve and remember the server's score is called first.
4. If your ball goes to the adjoining court, wait until their point is completed and politely say, "Ball, please."
5. Do not return bad balls that are out of court.
6. If others are waiting, play doubles or rotate, but don't monopolize the court.
7. Wait until a point is completed before walking behind players or across a playing court.
8. The server should begin each point with two balls in his possession.
9. Avoid unnecessary distractions and loud talking.
10. Return balls from an adjacent court after the point has been completed. Do so by tossing or rolling the ball to the nearest player.
11. You are responsible for calling balls on your side of the net, while your opponent calls his side of the net. If unsure of a call, play the ball and say nothing. If you play a ball, it is considered "good." If a ball is out, call it immediately.
12. The server should wait until the receiver is ready.
13. Avoid foot faults.
14. Control temper and expressions of anger.
15. If a service is obviously out, let the ball go past you instead of hitting it back to your opponent.

16. Call a "let" if interference occurs during play (e.g. a ball coming on your court).
17. Take all practice serves before the start of the match.
18. Call lets and faults (use hand signals) loud and clear so opponent sees and hears your calls.
19. Never question an opponent's decision regarding a rule or call. Respect each other.
20. Win or lose graciously.
21. Return balls directly to server after play on that point has been completed.
22. Try not to return a first serve which is a fault.
23. Recognize good play by your opponent.
24. Collect all balls on your side of the net after each point and return them directly to the server.
25. Congratulate opponent at the end of the match.

FUNDAMENTALS OF THE GAME

GRIPPING THE RACKET

The eastern or "shaking hands" grip is almost universally used for the forehand ground stroke. Hold the racket face perpendicular to the ground and grasp the handle as though you were shaking hands. The "V" formed by the thumb and index finger should be over the center of the handle on the top of the grip (Figure 7.3). The index finger is spread from the other fingers as the hand angles across the grip at approximately a 45° angle. The thumb rests between the index finger and the middle finger. To change to the eastern backhand grip, simply rotate the "V" of the thumb and index finger one-quarter turn to the left for a right-handed player. This will place the knuckle of the index finger on top of the grip (Figure 7.4). The "V" should now be slightly below the top left bevel of the handle.

The continental grip is a slight variation of the forehand and backhand. Actually, it's halfway between the two grips. The "V" is directly over the left bevel of the handle for a right-handed player. This grip is often used for both the forehand and backhand volley. It would be preferable to change grips for a volley, but often there is not enough time to switch, thus making the continental grip the best alternative.

The two-hand backhand grip is formed by the eastern backhand grip with the target hand and the eastern forehand grip with the rear hand. Although this grip reduces your reach, it often provides for greater control and power, thus improving confidence for the more difficult backhand stroke.

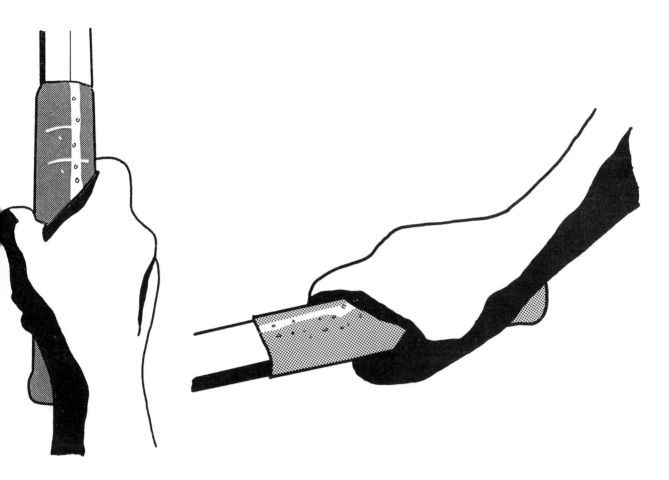

Figure 7.3 Forehand Grip

Figure 7.4 Backhand Grip

THE STANCE

The position used in tennis for receiving groundstrokes and serves is called the "ready position." In this position you should face the net with your feet approximately shoulder width apart. The knees are slightly bent with your weight on the balls of the feet. The racket should be held in front of the body and vertical to the court. The forehand or continental grip is used with the nongrip hand holding the neck of the racket (Figure 7.5). This is an alert, preparatory position and in singles, it is taken just behind the baseline near the center of the service mark. For receiving the serve, you should take a position according to the type and strength of the opponent's serve.

Figure 7.5 The Stance

THE FOREHAND STROKE

This is the most often used stroke in tennis and really forms the foundation for the entire game. The stroke begins as soon you can determine which side of the body you will hit from. As you become more experienced, your reading ability will become keener, allowing for much quicker stroke preparation.

Body Position--The backswing should begin immediately, after the ball leaves the opponent's racket. As the racket is taken back, the shoulders rotate so that the target side of the body faces the net. The hips rotate also, as you pivot on the rear foot, keeping most of the weight there. The target foot moves forward and forms a straight line with the rear leg. The target leg should be used as the "correction factor" and can be moved either left or right, depending on the position of the oncoming ball. The racket should be pointing toward the back fence at approximately hip level. The head of the racket should be tilted slightly down and the wrist held firm throughout the stroke.

Contact Point--As the racket moves forward from low to high, hip to head, the weight transfers from the rear to the front leg. The weight should be on the forward foot and the racket vertical at ball impact. Ball contact is made near the front foot or hip. The ball should be at approximately hip level whenever possible. The knees should be slightly bent and the wrist firm as the ball is stroked. You should watch the ball into the racket as long as possible and then as the racket meets the ball, keep the racket moving towards the net as long as possible.

Follow Through--As you make contact with the ball, do not look up to follow the ball immediately, but rather keep the head down as you follow through. The racket should continue forward, gradually rising toward the direction of the ball.

The wrist should stop at eye level with the racket pointing upward. The hips and shoulders have rotated and are now parallel to the net as you face the direction the ball was hit. The upper arm will be near the chin on a good follow-through. The trail leg will simply slide or drag forward to complete the swing and provide good balance to return to the "ready position" (Figure 7.6).

Remember that the body action activates the arm swing, and the swing plane from low (backswing) to high (follow-through) will give the ball natural topspin. Good preparation and a steady concentration on the ball are keys to a successful groundstroke. It's virtually impossible to get the racket back too soon in preparing for a stroke.

Figure 7.6 Follow-Through for the Forehand Stroke

THE BACKHAND STROKE

In most cases the forehand stroke is considered the "bread and butter" shot, but unless the backhand stroke is developed, you really cannot achieve the joy of a good all-round tennis game. Often the backhand becomes more of a mental block because it's on the non-dominate side of the body. There are, however, only a few basic differences between the forehand and the backhand strokes. Most of the same principles apply.

Body Position--The backhand grip is assumed as you begin the backswing. As in the forehand, you must "read" the returning ball as soon as possible in order to properly prepare the same set-up position for each shot. The pivot is made on the rear foot and simultaneously the racket is taken back until it's pointing toward the back fence. The racket should be held with both hands as it is taken back. The target hand grips the racket and the rear hand, holding the throat, guides it to the correct position. When the backswing is completed, the target arm is touching the body and the thumb rests on the thigh. As you can see, the arm is held closer to the body than for the forehand stroke. The shoulders and hips rotate to place the body sideways to the net. Also, as in the forehand, the knees are bent, the wrist firm, and the racket face is tilted slightly downward at the completion of the backswing. With the weight on the rear foot and the target shoulder near the chin, you are ready to stroke the backhand (Figure 7.7).

Figure 7.7 The Backhand Stroke

Contact Point--As the weight shifts to the target foot, the racket is released by the rear hand and starts forward in a low-to-high plane. The hips and shoulders rotate as they move toward the net. The target shoulder is pointing toward the ball as the weight transfers to the target foot. Just as in the forehand, the target leg can be used as a "correction factor" to allow you to step farther left or right, depending on the position of the ball. The ball should be contacted slightly in front of the target foot at approximately hip level. On meeting the ball, the racket face should be vertical, the wrist should be firm, and the arm firm and extended (do not bend the elbow). The racket is moving from the thigh slightly upward as the ball is contacted.

Follow-Through--The follow-through, as in the forehand, is fluid and high. The racket should be pointing up and the wrist should be at eye level. The racket and arm will finish slightly past perpendicular to the net, and the racket face should still, as it is throughout the stroke, be perpendicular to the court. Both knees are slightly bent throughout the stroke and the rear leg drags forward in contact with the court for better balance. Many of the key fundamentals previously mentioned; i.e., watch the ball as you stroke it, apply to the forehand and backhand ground strokes.

Two-handed Backhand--For some, the two-handed backhand is easier and allows for much greater stroke confidence. Often those with weak wrists find it to be more efficient and powerful. The two-hand grip should be used and the stroke fundamentals are the same as for the forehand. The reach is somewhat restricted because of the rear hand gripping the racket, but the additional power and control that are often gained make it worthwhile.

THE SERVE

The serve is probably the most important skill to learn because it is the only time that you have complete control over the ball. You can toss the ball up exactly where you want it and hit it with your choice of spin and speed. The best strategy for learning to

rve consistently is to **master the basic motion** before trying to serve with speed and
lacement.

The forehand grip, or the continental grip, should be used for serving (Figure 7.8).
he continental grip is usually more effective for putting spin on the serve.

Figure 7.8 The Serving Grip

Body Position--When serving to the deuce court, you should stand slightly
behind the baseline and approximately one to three feet from the center service
mark. The front foot should point toward the right net post for a right-handed
service from the deuce court. It should point six to eight feet past the left post for
a left-handed serve. When serving to the add court, the front foot should point six
to eight feet past the right post for right-handers and directly at the left post for a
left-hander. The feet should be comfortably spaced about shoulder width apart.
Hold the racket at the throat with the ball hand (Figure 7.9). Keep the elbows in
and point the racket in the direction of the serve.

The toss is the most critical part of the serve. For the flat serve, the toss is
made in front of the front foot (six to twelve inches), and slightly higher than the
extended reach of the racket. The toss begins with ball held in the fingertips. To
begin the action, both arms drop, with the ball hand going to hip level before
starting up. To avoid spin on the ball, you should open the fingers and push the ball
straight up with a firm arm and wrist movement. The weight is shifted to the back
leg and foot as the toss is made. As the ball hand goes up, the racket hand goes
down and around in a wide arc until it is curled back up into the "back-scratch"
position (Figure 7.10). The hips and shoulders have rotated away from the net as
the ball reaches its apex.

Fig. 7.9 The Serving Stance   Fig. 7.10 Serving Back-Scratch Position

Contact Point--From this position, with the weight on the rear foot, you will transfer your weight to the front foot as your racket hand starts the racket up to the ball. The hips and shoulders are rotating back toward the net, and the ball hand should pull down and around to help generate more speed for the racket. It is very important to remember during the toss and especially as you move toward contact, to watch the ball. It's easy to fall into the bad habit of only "seeing the ball" and not really concentrating on it. If you watch it carefully, this helps keep the chin up and prevents you from prematurely looking at the service court.

The ball should be contacted slightly in front of the front foot. The arm and body should be at full extension and, upon contact, you should snap your wrist forward and down. The wrist action is a pronating or rolling type movement, rather than a "waving goodbye" type.

Follow-Through--After contact the racket arm continues down and across your body to finish up on the opposite hip. Force from the swing is dissipated on this nonracket side. Your weight has transferred forward again onto the racket leg as you step forward into the court to maintain balance. At the completion of the swing, the knees are flexed and the upper body should be bent at the waist (Figure 7.11).

Figure 7.11 The Serve Follow Through

Spin Serves--There are two basic types of spins applied, depending on where the ball is hit and the angle of the ball. For the slice serve, as the racket meets the ball, it's still perpendicular to the court but at an angle to the service court. The ball is contacted more to one side, than squarely, as in the flat serve. For the spin or topspin serve, the ball toss is more over the head. Contact is made with the racket face moving up and to the outside with a strong wrist snap. More spin can be achieved by using a greater racket angle and more power.

THE VOLLEY

The volley is a ball that is hit before it bounces. It is an excellent shot to handle a weak return by your opponent. With practice, the volleyer can hit the ball deep or at a sharp angle, out of reach. This skill is easier to learn than others because there are fewer things to consider. The key points for a volley are **STEP**, **TURN**, and **BLOCK**.

Body Position--As previously mentioned, the continental grip is more commonly used in volleying. Because you are close to the net, there are many occasions when you will not have time to change to a forehand or backhand grip.

You should face the net with both hands on the racket (ready position). You will pivot much the same way as you would for a ground stroke, turn sideways and then step into the volley with either foot (forehand or backhand side). The shoulders should turn sideways to the net for the volley even when you don't have to move laterally to make the shot. There is very little backswing. The racket should be taken back no further than the rear shoulder. The racket head should stay above the wrist.

Contact Point--The swing is short, compact, and firm. You should step toward and meet the ball with a punching or pushing type movement. The wrist is bent but firm as the ball is met at around shoulder height. The point of contact should be out in front of the body. For lower volleys, you simply bend more at the knees rather than dropping the racket head. It may be necessary to open the racket face more to allow the ball to clear the net.

Follow Through--The follow-through is short for a volley. Generally, the entire swing occurs within the width of the shoulders. Since the stroke is more of a jab, the racket should not go beyond the "ready" position. You should recover quickly and prepare for a return volley.

THE LOB

The lob is just another forehand or backhand stroke with one difference; it is hit in an upward trajectory. It is used as both an offensive and defensive weapon. The objective is to hit the ball over an opponent's head and out of their reach when they are at the net. Fundamentally, the major difference between the forehand and backhand ground stroke and the lob is the angle of ball ascent. The racket face must have approximately a 45 or greater degree of angle at the contact point, as compared to the other ground strokes which require the racket face to be perpendicular at impact. Another slight difference between the strokes is that the lob does not require much forward weight shift nor follow through.

Lobs should land deep in the backcourt of the opponent. They should always carry past the back service court line, and ideally land within four or five feet of the baseline. A good defensive lob should clear the net by 25 to 30 feet. Lobs are most effective if they are not played too often and are well concealed.

THE OVERHEAD

The overhead is considered to be one of the most dramatic shots in tennis. If you become proficient, your ability to put away short lobs will make your net play better. The overhead swing is patterned after the service motion. The only real difference is that you use a modified backswing. Since the ball will not be tossed by you, like a serve, you must position your body at the right place to make the stroke. As soon as the lob is hit to you, turn sideways to the net and bring your racket back to where the handle is at shoulder height. Use your nonracket hand to track the ball. This helps you in turning and provides better perception in following the ball on its descent. As the ball drops near the contact point, drop your racket into the backscratch position. The ball is then hit like a flat serve, in front of the body. The follow-through lets the racket swing through and around the body like the serve.

On high or long lobs, it is wiser to let them bounce and then hit them as they start down. Just be sure you make contact before it drops too low after the bounce.

STRATEGY FOR PLAYING

Singles--The best way to enjoy tennis is to "keep the ball in play." This may sound rather simplistic, but it is intended to accentuate the importance of consistent and safe groundstrokes. Make your opponent hit the bad shots or go for the "winners" to try and end a rally. It's estimated that 75 percent of points are lost on shots that could have been returned. Patience, tenacity, and hitting down the middle will prevent many problems and lead to many mistakes by your opponent.

Get to the ball and "set up" as early as possible. You should normally start from the ready position, just behind the baseline in the center of the court. As you read the returning shot, you should be quickly moving to the correct court position and simultaneously starting your backswing. Good position and racket preparation are vital to producing consistent ground strokes. Avoid getting caught in "no-man's land," the area between the service line and the baseline. Shots that are hit to you here will often land near your feet and are difficult to return.

Try to keep the ball deep in the opponent's court. A deep shot helps you in two ways: it forces you to hit the ball high over the net, two to three feet, and reduces the chances of a good return by your opponent. Many more points are lost from hitting the ball into the net than from hitting it too deep. By hitting deep shots, it keeps your opponent back and greatly reduces the angle returns that he/she might hit on a short shot.

If your opponent does move you from side to side with angle shots, it's often wise to change the rhythm with a lob. This forces them to change their pace, and it gives you time to get back into a good position for the return.

Attack at the net whenever you have the opportunity. Approach on a short shot by your opponent and then hit your shot deep. This gives you time to move up and take a "ready position." Take the volleys early so you can hit them down.

Don't keep hitting a hard first serve and a "dink" for a second serve. If you are hitting it hard and missing, then "take a little off" on the power in favor of accuracy. A weak second serve only sets your opponent up for a "put away." Serving is the only skill in tennis that you can practice effectively alone, unless you have a backboard. Develop a consistent, deep second serve that will not put you in a defensive position.

Doubles--Let the better server serve first in doubles. This will allow him/her two serves to one for the weaker server, in the first six games.

Assume the proper court position for serving and receiving. When serving, the server should stand behind the baseline midway between the alley and the center line.

218

is partner should take a position approximately two feet from the alley and five feet rom the net. For receiving, the partner receiving the serve should stand just behind the aseline at a point bisecting the angle where the ball may be served. The partner stands ear the middle of the service line on the other half of the court. From this position the artner should help call the service line.

As your tennis game improves and you develop confidence in your ability to volley, he strongest offensive position in doubles is for both players to be at the net. This osition gives you more opportunities to hit angles, place shots deep, and to "put away" reak returns. It also tends to intimidate the opponents who often feel they must hit erfect shots to avoid losing the point. Seventy-five percent of the points in advanced lay are won and lost at the net.

"Poaching" can be very effective, especially when your partner has a good first erve. The net player moves across the court to the server's side to attempt to intercept he return and volley it away. The server should move to the other side to cover the ourt vacated by his/her partner. Poaching is usually much more effective if it catches he opponents off guard and, therefore, should not be attempted on all or even most eturns. One of the best situations for poaching is when your partner serves deep to the pponent's backhand.

ERRORS AND CORRECTIONS

Illustrations of the <u>MOST COMMON</u> errors and how to correct them

<u>ERROR</u> (Forehand)
Wrist and arm are not <u>firm</u>
at contact

<u>ILLUSTRATION</u>

Figure 7.12

RESULTS AND CORRECTION
-    Spraying of ball in different directions, no consistency.
-    <u>Correct</u> this by imagining a cast on your arm and wrist to ensure they are firm on contact with ball. Also, you must practice contacting ball at the front foot. This helps alleviate the need to break the wrist.

<u>ERROR</u> (Forehand)
Improper position for stroke

<u>ILLUSTRATION</u>

Figure 7.13

RESULTS AND CORRECTION
-    This usually results in late racket preparation and hitting the ball into the net or too long.
-    <u>Correct</u> this by practicing "reading" the returning shot and move quickly to set up for the return. <u>Remember</u> that as you are moving, the arm should be starting the backswing.

RROR (Backhand)
lbow bent, weak wrist,
:hicken wing" backhand

Figure 7.14

RESULTS AND CORRECTION
- Very eratic shot, usually weakly hit, i.e., high and short
- Correct this by first checking the backhand grip to make sure that the wrist is behind the face of the racket. Keep the elbow close to the body on the backswing and at the start of the forward swing. Wrist and elbow are firm as you lean into the ball.

RROR (Backhand)
Iitting ball late

Figure 7.15

RESULTS AND CORRECTION
- Ball will usually slice off to the left for right-handers and off to the right for left-handers.
- Correct this by setting up sooner and contacting the ball slightly in front of the lead foot.

ERROR (Backhand)
Punching or pushing ball with
no body motion

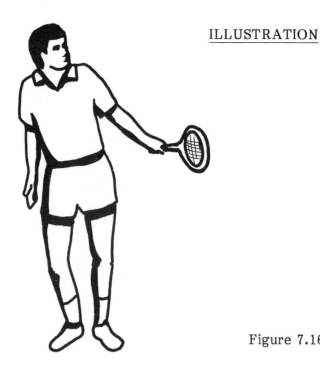

Figure 7.16

RESULTS AND CORRECTIONS
- Often results in a weak shot that is very short. Inconsistent return.
- Concentrate on a total body swing, with the legs, hips, and shoulders leading the way. Remember, swing from low and finish high, with the weight on the front foot.

ERROR (Serving)
Poor toss

Figure 7.17

RESULTS AND CORRECTION
- Ball is either hit too deep or into the net.
- Correct this by practicing toss until it becomes a consistent skill. If the toss is not where you want it, don't hit it; catch the ball and toss again.

ERROR (Serving)
Improper weight shift and
wrist action at contact point

Figure 7.18

RESULTS AND CORRECTION

- This usually results with the weight still on the back foot and the wrist not breaking or breaking too late. The serve will often be long and/or inconsistent.
- Correct this by putting your weight forward and breaking your wrist forward and down as you contact the ball. This is made much easier if the toss is in the correct position. Remember, the follow-through should carry you into the court.

OTHER PROBLEM AREAS

ERROR/FOREHAND	RESULT	CORRECTION
1. Shoulders not perpendicular to the net, thus producing a fading or "moving away" type stroke	Eratic ball flight-- no pace. This often causes the ball to slice off to the racket side of the court.	Step into the shot, leading with the non racket shoulder. Bend the front leg and stay down on the ball.
2. Backswing too high	Meeting ball with racket face open (pointing upward). Ball hit too far or too weakly (gives opponent easy put-away).	Point racket toward back fence (angling slightly below horizontal). Start low, finish high through ball.
3. Jabbing ball, no follow-through	Hitting ball into the net. Weak return that "sets up" opponent if it clears the net.	Swing forward low to high and exaggerate follow-through to "lift" the ball across the net.

ERROR/BACKHAND	RESULT	CORRECTION
4. Abrupt chop at ball	Eratic flight, usually hit poorly with backspin	Exaggerate the follow-through, keep the racket face perpendicular to court throughout the swing.

ERRORS/SERVING	RESULT	CORRECTION
5. Hitch or stall in swing	Inconsistent serve	Must work on a continuous motion from start to end of follow-through. The entire movement should be fluid, without stopping at the "backscratch" position.
6. Improper body rotation on back swing. Turning back toward service court too soon	Poor service direction	As ball is tossed, shift weight to rear leg and follow ball up with front hand and shoulder. Also, check your service grip and stroke.

ERROR/VOLLEY	RESULT	CORRECTION
7. Overswinging	Hitting ball into the net or too long	Use the pace of the oncoming ball to redirect it. Keep your stroke short and compact.
8. Poor body and arm position	Inability to put-away volleys or weak volleys that allow the opponent an easy put-away	Concentrate on shoulder turn and forward weight transfer. If time allows, step into every volley with the racket in front of the body.

ERROR/LOB	RESULT	CORRECTION
9. Using excessive wrist action	Often too long, usually inconsistent	The lob swing should be the same as the forehand or backhand. Keep a firm wrist and elbow. Simply open the racket face to achieve the desired height.

ERROR/OVERHEAD	RESULT	CORRECTION
10. Trying to "cream" the overhead	Hits either the back fence or the net	For this shot you must set up in the right position. You must be patient and wait for the ball. Then you should reduce your power by about 50 percent.

IMPROVEMENT DRILLS AND GAMES

Basic Progression Drills--Drills 1-4 for Forehand
1. Practice stroke without ball--20 times
    -- Pivot, turn sideways to the net with the racket back
    -- Make forward swing and follow-through
    Checkpoints for forehand stroke:
    (1) Backswing--Body Position
         Pivot on rear foot, sideways to net--racket face perpendicular to court-
         -racket head pointing toward fence and slightly below horizontal--
         racket at hip level--weight on rear foot.
    (2) Contact Point
         Racket face perpendicular to court--step forward to meet ball-contact
         ball at front foot--wrist and arm are firm.
    (3) Follow-Through
         Racket at head level--you can balance a dime on the top of racket (it's
         still perpendicular)--navel facing net--weight on front foot.

2. Self-Toss Forehand Drive
         Stand ten feet from the fence in a forehand position--using the fence as
    the net. With the racket back, toss the ball underhanded, out and just in front
    of your front foot. Step into the ball and use a forehand stroke to drive it
    into the fence. Keep the wrist and arm firm as you contact the ball. Use the
    checkpoints in Drill #1 to assist you in making corrections. Hit 40 balls--2
    sets (20 each).
         Turn and take the forehand position toward the net--toss and hit 20
    balls from the baseline toward the net. (Try to hit the balls over the net, but
    without opening the racket face--keep it perpendicular to the court.)

3. Partner Toss Drill (group)
    -- The hitter will stand near the baseline turned sideways to the net
        (forehand position).
    -- The tosser will stand a few feet across the net with a basket of balls.
    -- The retrievers, 1 or 2, will keep the tosser supplied with balls.
        The tosser will toss the ball underhanded, to the hitter's forehand side.
        The ball should bounce between the tosser and hitter and be a soft, easy
        ball to approach and stroke. The tosser will assist the hitter in
        correcting fundamental errors of the forehand stroke. The hitter will
        hit 25 balls and then become a retriever. The tosser will hit next.
    -- Each group member will hit twice (50 balls).

4. Partner Feeder Drill (group)
    -- The hitter will stand just behind the baseline in the ready position.
    -- The feeder will stand across the net at the back service line.
    -- The feeder will bounce and hit the ball to the hitter's forehand side.
    -- As soon as the feeder hits the ball, the hitter will begin taking the
        racket back as he/she moves and pivots for a forehand stroke (must
        have good position and racket preparation).
    -- The hitter will not attempt to hit balls that are misplaced to the
        backhand side.
    -- As in the Partner Toss Drill, the feeder will assist the hitter in
        correcting errors.
    -- One or two retrievers will gather balls for the feeder.

-- The feeder becomes the hitter, the retriever the feeder, the hitter retrieves--after 25 hits.
-- Each group member hits twice (50 balls).

Basic Progression Drills--Substitute Backhand for Forehand in Drills 1-4.

Checkpoints for Backhand Stroke:
(1) Backswing--Body Position
Pivot on rear foot, sideways to net--racket face perpendicular to court--racket head pointing toward fence and slightly below horizontal--racket arm is touching body--rear hand grips throat of racket--weight on rear foot--racket at hip level.
(2) Contact Point
Racket face perpendicular to court--step forward to meet ball--contact ball in front of front foot--wrist and arm are firm.
(3) Follow-Through
Racket at head level--you can balance a dime on the top of racket (it's still perpendicular)--navel facing net--weight on front foot.

5. Ground Stroke Drill (group)
This drill is the same as the Partner Feeder Drill for forehand or backhand, #4, with this exception:
-- The feeder will bounce-hit balls to both the forehand and backhand sides with alternating strokes.
-- It's important for the feeder to give the hitter enough time after each stroke to return to the ready position. As previously mentioned--the real key for good, consistent ground strokes, is early set-up and racket preparation.
-- The feeder will assist the hitter in correcting errors.
-- Each student will hit 15 shots and rotate--2 sets of 15 each (30).

6. Rally Drill
-- Begin with one student on each end of the court standing near the baseline--basket of balls behind each end of court near the fence.
-- One begins rally with a bounce-hit forehand and both continue to hit ground strokes until the ball is out-of-play. One student then starts another ball in play with a bounce-hit.
-- Students should become more keenly aware of the value of good stroke preparation and of the necessity of returning to a "ready position" after each stroke.
-- Continue drill for 10-15 minutes. As students become more proficient, the time can be increased.

7. Service Toss Drill
-- The server assumes the correct serving position near a court line (does not have to be the baseline). The server then places the racket on the court so that the throat of the racket is close to and curving around his/her front foot. The face of the racket should be just beyond and straight out in front of the server's foot. With a basket of balls within reach, the server practices tossing for the serve.
-- The server should toss the ball so that the ball will land on the racket face or within a few inches of it.
-- (NOTE) The server could begin with low tosses for accuracy and gradually toss to the correct height (just beyond the student's reach with a racket).

--   This drill should be practiced 5-10 minutes daily until the toss becomes accurate.

8.   Fence Service Drill (partners)
--   Students should assume the service position on the in-court side of the baseline facing the fence. The servers then practice the toss and serve, hitting the ball into the fence.
--   The non-serving partner should assist the server by supplying balls and indicating errors in their form.
--   Good form and fluid movement should be stressed with little concern about where the ball lands.
--   The server should hit 25 serves and rotate positions.
--   Each should serve 2 sets of 25 each (50).

9.   Service Line-Baseline Service Drill
--   Students should face the net and assume the service stance behind the back service line on either side of the court. They should attempt to serve the ball diagonally toward the correct service area, except they should consider the baseline as the back service line.
--   After 25 serves, they should move back to the actual service position, behind the baseline, and attempt to serve into the correct service court. They should also serve 25 balls from this position (50 total).
--   (NOTE) Server should be most concerned with these keys:
     (1)   a good toss
     (2)   fluid backswing into "Backscratch" position
     (3)   weight shift forward and body movement upward toward ball
     (4)   full extension of racket arm to meet ball
     (5)   wrist break to bring racket down and through ball
     (6)   arm with racket wrapping around body as you have moved forward into the court
--   (NOTE) The server should not be overly concerned about where the ball lands. As these fundamentals are learned and improved, the correct ball placement will be a natural outcome.

10. Toss-and-Hit Volley Drill (group)
--   The student should take a "ready position" to volley, 5 feet behind the net.
--   The tosser (feeder), standing just behind the back service line, tosses the ball to both the forehand and backhand sides of the volleyer. (The balls should be tossed close enough so that the volleyer can reach them in one step in either direction.)
--   After 25 tosses and volleys, the feeder moves back to the baseline and bounce-hits 25 balls at the volleyer.
--   One or two retrievers keep the feeder supplied with balls.
--   The feeder should correct errors in the volley.
--   (NOTE) Key points to look for in the volley are:
     (1)   shoulder turn (sideways to net)
     (2)   short backswing--short follow-through
     (3)   meet ball in front of body
     (4)   firm wrist and arm
--   Feeder replaces volleyer, retriever becomes the feeder, and the volleyer retrieves. Each volleyer hits 50 total balls before rotating.

TENNIS SKILLS TEST

GENERAL INFORMATION

The following test is designed for the beginning tennis player. It is designed to objectively assess ability in various situations.

1. Serve
2. Forehand/Backhand Drives

I. SERVE

Purpose--To measure the player's ability to serve a tennis ball with accuracy and power into the service court.

Equipment/Facilities--The tester provides a regulation tennis court properly marked (see Figure 7.19), balls in good condition, rope, and marking tape or ropes to mark the court. The student provides his personal racket.

Description--The student (X) attempts to legally serve into the right service court. Depending upon where the ball lands, 3, 4, or 5 points are earned. The serve must go between the net and a 9-foot rope, which stretches across the net above the ground.

Twenty (20) serves are taken into the right service court. Two practices are permitted.

Scoring--The student receives points based upon where the ball lands in the marked court. Balls landing on a line receive the higher value. Balls going above the 9-foot rope are scored "0." Let balls are replayed.

The sum of 20 serves is the official score. Maximum score is 100 points.

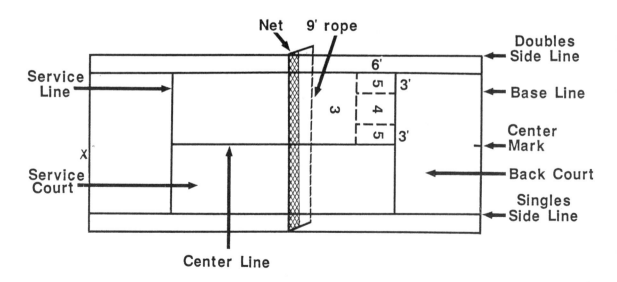

Figure 7.19 Serve

AAHPER, Tennis Skills Test, (Washington, D.C., 1966).

II. FOREHAND AND BACKHAND DRIVES

Purpose--To measure the student's ability to hit a forehand and backhand drive with accuracy and power into the opponent's court.

Equipment/Facilities--The student provides his personal racket. The tester provides rope of sufficient length to stretch 9 feet above the court and across the net, the balls, and regulation court properly marked (see Figure 7.20).

Description--The student holds his racket and assumes a position behind the baseline, then bounces the ball and hits it into the opposite court as deep as possible (see Figure 7.20). The ball must go between the rope and the net to receive the maximum score. Should a ball go above the rope, one-half value of the scoring area in which it lands is recorded.

The student completes 14 trials on the forehand side and 14 trials on the backhand side. Two practice trials are allowed for the forehand and two practice trials for the backhand.

Scoring--the sum of 14 trials taken on the forehand drive is recorded as an official score. The same is done for the backhand drive. Therefore, two official scores are derived from the drive tests. Maximum score is 112.

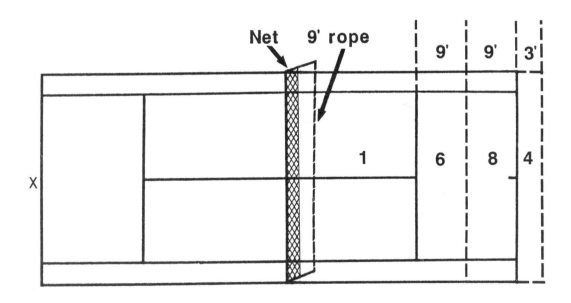

Figure 7.20 Forehand and Backhand Drive

Broer, M. R. and D. M. Miller, "Achievement Tests for Beginning and Intermediate Tennis," Research Quarterly, 21:303-321, 1950.

TENNIS
Skills Test Score Sheet

_____ Male/Female Date _____ Instructor _____
                           circle

_____ Section _____ Day/Time_____

| | | | RECORDER'S |
T ITEM	TRIALS	SCORE	T-SCORE	SIGNATURE
VE ord 5/4/3/0	── ── ── ── ── ── ── ── ── ── ── ── ── ── ── ── ── ── ── ──	── ── ──	── 	_____
EHAND ord 8/4/3/2/0	── ── ── ── ── ── ── ── ── ── ── ── ── ── ──	── ──	── 	_____
KHAND ord 8/4/3/2/0	── ── ── ── ── ── ── ── ── ──	──		_____

Total _____   Average _____
               Grade _____

TENNIS SKILLS TEST NORMS

	Serve		Forehand		Backhand	
T-Score	Men	Women	Men	Women	Men	Women
78	86↑	75↑	106↑	102	103	89
74	83	72	104	99	100	86
72	80	69	102	96	97	83
70	77	66	100	93	94	80
68	74	63	97	90	91	77
66	71	60	94	87	88	74
64	68	57	91	84	85	71
62	66	55	89	82	83	69
60	64	53	87	80	81	67
58	62	51	85	78	79	65
56	60	49	83	76	77	63
54	58	47	81	74	75	61
52	56	45	79	72	73	59
50	54	43	77	70	71	57
48	52	41	75	68	69	55
46	50	39	73	66	67	53
44	48	37	71	64	65	51
42	46	35	69	62	63	49
40	44	33	67	60	61	47
38	42	31	65	58	59	45
36	40	29	63	56	57	43
34	38	27	61	54	55	41
32	36	25	59	52	53	39
30	32	23	57	50	51	37

d

diate

r

231

TENNIS
Skills Test Score Sheet

_____ Male/Female Date _____ Instructor _____
circle

_____ Section _____ Day/Time_____

ST ITEM	TRIALS	SCORE	T-SCORE	RECORDER'S SIGNATURE

RVE
cord 5/4/3/0

REHAND
cord 8/4/3/2/0

CKHAND
cord 8/4/3/2/0

Total _____   Average _____
Grade _____

TENNIS SKILLS TEST NORMS

	Serve		Forehand		Backhand	
T-Score	Men	Women	Men	Women	Men	Women
78	86↑	75↑	106↑	102	103	89
74	83	72	104	99	100	86
72	80	69	102	96	97	83
70	77	66	100	93	94	80
68	74	63	97	90	91	77
66	71	60	94	87	88	74
64	68	57	91	84	85	71
62	66	55	89	82	83	69
60	64	53	87	80	81	67
58	62	51	85	78	79	65
56	60	49	83	76	77	63
54	58	47	81	74	75	61
52	56	45	79	72	73	59
50	54	43	77	70	71	57
48	52	41	75	68	69	55
46	50	39	73	66	67	53
44	48	37	71	64	65	51
42	46	35	69	62	63	49
40	44	33	67	60	61	47
38	42	31	65	58	59	45
36	40	29	63	56	57	43
34	38	27	61	54	55	41
32	36	25	59	52	53	39
30	32	23	57	50	51	37

TENNIS
Skill Analysis Score Sheet
(20 points)

Name _____ Date _____

Class _____ Evaluated By _____

POINT GUIDE

2 points -- Student appears competent
1 point -- Occasionally correct or minor errors
0 points -- Need more attention before ready to
            play

	POINTS SCORED		
	0	1	2
1. The Grip - the "V" *1) Forehand 2) Continental 3) Backhand	____	____	____
2. Stance *1) Ready position	____	____	____
3. Forehand Stroke *1) Body position 2) Contact point 3) Follow-through (low to high)	____	____	____
4. Backhand Stroke *1) Body position 2) Contact point 3) Follow-through (low to high)	____	____	____
5. Serving *1) Body position (deuce or add court) 2) Contact point (toss critical) 3) Follow-through	____	____	____
6. Volleying (step-turn-block) *1) Body position 2) Contact point 3) Follow-through	____	____	____
7. The Lob and Overhead *1) Lob past service line 2) Modify the serve for the overhead	____	____	____
8. Strategy for Playing *1) Singles (keep ball in play) 2) Doubles (know your partner)	____	____	____
9. Rules and Etiquette *1) Scoring - faults - tie breakers 2) Courtesy & respect in tennis (many poor examples)	____	____	____
10. Results *1) Tennis skill test results 2) General evaluation	____	____	____

*Points for evaluation

TOTAL SCORE _____

TENNIS
Skill Analysis Score Sheet
(20 points)

ame _____   Date _____

lass _____   Evaluated By _____

POINT GUIDE

2 points -- Student appears competent
1 point -- Occasionally correct or minor errors
0 points -- Need more attention before ready to
        play

	POINTS SCORED		
	0	1	2
The Grip - the "V"	____	____	____
*1) Forehand			
2) Continental			
3) Backhand			
Stance	____	____	____
*1) Ready position			
Forehand Stroke	____	____	____
*1) Body position			
2) Contact point			
3) Follow-through (low to high)			
Backhand Stroke	____	____	____
*1) Body position			
2) Contact point			
3) Follow-through (low to high)			
Serving	____	____	____
*1) Body position (deuce or add court)			
2) Contact point (toss critical)			
3) Follow-through			
Volleying (step-turn-block)	____	____	____
*1) Body position			
2) Contact point			
3) Follow-through			
The Lob and Overhead	____	____	____
*1) Lob past service line			
2) Modify the serve for the overhead			
Strategy for Playing	____	____	____
*1) Singles (keep ball in play)			
2) Doubles (know your partner)			
Rules and Etiquette	____	____	____
*1) Scoring - faults - tie breakers			
2) Courtesy & respect in tennis (many poor examples)			
10. Results	____	____	____
*1) Tennis skill test results			
2) General evaluation			

*Points for evaluation

TOTAL SCORE _____